ROUTLEDGE LIBRARY EDITIONS:
SOCIAL THEORY

Volume 29

THE HERMENEUTIC IMAGINATION

THE HERMENEUTIC IMAGINATION
Outline of a positive critique of scientism and sociology

JOSEF BLEICHER

LONDON AND NEW YORK

First published in 1982

This edition first published in 2015
by Routledge
2 Park Square, Milton Park, Abingdon, Oxon, OX14 4RN

and by Routledge
711 Third Avenue, New York, NY 10017

Routledge is an imprint of the Taylor & Francis Group, an informa business

First issued in paperback 2016

© 1982 Josef Bleicher

All rights reserved. No part of this book may be reprinted or reproduced or utilised in any form or by any electronic, mechanical, or other means, now known or hereafter invented, including photocopying and recording, or in any information storage or retrieval system, without permission in writing from the publishers.

Trademark notice: Product or corporate names may be trademarks or registered trademarks, and are used only for identification and explanation without intent to infringe.

British Library Cataloguing in Publication Data
A catalogue record for this book is available from the British Library

ISBN13: 978-1-138-79059-9 (hbk)
ISBN13: 978-1-138-99789-9 (pbk)

Publisher's Note
The publisher has gone to great lengths to ensure the quality of this reprint but points out that some imperfections in the original copies may be apparent.

Disclaimer
The publisher has made every effort to trace copyright holders and would welcome correspondence from those they have been unable to trace.

THE HERMENEUTIC IMAGINATION

Outline of a positive critique of scientism and sociology

Josef Bleicher

Routledge & Kegan Paul
London, Boston, Melbourne and Henley

First published in 1982
by Routledge & Kegan Paul Ltd
39 Store Street, London WC1E 7DD,
9 Park Street, Boston, Mass. 02108, USA,
296 Beaconsfield Parade, Middle Park,
Melbourne, 3206, Australia, and
Broadway House, Newtown Road,
Henley-on-Thames, Oxon RG9 1EN
Printed in the United States of America
© Josef Bleicher 1982
No part of this book may be reproduced in
any form without permission from the
publisher, except for the quotation of brief
passages in criticism

Library of Congress Cataloging in Publication Data

Bleicher, Josef.
The hermeneutic imagination.
Revision of the author's thesis (Ph. D.)
Bibliography: p.
Includes index.
1. Sociology - Methodology.   2. Hermeneutics.
3. Positivism. I. Title.
HM24.B555 1982   301   82-7522

ISBN 0-7100-9256-3
ISBN 0-7100-9257-1 (pbk.)

To

Fiona

CONTENTS

Preface		ix
Introduction		1
1	Scientism and hermeneutics: two claims to universality	3
	An outline of the socio-historical context of science and the science of society	4
	The meaning of science	7
	Science, meaning and the language of scientism	14
	Pragmatism between hermeneutic and scientistic thought	26
	Hermeneutics and the 'new philosophy of science'	33
2	The rise of a science of society and its normative presuppositions	37
	Positivist sociology and its metascience	39
	The use-context of positivist sociology	44
	From positivist to scientistic sociology	47
3	The development of a non-scientistic sociology in the context of the Geisteswissenschaften and Idealist philosophy	52
	Dilthey's founding of a hermeneutically informed sociology	55
	Verstehen between subjectivism and objectivism	64
4	Towards a hermeneutic paradigm for sociology	69
	The hermeneutic conception of understanding	70
	Science and language	77
	Objectivity and objectivism in the Geisteswissenschaften	80
5	Objective interpretation in macro-sociology and the hermeneutic dimension	88

viii *Contents*

Parsons's framework for the study of the objective meaning of action 89

The structural(ist) analysis of meaningful phenomena 92

System, structure and meaning 99

6 The dilemma of interpretive sociology 105

Symbolic interactionism 106

'Phenomenological' sociology and the analysis of the life-world 114

Winch and the linguistic conception of interpretive sociology 121

7 Between interpretive and hermeneutic sociology: the case of ethnomethodology 125

Ethnomethodology as the radicalization of interpretive sociology 125

Ethnomethodology as a hermeneutically oriented sociology 126

The ethnomethodological critique of sociology 130

Limitations of ethnomethodology in relation to the hermeneutic paradigm 133

8 Elements of a hermeneutic sociology 137

Metatheoretical perspective: what 'meaning'? 138

Methodological considerations 140

Metascientific issues: subjectivity, subjectivism, and the subject of science 144

Conclusion: between and beyond Idealism and reification - towards a hermeneutic-dialectical sociology 147

Hermeneutics and sociology in a capitalist society 147

Aspects of a hermeneutic-dialectical sociology 149

Notes 154

Bibliography 162

Name index 169

Subject index 171

PREFACE

In this book I have tried to apply some of the arguments developed in 'Contemporary Hermeneutics', in particular with reference to the subject-object relationship in the social sciences. The questions I asked myself were these: what is sociology? How is it possible? Why are there so many - conflicting - approaches to it? Can they be reconciled or interpreted in relation to their social context? What are the effects of a belief in the omnipotence of science on sociology and social practice? I can only hope the reader considers these questions relevant and finds my attempts at answering them at all enlightening.

'The Hermeneutic Imagination' represents a modified version of my PhD thesis. I am therefore pleased to be able to record my thanks here to Prof. Bauman who acted as my supervisor, and to Janet Wolff and Anthony Giddens from whom I received valuable advice. I am also indebted to students on my course in Sociological Theory on whom I tested out some of the ideas contained in this book and who responded in such an encouraging way. Dorothy Connor, who was one of them, also typed my thesis. Above all, I have to thank members of my family for the kindness and patience they have shown over the last few years.

INTRODUCTION

> This is one of the fundamental weaknesses - and perhaps also the fundamental greatness - of the human sciences: that all problems pertaining *to* mankind are ultimately problems *for* mankind. (Lévi-Strauss)

Never before has the fate of mankind been so precariously balanced. Its destiny seems intimately bound up with the questions of whether and how it can cope with accelerating scientific advance and channel its potential away from human self-destruction towards socially useful ends. The problems posed by science and technology had, therefore, best be seen as a challenge to the socio-cultural framework of society in the form of requiring us to understand their cultural significance and to create the social conditions in which their misuse - which seems to be programmed into our political order - can be avoided.

Such a task would necessitate learning processes in the sphere of the intersubjective determination of ends and purposes in line with the steady increase in instrumental knowledge. That the latter should have come to outstrip public control can be seen as symptomatic of the atrophy of the hermeneutic imagination which is being hastened by the encroachment of scientific rationality upon the communicative determination of a meaningful social existence.

It appears that sociology has, on the whole, not only failed to counteract this development, but has itself been instrumental in the demise of communicative rationality. It has largely failed to enlighten us about ourselves through widening our horizon to the point at which something qualitatively better, a more adequate way of organizing society, could have come into view. Instead it remained content with mirroring conditions in which individuals are fragmented both within and between themselves. I would argue that the tendency within sociology towards the gathering of instrumentally useful knowledge and away from the generation of practically relevant insight relates to the trained inability to take account of the hermeneutic dimension operative in the study of social phenomena and the reluctance on the part of sociologists to engage in hermeneutic (self-) reflection.

It is in this light that the following discussions should be seen. They take the form of a critique, i.e. an examination of the conditions of the possibility of sociology, in the hope of evidencing the social conditions, methodological and metascientific pre-

2 Introduction

suppositions, and practical implications of various approaches to it. I wish to argue that sociology contains a hermeneutic dimension which is both ineradicable and foundational. It is only on the basis of some pre-understanding that the study of social phenomena is possible; and since the latter are themselves meaningfully structured, the hermeneutic dimension in sociology takes the form of a 'double hermeneutic'. I argue further that there exists an internal relationship between the mode in which the object is projected - i.e. whether and how its meaningfulness is conceived of - and the possible use of research findings. Such an examination is itself hermeneutic in that it locates sociological approaches within their context, thereby making transparent their social and historical preconditions and consequences.

To anchor these discussions I develop a hermeneutic paradigm for sociology and on its basis examine the various approaches to this discipline: scientistic, functionalist, structuralist, and interpretive (symbolic interactionist, phenomenological and linguistic). The aim here is to evidence implicit background assumptions and their strengths and limitations on the level of ontological presupposition, methodology and the theory-practice nexus. From the perspective of the hermeneutic paradigm these approaches are challengeable and lead me to outline elements of a hermeneutic sociology via an analysis of ethnomethodology as a hermeneutically informed approach.

At this stage it will become necessary to inquire into the limitations of the hermeneutic paradigm itself in the light of a theory of society which stresses the continued efficacy of non-normative structures. In such conditions a hermeneutic-dialectical sociology would be more adequate since it considers and relates natural, quasi-natural and hermeneutic aspects of social reality. Such an approach is 'critical' in the sense that it aims to help realize the truth contained in the hermeneutic imagination - in contrast to scientism which represents the most radical denial of the hermeneutic dimension in socio-political practice, metascience and methodology.

I therefore commence my discussions with a critique of scientism in order to locate the various debates and indicate their significance in relation to both sociology and social existence.

1 SCIENTISM AND HERMENEUTICS: TWO CLAIMS TO UNIVERSALITY

> Is science the measure of knowledge, or is there a knowledge in which the ground and limit of science and thus its genuine effectiveness are determined? (Heidegger, 1967, p. 10)

Hermeneutic reflection aims at uncovering the conditions of science and its truth-claim by considering it as a 'project': a mode of mastering and using objectifiable processes which is linked to a particular way of viewing the world and of knowledge-acquisition. As such a project science serves as a point of reference for the emergence of sociology as a de-mystifying secularized perspective on social processes which are seen as amenable to rational investigation and control.

The realization that sociology has its roots within the project of science should not obscure the difference between the study and control of natural and social processes – even though the latter may, in given historical conditions, appear in a quasi-natural form. I shall term an approach to sociology 'scientistic' if it fails to recognize this difference and its implications for doing sociology. The self-understanding of sociologists working within such a framework is shaped by a view of science as a supra-historic, neutral enterprise and as the sole mode of acquiring true knowledge; these two aspects form the basis of scientism.

A concern with these metascientific issues should, of course, itself be seen in hermeneutic terms, i.e. in the historical context in which the rationality underlying science has become problematic in the sense that its spread is generating grave problems in social reproduction to the point where the survival of mankind is being threatened. The universality of scientific rationality refers both to the apotheosis of science and the reorganization of social existence through the application of technical reason at the expense of the hermeneutic dimension in social development. By the latter I understand the process of communication in which ends, norms, values are formulated dialogically in the determination of the course of social development, and that of science within it, in a hermeneutic-rational way. In claiming universal status for the latter I wish to argue that this dimension is not only ineradicable, but in fact fundamental, both to the establishing of societal forms and processes in which the intentions of members are realized and realizable as well as to the progress of science itself. It is this dimension

4 *Scientism and hermeneutics*

which allows me to speak of science as a social enterprise since
its course is ultimately set in view of the social will of members –
whether they be the public as a whole or self-interested and
powerful sections within it – and since it itself is possible only
on the basis of communication among those engaged in it directly.

This, then, is my purpose in evidencing the social, historic
and metascientific meaning of science: to consider the latter as
a project sustained by on-going processes of communication
within and around it in order to dispel the self-misunderstanding
of science which acts as a frame of reference for scientistic
sociology.

AN OUTLINE OF THE SOCIO-HISTORICAL CONTEXT OF
SCIENCE AND THE SCIENCE OF SOCIETY

Science acquired its social significance in the context of the rise
of that stratum of society that had most to gain from it in political and economic terms: the bourgeoisie. The entrepreneurial
class achieved political emancipation in conjunction with an increase in economic strength; this class had to

> calculate precisely in its activities in the fields of commerce
> and manufacture if it wanted to secure and extend its power
> in a newly emerging competitive market; the same applies to
> those who, so to speak, were its agents in the field of science
> and technology and whose inventions and other scientific
> work played such a great role in the incessant struggle be-
> tween individuals, towns and nations that runs through
> modern history. For these subjects it was a matter-of-course
> to view the world from a mathematical perspective. And be-
> cause this class came to characterize the whole of society in
> the course of social developments this perspective spread well
> beyond the bourgeoisie. (Horkheimer and Adorno 1973, p. 303).

In the course of the rise of the bourgeoisie the quest for a
more rational organization of society lost its critical edge and
turned into one of the mainstays of the preservation of the status
quo. As the strategic position occupied by the 'technostructure'
testifies, the belief in the omnipotence of science and technology
today is of central ideological importance. As ideology, this
belief rests not so much on a misrepresentation of the possibility
of science but on the exclusion of alternative conceptions of
the aims of social development and how they should be arrived
at.

As the production process is revolutionized through the application of instrumental rationality the socio-political framework
which should serve the democratic determination of policy is itself increasingly 'rationalized', as is apparent in the growth of
bureaucratic institutions in which the goals of efficiency and

Scientism and hermeneutics 5

instrumental rationality in general are paramount. That is to say that communicative interaction which is based on an evaluation of socially shared norms is supplanted by instrumental action which proceeds in relation to pre-given ends and follows technical, formalizable rules. 'Communication' here excludes the consideration of ends and refers to the monological flow of information from the centre of decision-making to the public under the control of 'experts'. This state of affairs represents a form of domination which is more subtle, and for this reason all the more effective, than brachial means. It operates, as mentioned, through the exclusion of public debate and the manipulation of language (e.g. through the re-definition of meaning and exclusion of meanings required for alternative interpretations of the good society). This development leads to the atrophy of practical reason through a lack of opportunity for exercising political judgment. To single out two important consequences: the economic subsystem may be deprived of its 'input' as members become gradually disillusioned with the material palliatives that they are offered in place of the opportunity to participate in the shaping of their own lives in accordance with their intentions and interests; left to its own device, the mindless expansion of science is even threatening the very survival of mankind. At the same time as society becomes more and more dependent on the instrumental-rational subsystem, the latter is increasingly escaping public control. To depict the gradual erosion of the democratic determination of social issues Feyerabend refers to '"Stalinist" (or "elitist")' (Feyerabend, 1980, p. 11) tendencies. These he equates with the disenfranchising of the public by cliques who arrogate the right and expertise to establish the standards to be employed for judging social institutions in general and science and its role in society in particular.

These trends act as a reminder of the ineradicability of the hermeneutic dimension in social evolution. Again, referring to the relationship between the progress of science and communication, it is today palpably clear that the former is to a large extent concerned with problems it generates itself rather than serving the needs of society. Science, where it is not directed at socially futile projects designed to enhance national prestige and military might, is transforming our habitat into an artificial environment that can only be maintained in the state of an - unstable - equilibrium through the plundering of non-renewable resources. This vicious circle is kept in operation by national elites who still consider economic growth as the most efficacious way of maintaining the present social arrangements.

It is difficult not to recognize the pressing need for informed public debate concerning the use science is to be put to. Such a debate can, of course, only be conducted in the form of an assimilation of knowledge of what is technically possible and necessary into the hermeneutic self-understanding of participants.

6   Scientism and hermeneutics

The debate between experts and public would, as Habermas (1973c, p. 127 and p. 136) argues, not only allow for the development of new technologies in line with the interpretation of existing needs, but it also acts as a means for checking the adequacy of existing value systems. This task would itself give rise to a hermeneutic problem of its own: the translation of technical knowledge into everyday language to facilitate its absorption into the pre-understanding of interested citizens.

To conceptualize the possible forms that the relationship between science and politics can take I would like to draw on a typology provided by Habermas which distinguishes between a technocratic, a decisionist and a pragmatic model.

The technocratic model approximates the use which some envisage for 'empirical sociology' which has its precursor in Saint-Simon. Starting from the conception of social progress as a scientific-technical development that follows its own internal logic, it assumes the virtually complete passivity of the individual in the face of external constraints. The role of the politician is here limited to the propagation of policies determined for him by scientific advisers - which also secures him the unenviable position as a scapegoat should any of the plans go wrong; he certainly has lost the capacity to generate his own initiatives. Scientized politics in this model can, consequently, only be thought of as 'the reduction of political domination to rational administration at the price of democracy altogether' (Habermas, 1973c, p. 128).

The decisionist model postulates the strict separation of expert and politician in the context of the guidance of politics by science: the scientist provides information on the basis of which the politician makes his decisions which introduces an element of 'decisive will' into the decision-making process that can not be subjected to rational analysis. The political climate conducive to the flourishing of such an approach to politics is one where 'democratic elections take the form of acclamation rather than public discussion. Here it is only the decision-makers that have to legitimize themselves in front of the political public rather than the decisions themselves which, in this conception, remain removed from public discussion' (1973c, p. 128). The political theories of Weber and Schumpeter provide a good formulation of this system.

Democracy can only remain intact in the pragmatic model while, at the same time, providing the prerequisite for it. In this model,

> in place of the strict separation of the functions of expert and politician we get a critical, reciprocal relationship which not only denudes the ideologically maintained domination of its basis of legitimation but which makes it accessible to scientifically informed discussions in toto and thereby alters it fundamentally . . . The development of new strategies . . . is here

Scientism and hermeneutics   7

directed by systems of values which themselves . . . are controlled through the testing of the technical possibility of their
realization. (1973c, pp. 126-7)

Since practical needs are involved in the orientation that is
given to social development as well as in the determination of
whether or not new strategies meet with the approval of the
public we are here dealing with a dialogical process of communication that

> is in both directions tied to what Dewey called value beliefs -
> that is, the historically determined and socially normed pre-
> understanding of what is, in concrete situations, practically
> necessary. This pre-understanding is an awareness that can
> only be arrived at by hermeneutic means and which is arti-
> culated in the process of communication engaged in by the
> communality of citizens. (1973c, p. 129)

It is the hallmark of technocracy as the socio-political expression of scientistic thought and practice that it should attempt
to impoverish or discredit the hermeneutic imagination required
for an adequate relationship between science and society. I shall
now trace the operation of this dimension within science itself
to counter the scientistic self-misunderstanding of science and
its sociological offshoot.

THE MEANING OF SCIENCE

The seventeenth century witnessed the rise of a new rationality
which found its first expression in the exposition of experimental science in the work of Bacon and in the redirection of philosophy as epistemology by Descartes. Embodying a radically
different outlook on man and nature within a quest for certain
knowledge, it heralded a shift from theological dogma to critical
analysis in which nothing could be taken for granted as the
source of truth and orientation of conduct.

With hindsight we can discern a dialectic within scientific
rationality in which its emancipatory potential is giving way to
a new form of dogmatism. The recognition of the liberating and
repressive moments of the rationality of science and the challenge
this offers to mankind has led to inquiries into the meaning of
science. I shall here refer to two of the most reflexive analyses
on this matter, those of Husserl and Heidegger.

Husserl and the Phenomenology of Science
I may be justified in focusing on Husserl's last work since it not
only represents a 'crowning achievement'[1] in his own view but it
also introduces a teleological-historical perspective which allows
for a more radical re-working of the Kantian problem with the

8 Scientism and hermeneutics

aim of evidencing the historical-practical basis of science.

Kant did not inquire into the ultimate grounding of science; by contrast, Husserl is led 'back to knowing subjectivity as the primal locus of all objective formations of sense and ontic validities' (Husserl, 1970a, p. 99). From the point of view developed in 'The Crisis of European Sciences and Transcendental Philosophy', Kant's own presuppositions, and with them 'the sciences to whose truths and methods Kant attributes actual validity, become a problem' (p. 104). Transcendental phenomenology, by contrast, has as its object what in

> the Kantian manner of posing questions, . . . is presupposed as existing - the surrounding world in which all of us . . . consciously have our existence; here are also the sciences, as cultural facts in this world, with their scientists and their theories. In this world we are objects among objects in the sense of the life-world, namely, as being here and there, in the plain certainty of experience, before anything that is established scientifically. (1970a, pp. 104-5)

Husserl's analyses are conducted within a framework that is of great relevance for the task-in-hand: to evidence the historic determinants of science. The whole issue is set within the crisis of Western thought, of which the sciences are a predominant part. Modern science derives from the Greek idea of knowledge and the concept of Reason which is dominant within it. The latter depicts man's ability to determine his own life and his environment which is made possible through the rational examination of a reality that is itself viewed as a rational system. At the same time, ontology and epistemology coincide in the recognition that objectivity is a correlate of subjectivity. On the basis of this assumed isomorphism between the structure of reality and rational thought it is possible to envisage that Reason, as theoria, can transform the world in its own image.

This specific 'project' finds its modern, and most fruitful, formulation in Galileo's mathematization of nature, with the result that only such interchanges with reality as can be fitted into this project came to be seen as 'rational'. Its very success spelled the gradual demise of the framework that had been its womb. Philosophy, now disregarded as metaphysical speculation, was no longer allowed to determine the ends for what by now has become the self-perpetuating, self-legitimating conquest of objectifiable reality. Scientific rationality separated itself from the autotelic interest of Reason that underpinned the initial success of philosophy.

What are the implications of these insights for the status of science?

From what Husserl has to say about the 'obvious' character of everyday occurrences it follows that the assumption of the self-evidence of scientific truths is an illusion that can maintain itself

Scientism and hermeneutics   9

only through the refusal to inquire into their constitution - and as such it is 'theoretically no better than an appeal to an oracle' (1970a, p. 189). The price the sciences have to pay for their 'naivety': 'Natural-scientific knowing about nature gives us no truly explanatory, no ultimate, knowledge of nature because it does not investigate nature at all in the absolute framework through which its actual and genuine being reveals its ontic meaning' (p. 189). Husserl goes on to argue that the crisis of Western civilization and its central cognitive mode derive from the uncertain foundations of the latter; that is to say, the inability of science to recover the experiences which underlie its empirical generalizations and analytic formulations. These procedures imply a loss of specificity, a loss of original insight into concrete objects which attends their progressive idealization and quantification. Mathematical symbols do not really symbolize, quite the reverse: they serve to suppress the original experience and gloss over its inconsistencies. But just as the internal coherence of the calculus is a poor substitute for new insight, so the clarity of the language of science is achieved at the expense of the reactivation of the original experience in the natural attitude of the referents of science. The solution Husserl offers for the crisis he diagnosed consequently rests on the contributions of a phenomenological description of the ultimate ground of - scientific - knowledge.

The first 'epoché' of objective science suspends, or 'puts in brackets', all scientific truth, so what we are left with is the 'natural attitude', our given everyday world and the unreflexive experiences which we make within it. This sphere provides the foundation for all objectivating thought, and therefore also for the 'objective sciences as subjective constructs - those of a particular praxis, namely, the theoretical logical' (p. 129).

However, pre-scientific experience cannot be the ultimate ground of knowledge since it itself presupposes something else: the very existence of objects in the world. Consequently, a second epoché has to be performed in relation to the universal horizon of experience of a pre-given world, the life-world (Lebenswelt). In the course of this last reduction we bracket our natural attitude, the common-sensical belief in the validity of everyday experience, since it is the latter which acts as a mystifying veil behind which science can appear as a neutral activity. The phenomenological-transcendental reflection on the possibility of science thus evidences the '"how" of the subjective manner of givenness of the life-world and life-world objects' through the 'investigation of the transcendental correlation between world and world-consciousness' (pp. 143, 151).

The second epoché reduces 'the world' to its correlate, 'transcendental subjectivity', in and through whose 'conscious life' the world, valid for us straightforwardly and naively prior to all science, attains, and always already has attained, its whole content and ontic validity. It is then, to this transcendental

10 Scientism and hermeneutics

subjectivity that the world is given as a phenomenon of and for
an absolute subjectivity. Objects are 'constituted' in specific acts
of synthesis in which objectivity and subjectivity are linked; it
is 'absolute' as the ultimate ground, as the condition of the
possibility of objectivity.

The central insight derivable from the transcendental reduction
shows that within our consciousness there functions the self-
given, absolute, or primal 'ego' as the carrier of all meaning-
horizons and of the Lebenswelt, 'the ultimately unique centre
of functioning in all constitution' (1970a p. 186).

Knowledge attained through

> the constitutive 'internal' method through which all objective-
> scientific method acquires its meaning and possibility cannot
> be without significance for the scientist of nature or any other
> objective scientist. It is, after all, a matter of the most
> radical and most profound self-reflection of accomplishing sub-
> jectivity; how could it not be of service in protecting the
> naive, ordinary accomplishment from misunderstandings such
> as are to be observed in abundance, for example, in the
> influence of naturalistic epistemology and in the idolization of
> a logic that does not understand itself? (p. 189).

This quote illustrates Husserl's powerful argumentation with
which he helped to dispel the misunderstanding which scientists
have of their own practices - a misunderstanding that permeates
the Logic of Science approach to metascientific questions and
the methodology of scientistic approaches to the study of society.

Heidegger's ontological argument
Husserl's analysis of scientific knowledge seems to parallel that
of Heidegger. Both consider the sciences as one possible way
of providing an interpretation of reality, i.e. as a project which,
like all historic projects, is grounded in a given mode of existence - and thereby accountable.

They differ in this: Husserl, the rationalist philosopher,
exempts philosophy from the particularly Western project of
domination and regards it as the domain in which the 'struggle
for the meaning of man' (Husserl, 1970a, p. 14) is to be conducted. For Heidegger, the tradition of Western philosophy since
Descartes is itself an expression of a project that is grounded
in Dasein and which also encompasses science. The transition
from Husserl to Heidegger consequently takes the form of an
abandonment of all forms of epistemology in favour of a transcendental ontology.

Heidegger's analysis centres on the 'ontological difference'
between 'Being' and the 'beings' it makes possible. By outlining
the basic features of Heidegger's transcendental ontology I hope
to show that the idea of presuppositionless activity is untenable
in general and to point out the implications of the groundedness

Scientism and hermeneutics   11

of science in Dasein[2] as the Being of mankind.

The synthetic a priori of knowledge has been conceived in different ways in transcendental philosophy from Kant to Husserl. Heidegger uncovers the final presupposition of Idealism: the conception of all constitution as self-constitution, through his explication of the meaning of Being as Dasein. He is thereby able to arrive at the *existentialist* a priori: all experience is made possible by the existential fore-structure of knowledge, yet remains tied to it.

Science, as a project in which the essence of things is disregarded in favour of their quantitative determination, can, consequently, no longer maintain its scientistic self-image. The historicality of scientific knowledge can best be illustrated by referring to the 'heremeneutic circle'. Formulated in terms of the process of science, the realization that the subject shares the world with his objects, and has a pre-understanding of them which guides his subsequent methodical inquiry, leads to the thesis that the purpose behind scientific research, the delineation of the subject-matter, the formulation of the criteria and standards of scientific work, are permeated by the historical situatedness of science.

In the case of sociology or any other social or human science the following, a fortiori, case can be established: since the study of natural phenomena is already imbued with historically derived significance, how much more must this be the case in relation to phenomena which not only 'affect' us more directly but which are signficant, i.e. they are meaningfully structured themselves. However much we may objectify our object, as socio-historically situated observers we cannot but approach it with some pre-understanding. This kind of understanding does not vie with accepted empirical procedures as merely another method, but it represents a kind of knowledge that objectifying explanation may help us to improve.

This last point will be developed further in the context of an inquiry into the possibility, or rather the conditions of the possibility, of the social sciences. In the following sections of this chapter I would, however, like to pursue the theme underlying these last remarks: how 'objective' is science? How can its historicality be shown more concretely?

Heidegger refers to his ontological analysis as 'hermeneutic' in contradistinction to ontic investigations. The 'ontological difference' implied is also apparent in a theme that occupied Heidegger after Being and Time and which is of relevance to the task-in-hand: to evidence science as a specific project that issues from within an existential understanding which forms the 'pre-understanding' that guides all objectifying thought.

In Heidegger's work we do not find an explicit philosophy of science. It appears, however, that his dealings with this field are related to his concern with the meaning of metaphysics and

12 Scientism and hermeneutics

of technology. These three areas are considered together in terms of their 'mathematical' essence, which itself is 'the execution and consequence of the historical mode of Dasein' (Heidegger, 1967, p. 95).

'The mathematical', as a project, itself brings forth the experimental and mathematical procedures of science. All questions posed in relation to nature are now seen as developing in accordance with the initial project. It is only on account of the latter that science can achieve its exactitude since the project opens up that field of pheonemena which can then be located within the co-ordinates of space and time and be subjected to experimentation. The appropriate conception of the object is one that admits only those aspects that fit into the original projection - which implies a view of things that takes them to be what they show themselves as. Knowledge is now no longer one of the essence of the laws of Being but only of the laws of their appearance.

Heidegger regards attributes given to modern science which are supposed to distinguish it from medieval science, such as factual, experimental, and measuring, as insufficient since they also apply to earlier forms of science.[3] Instead, 'the fundamental feature must consist in what rules and determines the basic involvement of science itself' (1967, p. 68). This, 'the mathematical', allows modern science to supersede the previous orientation on the authority of the Church in matters concerning knowledge and truth. It liberates and, at the same time binds, the investigator to new, but self-imposed, principles. It is essentially axiomatic and provides a basic outline of the structure of the object and its relation to it in advance. The mathematical nature of mathematics itself resides in the fact that its application is possible on the basis of something that is known in advance: 'mathesis', Heidegger tells us, is a process in which we learn something we already have some knowledge of.

Apart from mathematics and mathematized science Heidegger also includes metaphysics within the mathematical project. Modern philosophy is here seen as the axiomatic pursuit of knowledge that insists on the methodical progression from immediate and absolute self-certainty. The emphasis on, and use of, the faculty of Reason is a putting to work of axiomatic propositions. Taking nothing for granted but itself, Reason projects itself on to its object which takes the form of the determination of something as something. What the object 'is' depends, therefore, on what attributes it is given and is for this reason intimately connected with the structure of assertions. Reason, as the translation of ratio and logos, originally means 'addressing something as something': 'the basic form of thinking, and thus of thought, is the guideline for the determination of the thingness of the thing' (Heidegger, 1967, p. 64).

The third component of the mathematical project, technology, is seen by Heidegger as closely related to metaphysics and his

Scientism and hermeneutics 13

analysis of it provides us with a deepened understanding of the meaning of science.

Heidegger notes a close affinity between rational comprehension and technological application in that they both are seen as processes of dis-covery ('Entbergen'). Technology brings to light something that has so far remained latent. Such a real-ization leads to the discovery of truth for which Heidegger employs the Greek word 'aletheia' and which he renders as 'that which is not hidden'. Consequently, 'technology - so it is said - dwells in that sphere where discovery and openness, where 'aletheia', where truth takes place' (Heidegger, 1962, p. 13). It follows that technology is not a mere application of knowledge for a given purpose, and neither is it a neutral phenomenon; it is rather a process of realization, of making real something that, as the structure of nature, is real but has remained hidden, un-dis-covered.

Man's progressive discovery of nature gives rise to a challenge as he finds himself confronted with his realizations. This challenge consists in trying to use them wisely and to be mindful of the fact that they do not exhaust Being. Using them wisely implies not being taken-in by them or losing one-self in them or 'to remain at the periphery of the possible, only to pursue and deal with dis-coveries which can be made and used, and to take them to be the measure of all things' (1962, p. 25).

Having outlined Heidegger's analysis of the intimate relationship between 'teche' and 'episteme' I would wish to indicate briefly two further implications of man's new relationship with his environment: the separation of subject and object in philosophy and the particular conception of truth connected with scientific knowledge in scientistic discourse.

The thinking subject as 'subjectum', meaning that which provides the basis, found its ultimate source of certainty in the self-evidence of the cogito. Heidegger now traces the movement towards a separation of subject and object by, first, stating that knowledge has come to be seen as identical with the process of presenting to itself what is known. Yet what can be presented in this way is only that which can be objectified in the course of such a process. Finally, the certitude associated with this kind of knowing and with these objects of knowledge assumes the status of truth; truth, consequently, comes to be seen as being assured to the extent to which exact calculation is possible - which is itself dependent on the objectifiability of its object. Descartes, having separated thinker and object has in this way established the theme of modern philosophy which still reverberates in scientistic philosophies of science.

In conjunction with this 'forgetfulness of Being' a conception of truth achieved prominence which did not link the process of thought with Dasein and which for this reason allowed itself to be used all the more in the heedless domination of not only natural but social processes as well.

14 *Scientism and hermeneutics*

SCIENCE, MEANING, AND THE LANGUAGE OF SCIENTISM

Hermeneutic reflection on the status of science interprets the latter as a specific mode of interchange between man and nature within a historic and social context. In emphasizing the historicality of science, hermeneutic thought provides a critique of and alternative to 'scientism'. In the present context, this term should denote a methodic unwillingness to acknowledge the historicality of science. The result of such a metascientific approach is a peculiarly truncated conception of the development of scientific knowledge and of its epistemological status. Scientism, as I use the term, would entail a commitment to one or more of the following tenets:
science deals with 'facts' given independently of the researcher; the empirical-analytical method is the only valid mode of knowledge-acquisition;
that this method should be extended to all spheres of cognitive activity;
that its results are the only true form of knowledge.

While some of these tenets have entered everyday conceptions concerning the process and status of scientific knowledge, the monopolistic and imperialistic trends of scientistic doctrines are, perhaps, most clearly expressed in the neo-positivist philosophy of science - which takes the form of a Logic of Science.

The most promising strategy for conducting a *positive* critique of scientism - in which I would hope to evidence the hermeneutic dimension in scientific activity - is to engage it on its own ground: the neo-positivist concern with language.

Here, the core of the argument centres on a theory of communication which serves to define science in relation to the complete intersubjectivity of statements about reality. This approach found its programmatic formulation in a 'Manifesto' issued in 1929 by a group of thinkers which came to be known as the Vienna Circle under the title: 'The Scientific Conception of the World: The Vienna Circle'.[4] This programme, which informed the Logic of Science, rests on two main tenets: knowledge derives from experiences gained from observations and experiments and as such also 'sets the limit for the content of legitimate science' (Neurath, 1973, p. 309); two, the call for a unity of science which is to be achieved 'by the application of a certain method, namely logical analysis' (ibid) to all disciplines claiming to produce valid knowledge on the basis of a unitary language. Logical analysis and employment of an approved language also help to demarcate science and metaphysics, meaningful and meaningless knowledge (or, more accurately, statements).

Logical analysis   The concern with logic entered the discussions of the Vienna Circle through their shared interest in the 'Principia Mathematica'. In this seminal work Russell continued the work of Frege, in particular the latter's view that the con-

Scientism and hermeneutics   15

cepts of mathematics should be defined on the basis of the concepts of logic. This endeavour already occupied Leibnitz, who saw great promise for the advance of mathematics and science in the calculability of all the consequences following from given preconditions. The device to be employed for this purpose was the construction of a calculus formed by a rule of inference and a system of signs which represent the object. Together, these would result in the famous 'mathesis unversalis', the sign language comprehending all sciences in the form of a strictly deductive system.

Russell and Whitehead referred to their logistics as 'mathematical' or 'symbolic' logic, which already indicates that its construction was guided by the example of mathematics and the sign language employed in it, and that it received its decisive impetus from the project of reducing each mathematical statement to the axioms of logic.

Mathematical logic attracted the interest of the members of the Vienna Circle because of its apparent unambiguity and certainty of deduction. As such it has been regarded as paradigmatic and attempts were made to approximate the standards achieved by its axiomatic and formalizing procedures. Given a certain stage of development, the material accumulated within a field of study could be arranged in an axiomatic form, i.e. as a 'theory'. Theory is regarded as representing a system of statements, hypotheses, laws, explanations, etc. Formalization, in this context, consists of the replacing of descriptive signs by mere marks and has the advantage of preventing any oversight in the process of deducing any theorems from these axioms. The latter now no longer take the form of statements but consist only of schemata of such which in turn need to be 'interpreted', i.e. the symbols of the calculus have to be correlated to observable or measurable magnitudes; as this allows for a number of possible interpretations of abstract theory, it can lead to the formulation of a number of different 'models' – in particular conceptual and factual ones. The connection between abstract theories or conceptual models of such on the one hand and reality on the other is achieved via a set of assumptions usually referred to as 'rules of correspondence'; in the context of the methodology of social science one finds the term 'operationalization' for the interpretation of an abstract theory, and that of 'operational definition' for the interpretation of basic concepts, or 'primitives'.

Despite warnings concerning the 'current ideological concern with formalization in the behaviour sciences' (Hochberg, 1959b, p. 434) such attempts have been, and are still being made, especially by philosophers who were also influenced by Hilbert's[5] formalistic conception of logic and mathematics in which the basic concepts are defined in reference to axioms which are interpreted only later in the course of their application. In 'The Foundation of Logic and Mathematics' Carnap then made the distinction between a logical-mathematical basic calculus and a

16 Scientism and hermeneutics

specific deductive system – a distinction that is paralleled by the
separation of logical and factual truth already referred to by
Leibnitz and taken up by Carnap. Theories in natural science
would then exhibit the following pattern: a calculus is constructed on the basis of a logico-mathematical calculus in conjunction
with the formulation of high-level generalities, or axioms, which
have no empirical meaning attributed to them. One then proceeds
to interpret this syntactic system through the use of semantic
rules and is now in a position to deduce statements about the
object of investigation. Once they have been verified, these
theorems are acceptable as valid.

Scientism and the problem of meaning

The 'linguistic turn'[6] in neo-positivist philosophy refers to a re-
orientation of empiricistic epistemology from sense-impressions
to intersubjectively verifiable statements of such. Science, as
true knowledge, could now be distinguished from metaphysics in
reference to the language employed: only statements which conform to certain formal requirements are to be regarded as meaningful.

Wittgenstein's 'Tractatus Logico-Philosophicus' provided the
catalyst that sparked off and sustained the Vienna Circle in its
rejection of metaphysics.[7] It establishes the 'principle of verifiability' which states that the meaning of a sentence is given by
the conditions of its verification. A sentence is meaningful only
if its verification is in principle logically possible. That is to say
that its meaning consists solely in its verifiable content. With
this principle in hand, it should be possible to distinguish between scientific and metaphysical sentences, the latter having
no meaning since they do not admit of verification; only empirical
statements can be meaningful.

One startling consequence of this view is the fact that now
logic and mathematics in particular, and philosophy in general,
too, have to be regarded as consisting of 'meaningless' statements! They are trivial, i.e. they are used for purposes of
description without describing anything themselves – in contradistinction to informative, synthetic statements. Wittgenstein
acknowledged this conclusion and came to view philosophy as a
ladder to be discarded once one had ascended it. Neurath, on
the other hand, still discerned a residue of metaphysics in such
a conclusion and supported Carnap's transformation of philosophy
to the 'Logic of Science' which did not yield any new knowledge.
To understand the crucial restriction of all meanings to empirical
meaning it is necessary to refer to Russell and Whitehead's
'Principia Mathematica', which came very close to establishing a
theoretically perfect language through the purely logical reduction of all propositions to 'elementary' ones, i.e. those that can
immediately be compared with reality.

The language established in the 'Principia' can be characterized
as 'extensional' and 'truth-functional'. Wittgenstein, in the

Scientism and hermeneutics   17

'Tractatus',[8] accepts this view of language and goes on to establish the relationship between language and the world. This world 'is all that is the case' (1), and shows itself in language since 'a proposition is a picture of reality' (4.021) and asserts, in its simplest form, 'the existence of a state of affairs' (4.21). 'If an elementary proposition is true, the state of affairs exists' (4.25) and 'if all true elementary propositions are given, the result is a complete description of the world' (4.26).

Russell had already distinguished among elementary propositions between 'atomic' and 'molecular' propositions. The former are characterized by a subject-object relation in which the 'subject' denotes an individual thing and the 'object' refers to a characteristic of it; they therefore provide information about reality that may be true or false. 'Reality' itself consists of 'facts', themselves made up of an individual thing plus its characteristic and which are described by atomic propositions. Molecular propositions can be reduce to atomic propositions plus logical connectives and they are 'truth-functional; i.e. their 'truth-value' depends on the truth or falsity of their constituent propositons. The concept of truth-value underlies the thesis of 'extensionality' that determines the 'domain of relevance' of propositions. The meaning of a proposition, then, depends on elementary propositions which picture empirical facts. It can be determined by comparing the elementary proposition with the 'fact'; non-elementary propositions depend for their truth on the truth-value of the elementary propositions from which they are derived. An 'ideal language' can now be defined as one that is based on elementary propositions - and in which metaphysical speculation is logically impossible.

Wittgenstein's central legacy to the Vienna Circle consists, consequently, in the idea of an 'ideal language' and the use of logical analysis for the determination of the significance of propositions. Through the work of Moritz Schlick his conception of 'meaning' as the 'empirical-meaning requirement'[9] became the basis of the 'criterion of verifiability' which was formulated in this way: 'stating the meaning of a sentence amounts to stating the rules according to which the sentence is to be used and this is the same as stating the way in which it can be verified (or falsified). The meaning of a proposition is the method of its verification' (Schlick, 1949, p. 148).

It is now possible to give a more precise characterization of what logical empiricists understand by the term 'metaphysics': its sentences do not meet the condition of 'verifiability which is the sufficient and necessary condition of meaning' (Schlick, 1949, p. 155). The statements of metaphysics are non-empirical, i.e. no empirical method can be given for the determination of their meaningfulness; they are thus 'meaningless', non-significant 'pseudo-propositions' (Carnap). 'Metaphysical aberration' can be traced back to two sources:

one, the well-known confusions inherent in traditional, every-

18 *Scientism and hermeneutics*

day languages and, two, the notion that thinking can either
lead to knowledge out of its own resources without using any
empirical material, or at best arrive at new contents by an
inference from given states of affairs. (Neurath, 1973, p. 308)

Logical analysis can provide a cure for both ills. Based on
nominalist conceptions, it rejects hypostatizations apparent in
ordinary language which have been traced to the unclear usage
for different purposes of given parts of speech.

The task ahead, clearly, lay in the establishing of a language
that avoided these pitfalls - and then the way would be open for
the spreading and accumulation of true knowledge. By the time
this task came to be perceived and steps were undertaken to
tackle it, the means for doing so had suddenly lost their appeal.
Weinberg has pointed at two difficulties that rendered the
Wittgensteinian route to true knowledge unviable:

> First, the criterion of meaning depends on an assumption for
> which there is neither logical nor empirical justification.
> Second, the theory of language which depends on the criterion
> of meaning cannot be expressed. Thus there is the paradox of
> a theory of logical syntax which cannot be formulated.
> (Weinberg, 1936, p. 195).

The first point here concerns the impossibility of providing a
basis for elementary propositions from the logical point of view;
i.e. the existence of propositions wholly determined by atomic
facts cannot be demonstrated - which leads to the insight that
'the elimination of metaphysics rests on unproven dogma' (p. 195).
The second objection brings to light Wittgenstein's rejection of
any metalanguage in consequence of his view that propositions
mirror or picture facts without being expressible in them.

If one wishes to follow the development of scientism after the
impasse reached by the early Wittgenstein it is necessary to
consider more closely the work of Neurath and Carnap and with
it the development of the Vienna Circle.

Wittgenstein's theory of verifiability and the criterion for the
meaningfulness of statements had led to the search for 'basic'
statements. Protocol statements were considered as the rock
bottom of knowledge by providing intersubjective accounts of
the immediately given. In the course of discussions conducted
around the Vienna Circle it was found that even protocol sentences themselves were not completely verifiable - a difficulty
that was even more apparent in general sentences, such as
natural laws. A modification of the thesis of verification and its
equation with meaningfulness became an urgent task and proceeded via the liberalization of Empiricism. The asymmetry
between verification and falsification which derives from the fact
that the latter require only one instance whereas the former can
never be completed due to the infinity of possible instances,

Scientism and hermeneutics   19

one of which may be a falsifying one, has been recognized by
Carnap's reformulation. With this liberalization of the tenet of
Empiricism it was possible to move away from the original project
of the Vienna Circle, viz. the construction of a scientific world-
picture in conjunction with the idea of Encyclopedism – a move
that is also manifest in the replacement of the principle of verifiability with the concept of degrees of confirmation or logical
probability. It also re-opened the debate about the status of
induction.

J.S. Mill had hoped to provide a postulate of induction by which
it would become possible to justify the step from a number of
instances to general laws by introducing 'the law of universal
causation' which was to function as the major premise in the
formulation of a syllogism. While remaining on the firm ground
of Empiricism Mill still relied too much on some metaphysical
assumptions in his endeavour to save the certainty of knowledge.
   Within Logical Empiricism two possible solutions to the problem
of induction were put forward. Reichenbach, following some of
Peirce's[10] suggestions, held that inductive statements can never
serve as the basis for deduction; but even though they may
not be verifiable they can at least be 'vindicated'. Carnap, on
the other hand, hoped to build on the calculus of probability for
his 'inductive logic', or 'theory of probability', including also
a 'theory of estimation' since he 'believe(d) that if it were
possible to find a satisfactory definition and theory of probability
this would at last supply a clear rational basis for the controver-
sial procedure of inductive inference' (Carnap in Schilpp, 1963,
p. 72). By his own admission this theory is not yet fully established, but his friends are already asking: 'is this not the be-
ginning of a dangerous apriorism or rationalism?' Clearly,
scientism has moved a long way from its Vienna days.
   The insight that 'all empirical knowledge consists of the
formulation of hypotheses which always go beyond the given,
always assert more than the latter, even if they are singular
statements' (Kraft, 1953, p. 131), has even more far-reaching
consequences if applied to universal statements. Laws of nature
claim to be operative for all processes under consideration and
are, therefore, not amenable to complete enumeration. The
quantifier 'all' renders immediate verification impossible – and so
commits empirical statements making up science to the metaphysical rubbish heap? Whereas Schlick attempted to save the
principle of verifiability by regarding the laws of physics no
longer as general statements, i.e. as truth-functions of similar
statements, but as rules for the derivation of singular statements, Carnap searched for a new criterion of significance.
The essay on 'Truth and Confirmation' introduced the concept
of 'confirmation'.
   The 'distinction between truth and knowledge of truth (verification, confirmation)' (Carnap, 1936, p. 120) has opened the

20   *Scientism and hermeneutics*

door to the penetration of relativistic strands into what once
appeared as a monolithic, if not petrified, system. Confirmation,
in contradistinction to truth, is essentially related to a given
state of scientific knowledge; it is, furthermore, divisible into
degrees. Confirmation can be attained by 'the formulation of an
observation and the confirmation of statements with each other'
(Carnap, 1936, p. 127). The former procedure maintains the
link with Empiricism and is given greater weight than the latter
which Neurath had considered sufficient for deciding whether
or not to accept any new statement.

These views received their most cogent expression in his essay
on 'Testability and Meaning[11] where he further distinguished
between confirmability and testability. 'A sentence which is confirmable by possible observable events is, moreover, testable if
a method can be specified for producing such events at will'
(Carnap in Schilpp, 1963, p. 59). It is here quite apparent how
pragmatist strands of thinking have led to a softening-up of the
Vienna Circle's initial criterion of meaningfulness. As a consequence, the continued crusade against metaphysics could be conducted with more flexible means. After the broadening of a
narrow empiricist conception of knowledge that demanded a tight
connection between non-analytical statements and observables it
became possible for this relationship to take the form of confirmability. This would also lead to a new criterion of significance:
metaphysics is distinguished from scientific knowledge in that
the latter is, in principle, confirmable.

Language and the unity of science
Contemporary discussions concerning the status of science and
appropriate scientific procedures are conducted largely on the
basis of the language employed - in contrast to references to an
idea of the object. Consequently, the dichotomy of verstehen
and erklären has given way to the question of whether the social
sciences should use the language of natural science or whether
an investigation of social phenomena necessitates the use of
such concepts as will, intention, meaning. On this basis, the
hermeneutic critique of scientism can avoid taking a merely
opposing standpoint, and thereby be more easily shrugged-off,
since it too has experienced a 'linguistic turn' and can therefore engage scientism on its own ground. This ground has
largely been staked out by discussions about the language of
science which originate in the Vienna Circle and it acts as the
terra firma from which scientistically oriented approaches launch
their offensives against such recalcitrant disciplines as sociology.

A brief look at the emergence of the linguistic underpinning of
the imperialism of scientism should commence with a reference to
Neurath's contribution. It was he who first raised objections
against the metaphysical elements introduced into the discussions
by Wittgenstein's closest associate, Schlick,[12] which he feared
might lead to a 'philosophy of the inexpressible'. Neurath termed

Scientism and hermeneutics 21

his alternative to the distinction between statement and fact, and the attendant view that the ultimate propositions of the philosophy of science were not open to further analysis, 'physicalism' and regarded it as the core of his projected 'unity of science'.

The main point in favour of a 'physicalist language' as the language of unified science concerns its ability to satisfy the two central aspects of science: intersubjectivity and universality. The formulation of such a language could either be undertaken by constructing a public language from the private languages of individuals[13] or on the basis that all linguistic expressions are public at the outset. Both approaches differ in significant aspects but converge on some significant points, especially the role of 'protocol-sentences'.

Carnap has rightly viewed the status of protocol sentences as the central issue in the 'Logic of Science (theory of knowledge)' (Carnap). Questions concerning the status of knowledge - facti and iuris - are solved within the context of the formalization of the process of science and its reconstruction. The implications of this position have a direct bearing on the twin concerns of scientism, physicalism and unity of science, which are linked in the following way: 'the thesis of Physicalism is a syntactical doctrine which states that every significant statement is, or is equivalent with, a physicalist sentence. An intersubjectively valid and unified science results from the rigorous application of the principles of the physicalisation of languages' (Bergmann, 1954, p. 280).

Neurath's conception of the unified science programme contrasts with the phenomenalist language developed in Carnap (1928) in its insistence on a thoroughly physicalist approach. Even though the latter recognized the motivation behind Neurath's position to be his commitment to (dialectical) materialism - 'itself as much a pseudo-thesis as idealism' (Carnap in Schilpp, p. 51) - he eventually followed Neurath's lead and endorsed the view that the 'intersubjectivity' of language is guaranteed by 'the fact that the events described in the language are, in principle, observable by all users of the language' 'Carnap in Schilpp 1963, p. 52).

The first result of this change of heart appeared in 1932 in an essay entitled 'Physicalist language as the universal language of science' where he introduced the term 'protocol sentences'. These he regarded as providing the basis for all other scientific sentences and, as such, they represent the physicalist reformulation of the 'elementary experience' referred to in the Aufbau as the most basic form of apprehending the given. Neurath, while on the whole favourably inclined towards this conception, nevertheless introduced some conventionalist elements to attenuate the vestiges of absolutism inherent in claims to certainty as embodied in 'basic statements'; for him, there are 'no means for using definitely ascertained and purified protocol sentences as

22 *Scientism and hermeneutics*

the starting point of science. There is no "tabula rasa". We are
like seamen who have to rebuild their ship on the open sea without being able to dismantle it in a dry-dock and reassemble it
anew from its components' (Neurath, 1933, p. 206). No knowledge
is devoid of imprecisions - 'they always remain somehow part of
the ship . . . only metaphysics can disappear completely' (1933,
p. 206). In the same paper Neurath also gives an outline of the
form of protocol sentences. They always include the name of a
person and reference to time, space, and perceptions. The
question of how one is to distinguish between acceptable and
unacceptable statements Neurath could only answer by demand-
ing that new protocol sentences should fit in with already established ones - thereby taking the first step away from a hard-
line inductivist stance and introducing an element of arbitrariness
into metascientific discussions.

Carnap quickly accepted that protocol sentences cannot be
regarded as somehow privileged - in fact, 'there are no absolutely
basic sentences in the construction of science' (Carnap, 1933,
p. 22). That also means that there is no definite point beyond
which reduction is no longer possible. In this essay, which
followed that by Neurath in the same issue of 'Erkenntnis',
Carnap also draws out the differences in approach between himself and Neurath - while acknowledging that both forms are
justified. In his version, protocol sentences are situated outside
a systems language (i.e. the language of physics) and are translated into the latter with the help of rules of transformation.
Physicalist language represents the intersubjective means of
formulation sought by Logical Empiricism and includes, as universal language, protocol language as a part. The point about such
a universal language is that every sentence can be translated
into it, i.e. reduced to merely quantitative concepts. Neurath,
sensing remnants of an earlier dualism, preferred to regard all
sentences as intersubjective and as part of a unitary language.
The form of protocol sentences could, therefore, no longer remain arbitrary. They have to conform to the rules of syntax
as laid down in the systems language; as a consequence, rules
of transformation would no longer be required either. A third
possibility mentioned by Carnap is an extension of Neurath's
view; here, 'every concrete sentence of the physicalist system
language can, potentially, serve as a protocol sentence' (1933,
p. 224).

These points of difference are really only of peripheral
importance for my purposes and I shall refrain from discussing
them. Instead, I find the area of agreement between the dis-
putants of more relevance. As has been indicated, Logical
Empiricism treats problems of knowledge, whether they emerge
in the context of philosophy or science, as soluble through
language analysis. The physicalist quest for the unity of science,
keeping in line with this approach, takes the form of establishing
an ideal language by means of which all scientific findings can

Scientism and hermeneutics   23

be meaningfully expressed. The possible form of such a language suggested by Carnap and Neurath has already been referred to. I would now like to outline the methodological consequences of physicalism, keeping in mind that Neurath quite specifically put forward this approach in an attempt to render nonsensical Dilthey's distinction between the natural and human sciences. I shall hereby, however, follow Carnap's position since it seems to have had greater resonance among like-minded philosophers of science while also providing a reformulation of the original tenets of physicalism.

The immediate problem confronting the attempt to translate all protocol sentences into physicalist language concerns the possibility of translating mental phenomena into quantitative concepts. Hempel's essay on 'The Logical Analysis of Psychology'[14] provides an exposition of what he very aptly calls 'logical behaviourism'. As the physicalist interpretation of psychology it insists on intersubjectivity in the investigation of mental phenomena through the use of 'physicalist terminology of observations' which were made at specific points in space and time. Hempel demonstrates how a statement of this kind: 'Paul has a toothache' can be reformulated so that 'all the circumstances which verify this psychological proposition are expressed by physical test sentences' (Hempel, 1949, p. 377). Such a reformulation can be achieved without any loss of content, which goes to show that 'the propositions of psychology are consequently physicalist propositions. Psychology is an integral part of physics. . . . This logical analysis of which the results show a certain affinity with the fundamental ideas of behaviourism, constitutes the physicalist conception of psychology' (1949, p. 378).

This radical formulation of physicalism did not escape severe criticism, forcing Carnap to modify his early stance and to suggest a new version: the reducibility of psychological terms to those of the 'thing-language'. Carnap expounded this view in a clear way in 'Logical Foundation of the Unity of Science'; this essay appeared after 'Testability and Meaning' and exhibits traces of pragmatistic, conventionalist, and operationalist influences. The treatment methodological issues have received here does not seem to have undergone any serious alteration since and can remain as a central tenet of scientism - and, in turn, scientistic sociology.

The empirical sciences are composed of physics and biology. One can distinguish among the latter between biology in the usual sense and another part that contains psychology and social science. The question arising now concerns, first, the characteristics separating the various branches of science and, second, the common denominator that allows them to be introduced into the fold of unified science. Following the strategy of the Vienna Circle the answer to these questions may only be given in logical terms, i.e. through the analysis of language; ontological

24 *Scientism and hermeneutics*

references to a distinction or unity within the object of science -
such as the mind/matter dualism - cannot be considered. As to
the first question, Carnap states that the boundary lines between
the various branches of biology are still not clearly determined;
this is mainly due to the difficulty of allocating specific areas of
investigation to specific scientific disciplines and to the fact that
new branches of science are continually emerging. Be this as it
may, the eventual solution to this question will ultimately be
found on linguistic grounds - as is already the case in the way
biology is distinguishable from physics.

The language of physics, containing terms 'for the description
of processes in inorganic nature', forms a 'sublanguage of the
language of science' (Carnap, 1936, p. 411). The laws of physics
formulated in this language are valid universally and are, therefore, also apparent in the phenomena which constitute the subject
matter of biology. In fact:

> the biologist has to know these laws of physics in studying the
> processes in organisms. He needs them for the explanation of
> these processes, but since they do not suffice he adds other
> laws not known by the physicist, viz. the specifically biological
> laws. Biology presupposes physics, but not vice versa. (1936,
> p. 411)

The formulation of the thesis of physicalism now offered is clearly
different from the one expounded by Neurath, Hempel, and the
early Carnap: the terms of biology, psychology and of social
science - or, rather, 'individual' and 'social behaviouristics' -
no longer have to be definable on the basis of a physicalist
language which usurped the role of the language of science;
physicalist language is now considered as a sub-language of science.
and its terms are reducible to those of the thing-language. The
latter provides the basis of everyday pre-scientific as well as
scientific sentences and is used for speaking about the properties of the observable (inorganic) things surrounding us. The
terms contained in it either 'designate what one may call observable properties, i.e. such as can be determined by direct observation . . . , observable thing-predicates', or they may express
'the disposition of a thing to a certain behaviour under certain
conditions . . . , disposition-predicates' which, however, 'are
reducible to observable thing-predicates because we can describe
the experimental conditions and the reactions characteristic of
such dispositions in terms of observable thing-predicates' (p. 416).

This thing-language, Carnap hoped, could avoid the pitfalls
of physicalist language when used for the description of phenomena in individual and social behaviouristics as advocated by
Neurath by providing an even narrower, or more basic, foundation for the language of science, i.e. 'a common reduction basis
for the terms of all branches of science' (p. 422).

The meaning of a term is known when 'we know under what

Scientism and hermeneutics 25

conditions we are permitted to apply it in a concrete case' (p. 413). Such knowledge can either be of an immediate, practical kind or involve the ability

> to give an explicit formulation of the conditions for the application of the term. If we now ascertain that term x is such that the conditions for its application . . . can be formulated with the help of the terms y, z, etc., we call such a formulation a *reduction statement* for x in terms of y, z, etc and we call x reducible to y, z, etc. . . .' (pp. 413-14)

Such statements, in their simplest form, can take the form of a definition or be of the 'if . . . then' kind.

With this conception of the unity of science, as brought about by the reduction of concepts used in any branch of science as well as those of everyday language to those of the thing-language, Carnap established an ingenious way out of the methodological difficulties Neurath's brash physicalism had run into. Instead of using physicalist terms for the description of processes, Carnap preferred the use of terms of observable properties - which led to the important consequence of allowing qualitative predicates into the language of science in addition to the quantitative space-time 'slang' (Neurath) of physicalist language; the only condition being that each term was to be reducible to 'observable thing-predicates'; that is, 'we can apply it either on the basis of direct observation or with the help of an experiment for which we know the conditions and the possible result determining the application of the term in question' (p. 416).

As Carnap states,[15] these views were further developed in communication with Hempel and Feigl and eventually clarified on the basis of the distinction between observation language and theoretical language referred to earlier. This modification is based on the recognition that scientific concepts cannot be interpreted completely and that the statements of scientific language cannot be translated into observational terms. Carnap suggested the construction of a language of science consisting of two parts:

> the observation language which is presupposed as being completely understood . . . speaks about observables, and the theoretical language of the network. The partial interpretation for the theoretical language is then given by rules of correspondence which permit the derivation of sentences of the one language from sentences of the other. (Carnap in Schilpp, 1963, p. 78)

On balance, Carnap considered that the disadvantages of his scheme, viz. the incomplete interpretation of theoretical terms and the impossibility of translating theoretical sentences into the observation language, as being outweighed by 'the greater

26 *Scientism and hermeneutics*

advantage of the theoretical language, viz. the great freedom of concept formation and theory formation, and the great explanatory and predictive power of a theory' (p. 80). If anybody should still be in doubt, it would only be necessary to point to

> the prodigious growth of physics since the last century . . . [which] . . . depended essentially upon the possibility of referring to unobservable entities like atoms and fields. In our century, other branches of science such as biology, psychology and economics have begun to apply the method of theoretical concepts to some extent. (p. 80)

PRAGMATISM BETWEEN HERMENEUTIC AND SCIENTISTIC THOUGHT

Carnap's later formulation of the criterion of meaningfulness bears witness to the fusion that occurred between neo-positivist and pragmatistic thought upon the emigration of members of the original Vienna Circle to the United States.[16] This development is most clearly expressed in the work of Morris who continued the project of a unified science in the course of editing the 'Encyclopedia of Unified Science' founded by Neurath.

I should like to refer briefly to the contributions of the founder of pragmatism, Peirce, and its most famed contemporary representative, Quine, to indicate a related, though different and possibly more influential, formulation of the criterion for meaningfulness.

As a philosopher of science, Peirce had anticipated the concerns of the Vienna Circle, viz. the explication of the meaning of general terms, and had introduced a solution that proved rather more fruitful than the construction of metalanguages.

The hermeneutic dimension in the thought of Peirce and Quine
Peirce's theory of meaning developed as an attack on the Cartesian method of doubt and it is worth singling out two aspects. First, the method of doubt cannot lead to the alteration of belief and merely terminates in the reaffirmation of the original belief; second, individual consciousness cannot assume the role of the ultimate test of certainty. The pursuit of knowledge is a communal task and reference to the clarity and distinctness of ideas does not suffice for determining the truth of knowledge. The certainty seen as attaching to science due to the presentation of its accumulated knowledge in axiomatic or deductive form neglects the provisional character of its fundamental theoretical axioms. Rather than forming a finalized body of knowledge, science is always open to reformulation and its progress owes more to the perfection of its methodological rules than to the unshakeable certainty of its axioms. In place of the rationalist conception of meaning Peirce formulates what has come to be

Scientism and hermeneutics   27

known as the 'pragmatic maxim': 'consider what effects, which might conceivably have practical bearings, we conceive the object of our conception to have. Then, our conception of these effects is the whole of our conception of the object.'[17]

The practice-oriented approach is concerned not with a theory of the language of science, but with a theory of inquiry: the statements of science contain nouns and adjectives the meaning of which can be ascertained by observing their effects in a test situation. Meaningful statements are in turn identified by the application of the criterion of practical effectiveness. Peirce also places great emphasis on the existence of a 'community of investigators' which decides on whether a hypothesis can be regarded as confirmed and eligible for being incorporated into the body of existing knowledge.

In the work of Quine the scientism of the neo-positivist philosophy of science is challenged in two of its central tenets. Focusing on the impossibility of explicating analyticity – whether this can be attempted through definition, interchangeability of synonyms, or employment of semantic rules – on account of the circularity of this attempt, Quine concludes that 'for all its reasonableness, a boundary between analytical and synthetic statements simply has not been drawn. That there is such a distinction to be drawn at all is an unempirical dogma of empiricists, a metaphysical article of faith' (Quine, 1961, p. 37).

A second dogma that Quine sets out to refute is the verification theory of meaning. In keeping with the difficulty Quine is known to be experiencing in trying to make sense of the term 'meaning' such a theory proves welcome gist to his logical mill. 'Radical reductionism', as exemplified by the early Carnap, states that meaningful statements have to be translatable into statements about immediate experiences which are formulated in a physicalist language. Even though Carnap himself revised this position, the dogma continues in existence in the belief that each statement 'taken in isolation from its fellows, can admit of confirmation or infirmation' (p. 41). Following Duhem, Quine puts forward the view that 'our statements about the external world face the tribunal of sense experience not individually but only as a corporate body' (p. 41).

Quine traces the dichotomy of analytical and synthetic truths and the reductionism of the verification theory of meaning to the same root: the attempt to differentiate between language and experience by reference to individual statements. Statements in which the linguistic content only is relevant, i.e. 'analytical' statements, represent a limiting case of factual statements the truth of which depends on confirmation by experience. The consideration of statements as units of critical examination represents an intermediate stage between the term-by-term approach of Locke and Hume and Quine's view that 'the unit of empirical significance is the whole of science' (p. 42). Reaffirming the pragmatistic stance, Quine goes on to reject the central tenet

28 Scientism and hermeneutics

of the Vienna Circle – the possibility of distinguishing clearly
and at all times between speculative metaphysics and natural
science. He does so in only four pages and in a style so vivid
and lucid that one hesitates to attempt a summary of his argument. I shall only note two points: one, science, as a total
field of force, is underdetermined by its boundary conditions,
experience. Contrary experiences can therefore be accounted
for by more than one revised statement and no statements, even
those constituting the core of science – e.g. analytical statements such as logical laws – can be regarded as immune to
revision. Two, science is a continuation of common sense and as
such exhibits a certain trait that is shared by atomic physics
and an Homerian epos: the introduction of entities in order to
simplify theory. Quine's radical instrumental pragmatism leads
to the view that:

> in point of epistemological footing the physical objects and the
> goods differ only in degree and not in kind. Both sorts of
> entities enter our conception only as cultural points. The myth
> of physical objects is epistemologically superior to most in that
> it has proved more efficacious. (p. 44)

Pragmatism, science, and the behaviourist theory of language
As was mentioned earlier, pragmatist philosophy of science
emphasizes the judgment exercised by the community of scientists
in the conduct of scientific inquiry, thereby following the lead
given by Peirce. It can, however, be argued that both Peirce
and Quine fail to recognize fully the hermeneutic dimension and
its consequences on account of their preoccupation with instrumental language at the expense of everyday language.
Peirce's recognition of the social context of knowing in general
and the 'quasi-transcendental' status of the 'community of investigators' for science helped to supersede the merely logistic
approach of the Logic of Science. Apel and Habermas have
referred to this position as the transformation of Kantian epistemology into a critical semiotics and a transcendental logic of
inquiry. To summarize Habermas' argument: Peirce ultimately
fails to avoid a 'hidden positivism' in his logic of inquiry. At the
root of this lies Peirce's application of the 'maxim of pragmatism'
to both mind and matter. By taking this route, i.e. the formulation of an operationalist conception of mind, Peirce is prevented
from engaging in a full self-reflection of the pragmatist conception of science which became possible with the recognition of the
community of investigators. He can analyse the conditions on
the basis of which investigators arrive at a consensus only in
terms of purposive action and fails to realize that their discussions proceed on the basis of intersubjectivity, conceived
not in monological terms – as in the Logic of Science – but in
dialogue through the 'symbolically mediated interaction of social
subjects who recognize and accept each other as individuals.

Scientism and hermeneutics   29

This *communicative action* represents the frame of reference that
cannot be reduced to that of *instrumental action*' (Habermas,
1968, p. 176). The relationship between scientists is

> constituted on the basis of intersubjectivity that reaches
> beyond the transcendental frame of instrumental action. The
> communication between scientists draws on insights which are
> tied to the frame of symbolically mediated interaction for the
> dialogical clarification of metatheoretical issues; these insights
> are prerequisites for the acquisition of technically utilizable
> knowledge - even though they cannot be legitimized through
> the categories of this knowledge. (p. 178)

The normative basis of science, its hermeneutic dimension, is
still proving a major irritant to scientism. Contemporary pragmatistic thought on this matter has followed the 'linguistic turn'
and now tries to reconcile the status of the community of scientists and the centrality of communicative processes within it
through recourse to a behaviourist theory of language-acquisition.
Quine's reformulation of empiricism

> comes of the old empiricism by a drastic externalization. The
> old empiricist looked inward upon his ideas, the new empiricist
> looks outward upon the social institution of language; . . .
> talk of ideas comes to count as unsatisfactory except insofar
> as it can be paraphrased into terms of dispositions of observ-
> able behaviour. (Quine, 1969, pp. 97-8)

With the help of this conception, the objectivity of scientific
knowledge can again be accounted for through reference to the
intersubjectivity of observation sentences. A speech community
can agree on the meaning of a scientific statement and thereby
judge whether it can be incorporated into the body of scientific
knowledge or not: 'Observation takes its provisional place as
arbiter of science. Observation sentences for the arbitrating
community are the sentences on which that community can reach
immediate agreement' (Quine, 1970, p. 19). So far, Quine would
seem to be in agreement with other philosophers of science who
equally stress the communicative aspect in the development of
science and who see in linguistic communication the a priori of
scientific knowledge. Any notion that Quine may have the
slightest sympathy with hermeneutic philosophy is quickly and
incisively dispelled by completing the above quotation which
ends with the qualification 'under appropriate stimulation' (p. 19).
The view of language-acquisition and development implied in
this statement has, of course, nothing to do with the capacity of
language to disclose our world or with its being tied to 'forms
of life' (Wittgenstein). Any meaning a statement may possess is
due to its publicly accessible depiction of reality in a true way.
Reflexivity in and through language merely leads to a clouding

30 *Scientism and hermeneutics*

of the picture we gain of the world; Quine prefers his knowledge neat. Scientists can agree because they are stimulated in a corresponding way and science is possible as an objective activity because observation sentences agreed upon give a true account of reality. The consensus achieved is therefore a post festum affair: a consequence of being confronted with true statements. As Quine remarks in his critique of Hanson, 'as dissident theorists converge toward observation sentences they converge to agreement' (1970, p. 16). But what guarantees that different scientists will interpret the evidence in front of them in identical ways? Obviously an identical way of using language - as conceived of in a behaviourist theory of language-acquisition.

Watson (1928) applied a physicalist language to the study of human actions in contrast to the then dominant introspective psychology. In conjunction with the conceptualizations provided by Pavlov (1927), this approach gave rise to behaviourism and experimental psychology. Even though it has its origins in the study of animal behaviour, this approach soon proved successful even in the field of human phenomena and it found its most ambitious application in the study of the most distinctly human characteristic: the acquisition of language. Skinner (1957) developed classical behaviourism by refining its basic vocabulary which centred on the stimulus-response schema. His concept of 'reinforcement' stresses the importance of rewards in the habitualizing of approved behaviour; the concept of 'operants', which refers to spontaneously emitted motor responses and which led to the 'Skinner Box', replaces the concept of 'reflexes'. With this apparently simple conceptual apparatus Skinner then constructed a theory of learning which depicts the processes involved in an organism adapting to its environment. Certain responses to given stimuli would, if successful, be reinforced. Linguistic behaviour can equally be seen as a - particularly successful - mode of adapting to the environment and it develops in ways that can be explained by reference to observable causal mechanisms.

In my view, Quine's recourse to a behaviourist theory of language and language-learning does not eliminate the hermeneutic dimension in science but merely shifts the debate on to a different ground. I shall follow the argument on to this ground and, very schematically, indicate the ineradicability of the hermeneutic dimension even on the level of language-learning and use.

The locus classicus for the rationalist critique of behaviourism is Chomsky's (1959) review of Skinner (1957). In linguistic terms, a rationalist approach to the study of language assumes 'that various formal and substantive universals are intrinsic properties of the language-acquisition' (Chomsky, 1971, p. 136) and focuses on theoretical accounts of transformational grammar as specific forms of generative grammars.[18] The latter refer to the celebrated distinction between 'surface' and 'deep structures'

Scientism and hermeneutics 31

which Chomsky developed in order to account for the fact that:

a child will be able to construct and understand utterances which are quite new, and are, at the same time, acceptable sentences in his language. Every time an adult reads a news-paper, he undoubtedly comes upon countless new sentences which are not at all similar, in a simple physical sense, to any that he has heard before, and which he will recognize as sentences and understand; he will also be able to detect slight distortions or misprints.' (1971, p. 137).

Phenomena like these, and the realization that all existing languages can be reconstructed on the basis of a limited matrix of elements, would suggest that 'talk of "stimulus generalization" simply perpetuates the mystery under a new title. These abilities indicate that there must be fundamental processes at work quite independently of "feedback" from the environment' (p. 137).

Put briefly, the human mind is pre-programmed in the sense of containing a deep structure which allows the generation of every possible language. Consequently, behaviourist reference to the role of reinforcement in language-acquisition is unable to account for the rules that competent speakers employ in formulating or understanding completely original sentences, that is, the creative capacity inherent in language.

If the rationalist critique is valid in its central points then it would appear that the empiricistic-behaviourist underpinning of scientism is insupportable because knowledge-acquisition in general and science in particular have now to be conceived of as a rational-empirical activity in which such imponderables as predisposition, reflexivity, imagination, genetic structuration play a central part.

Outline of a hermeneutic theory of language
In the debate with behaviourism Chomsky occupies a somewhat extreme rationalist position as is exemplified in his stress on the innate, aprioristic preformation of the human mind. This is not to deny that 'as far as acquisition of language is concerned, it seems that reinforcement, casual observation . . . are important factors (Chomsky, 1971, p. 137). Yet Chomsky does not seem very successful in relating continuity and change apart from asserting that a determined structure provides both the pre-conditions and limitations of any surface manifestation.

A more flexible account is apparent in the work of Piaget who, like Chomsky, fervently attacks empiricist dogma but who also rejects the latter's 'innatism'. Piaget is highly topical, in particular because he tries to settle the age-old conflict between empiricist and rationalist, or 'nativist' as he calls it, conceptions through the study of how we actually come to acquire knowledge; here the stress is firmly placed on the active part played by the child in the development of his knowledge of the world.[19] In par-

32 Scientism and hermeneutics

ticipating in practical life activities the child not merely acts on the basis of given structures but also creates new ones. It is the dynamic aspect characteristic of Piaget's theory of knowledge that is of particular interest. Whether the conception of thought as interiorized action, as the product of the interaction between biological substratum and concrete experiencing, does in fact do justice to all forms of knowledge, and I am thinking here in particular of normative knowledge which develops in interaction with other subjects, is a question which can be pursued a little further.

The communicative element in language-learning relates to the pragmatic dimension of language itself which remains unaccounted for in Chomsky's reconstruction of the system of abstract rules which is presupposed in the use of language. I can turn to linguistic philosophy for an account of this dimension.

Austin's early theory of speech acts recognized that there exist utterances which do not aim to be true or false ('constatives') but where saying something is doing something. Among the latter, which he called 'performatives', fall utterances such as 'I promise'.

Austin's later general theory of speech acts considered all utterances as ways of 'doing', an insight which Searle developed further by considering the speech act as the basic unit of meaning.[20] Utterances are now seen to contain 'propositional content' and 'illocutory force' which is to say that the referential (semantic) and pragmatic components of an utterance are fused in an utterance such as 'I promise you that . . .'. Here the illocutory force which establishes the terms on which the speaker and listener interact is contained in the dominant sentence, the 'performative', and the 'what' of the communication in the dependent sentence which usually contains a referring and a predicative element. Communication in this view entails that speaker and listener not only apprehend what is being said but they also identify given pragmatic intentions. This theory of language-use overarches linguistic competence - which allows a speaker to construct and comprehend grammatically correct and semantically meaningful elements of a natural language - by pointing to the pragmatic dimension in which language as a structured system is transformed into speech.

Incorporating both the work of Chomsky and Searle, Habermas adumbrates a hermeneutically - oriented theory of language-development.

Linguistic competence refers to a monological capability in the development and use of language which is here seen as being stimulated, rather than formed, in the process of socialization. 'Communication' can consequently only be considered as an exchange of information in which participants encode and decode sounds with the help of a shared competence - that of constructing and comprehending grammatically meaningful sentences. If communication is, however, to be seen as a dialogical

Scientism and hermeneutics 33

process, then Chomsky's approach has to be complemented by a theory which evidences the pragmatic rules employed in the uttering of sentences in a speech act. These rules are the object of a universal pragmatics which assumes that communicative competence is based on a competence equally as universal as the ability to construct grammatically correct sentences. The emphasis on such 'dialogue-constitutive rules' which are regarded as the 'universal conditions of possible agreement' (Habermas, 1976, p. 20) acts as a strong reminder of the hermeneutic dimension of language. Monological conceptions which exclude the pragmatic element in language cannot account for the intersubjectivity of the meaning of statements.

HERMENEUTICS AND THE 'NEW PHILOSOPHY OF SCIENCE'[21]

Through focusing on formalized language, scientistic philosophy of science attempts to account for the intersubjectivity of the meaning-content of scientific statements. To put the same point differently, scientific knowledge is objective to the extent to which it achieves the elimination of all factors pertaining to the subjectivity of the participants in the enterprise and the socio-historic context of science. A hermeneutic critique of scientism would consequently aim at evidencing the hermeneutic dimension presupposed in this view, to show that 'theoretical Reason has itself a normative basis' (Lorenzen, 1970, p. 60).

This normative basis refers to the use of everyday language in establishing the norms of scientific procedures within the scientific community and forms the 'communicative a priori' (Apel) or the 'a priori of argumentative reasoning' (Habermas). As such, it makes possible the establishing of a consensus concerning empirical statements; or, rather, it grounds forms of argumentation in which experiences act only as supports but not as final arbiters. Such a grounding 'has nothing to do with the relation between individual statements and reality, but refers to the coherence between sentences within a system of speech' (Habermas, 1973e, p. 245). Communication, in Habermas' view, aims at the formation of a 'rational consensus' among participants; as such, it has to satisfy a number of 'validity claims': intelligibility (utterances have to be comprehensible); truth (their propositional content has to be true); correctness (they are formulated in an acceptable way in given circumstances); sincerity (the speakers are interacting in good faith). These validity claims are, in fact, presupposed in every communicative act and they can be substantiated if so required. In the case of claims to truth and correctness this takes the form of a 'discourse' in which, given an 'ideal speech situation', the force of the better argument will prevail.

As far as the hermeneutic dimension in the scientific process

34 Scientism and hermeneutics

is concerned, this position would allow the following argumentation: Statements referring to the world of perceived and manipulatable objects can be examined in relation to their truth content in the context of a 'theoretical discourse'. In such a 'co-operative search for truth', as a communicative enterprise, the validity claims underlying all communication will again be operative - including not merely the theoretical-empirical but also the normative-practical ones.

Habermas's explication of the communicative basis of science would provide a further argument against scientistic conceptions which rely, generally, on a correspondence theory of truth and the assumed possibility to distinguish at all times between facts and statements of facts. In Habermas's view, 'facts' are not entities 'out there' but exist only as correlates of propositions on the level of argumentative reasoning. Their meaning cannot be ascertained outside the process of theoretical discourse. Habermas would seem to support Gadamer's view on this point when he states that we can 'never move outside of the sphere of language' (Habermas, 1973a, p. 216).

Considering again the language employed in the scientific process we recall that the - formal - language advocated in the Logic of Science approach is constructed solely along syntactic-semantic lines, thereby filtering out the unexpressed field of meaning surrounding the concepts of everyday language. Yet, because the artificial (mathematical or the thing) language employed in the description of objectified processes is the result of an abstraction from the practical use of language it remains, by this fact, tied to it. These instrumental languages

> have no community of speech or life as their basis but are introduced and employed merely as means and tools of communication. It is for this reason that they have to presuppose actually practised understanding. . . . As we know, the agreement through which artificial languages are introduced belongs to a different language (Gadamer, 1975, p. 422).

Everyday language is the last metalanguage. This insight has also been expressed by Kaplan, who is himself associated with the pragmatist tradition, in a succinct way: 'every scientific language, however technical, is learned and used by way of the common language of everyday life; it is everyday language to which we inevitably turn for the clarification of scientific meanings '(Kaplan, 1964, p. 45).

The centrality of communication in the development of theoretical-instrumental knowledge provides also the starting point for a critique of two aspects of contemporary scientism which is presented in its most enlightened form by Popper.

Popper's falsificationism contains an important critique of some tenets of empiricistic metascience - in particular its inductivist conception of the development of scientific knowledge -

Scientism and hermeneutics   35

while remaining itself within the orbit of scientism. He recognizes that scientific statements cannot be verified once-and-for-all but are accepted only after rigorous attempts at falsifying them have been negative. The acceptance of statements thus 'corroborated' is still provisional and is also subject to the consent of the scientific community. Scientists are able to come to an agreement on account of their mutual application of rational criteria as embodied in logically coherent argumentation. In this sense, the 'rationalism' advocated by Popper is a 'critical' one in that any statement purporting to be scientific is made available, and lends itself, to refutation in the course of argument or empirical testing; but the rationality of this procedure is itself not amenable to further justification resting, as it does, on the 'irrational' opting for Reason in an 'act of faith' (Popper, 1966, vol. II, p. 232).

This conception locates Popper between scientism and the new philosophy of science in that he rejects the myth of theory-free observation while also denying truth value to statements that form, and ongoingly reaffirm, the normative basis of science. The former point can be illustrated in reference to Popper's rejection of the criterion of meaningfulness suggested by the Logic of Science in favour of 'a criterion of demarcation, designed to demarcate systems of scientific statements from perfectly meaningful systems of metaphysical statements' (Popper, 1959, p. 312). This solution to the 'Kantian problem' which re-admits metaphysics as a cognitive mode of thought with hypothesis-generating potential in the course of welcoming any bold, imaginative thought to the process of scientific inquiry, has two important ramifications: one, all statements of science remain provisional; if determined attempts at falsifying them have failed they can still only provisionally be accepted as 'corroborated'. Truth can be approached only asymptotically and we have to settle for 'verisimilitude'. Two, with the rejection of the inductivist view of the growth of knowledge we have to jettison the 'bucket theory of knowledge' as well in favour of a rationalist position. A methodological upshot from this viewpoint then leads to the advocacy of a 'hypothetico-deductive' model of explanation.

Popper has from the outset acted as the 'loyal opposition' (Popper) to the Vienna Circle and his loyalty to the scientistic programme[22] is not only evident in his abandoning the normative basis of science to irrationality but also in his assumption that the falsification of hypotheses can avail itself of 'independent evidence' against which scientific statements are 'independently testable' (Popper, 1974, p. 24, p. 67). This view clashes with one of the central tenets of critical rationalism 'that the apparent "data" of experience were always interpretations in the light of theories, and therefore affected by the hypothetical or conjectural character of all theories' (1974, p. 387).[23]

The embeddedness of science in everyday language can appear to the Logic of Science and Popper's Logic of Inquiry only as a

36 *Scientism and hermeneutics*

threat to the objectivity of science - as Bacon already anticipated in his exhortation to beware of the various 'idols', including those introduced through the language employed. Yet, as the argument so far has revealed, scientism can be overcome only in the recognition of the hermeneutic dimension in science itself.

Post-Popperian philosophy of science and hermeneutic philosophy have arrived at similar insights about the process and status of science, even though they proceeded from different intellectual traditions. The startling congruence of the results of their investigations may, perhaps, be due to their common approach to metascientific problems: the preference for a description - phenomenological or historical - of what actually happens, as opposed to the 'philosophic' prescriptions characteristic of the Logic of Science approach and its concern with the logic of verification rather than that of discovery. The reconstruction of the possibility of science has uncovered the historic, social and psychological conditions for the growth of knowledge, i.e. the pragmatic dimension in addition to the mainly semantic and syntactic analyses of the previously dominant approach, and it has given rise to the new philosophy of science.

Kuhn's notion of 'paradigms' underlying the work of scientists redirected the focus from the internal development of the cumulative growth of knowledge towards the socio-historical embeddedness of science and the occurrence of gestalt-switches which underlie major redirections in the conceptualization and investigation of the object of science. New conceptual frames form different language-games which allow not only the discovery of new facts but also the re-interpretation of previously established ones. New theories do not 'speak the same language'[24] as previous ones and contain different standards of rationality. The normative function of paradigms precludes the possibility of judging their relative superiority from the outside since that would only constitute the unwarranted application of external standards originating in a different language-game.

This view could be expressed in hermeneutic terminology as a confirmation of the universality of the hermeneutic dimension, i.e. of language and communication as the basis of the growth of science.

2 THE RISE OF A SCIENCE OF SOCIETY AND ITS NORMATIVE PRESUPPOSITIONS

With the evident success of science as a mode of knowledge-acquisition it comes as no surprise to find its rationality extending on to spheres other than the natural. Weber's reference to the 'disenchantment' of the world attending the rationalization of cultural and social processes describes this development well. Concomitant with it the study of society also hoped to reach the 'secure path of science' through adopting the methods of the natural sciences – once social processes came to be seen as important topics of research and being qualitatively similar to natural ones.

The Enlightenment saw the emergence of a 'social physics' at a stage of economic and socio-political development which made it possible to conceive of society in mechanistic terms as propelled by ascertainable laws which could themselves be brought under rational control on the basis of sound knowledge. The realization that society itself could be re-established on a rational basis provided the impetus for a thorough critique of existing institutions which did not conform to rationalist conceptions – as they found expression in the entrepreneurial stress on wealth-creation and self-determination in opposition to the parasitism and authoritarianism of the feudal establishment. Philosophers gathered around the 'encyclopédie' articulated this new way of seeing which placed rational and active man at the centre of the historical stage. They could consider themselves as the teachers of society.

The elitism inherent in such an educational programme foreshadows the role of sociologists as the new 'priests' of society and the 'experts' in the technocratic steering of society.[1] This tendency towards a new form of dogmatism, exemplified by sociology replacing theology as the 'queen of the sciences', became manifest in post-revolutionary France as positivist thinkers attempted to weld together an emphasis on certain and constructive knowledge and a socio-political programme that envisaged the reconstruction of society along sound and harmonious lines. It is therefore in the programme of Positivism that a characteristic unity between a normatively oriented theory and a technocratically oriented practice is achieved which is underpinned by a focus on scientific rationality.

Sociology replaced the normatively oriented critique of political philosophers in an epoch in which the upheaval associated with the industrial and political revolutions called for the attempt to

37

38 *The rise of a science of society*

reintegrate society in the face of systematic social conflict. During this period social processes became progressively less transparent as social relationships came to be mediated by, and subordinated to, the market mechanism. In these conditions sociology promised to provide the know-how for the steering of society.

The history of sociology shows the integration of empiricist tenets into a normative framework in positivist sociology to have been followed by the outright rejection of any 'preconceived ideas' in favour of the unbiased accumulation of facts. In this chapter I wish to trace the development from positivist to scientistic sociology in the course of which sociology gradually and conveniently 'forgot' about its normative context of origin and present-day use.

I consider scientistic sociology as the heir to positivism, yet being underpinned by the rejection of any obvious socio-political commitment. The scientistic self-understanding of contemporary sociologists is, however, only the 'false consciousness' of servants of the powers-that-be and only acts to facilitate the use of the fruits of their labour for the purpose of control, and sometimes manipulation, in 'the best interest of society' - as defined by the most powerful groups within it. How is the 'false consciousness' maintained, though?

Here I would argue that the conflict between the purported value-free reflection of what is 'given' and the normative aspects of such an approach to social phenomena - which invests facticity with moral justification - is 'resolved' through being ignored. In this context empiricist methodology serves as the ideology of scientistic sociology, making a virtue out of the disinclination to reflect upon the presupposition and use-context of scientistic sociology.

Yet, support of the status quo and an interest in control, which is reflected in the monologically conceived relationship of subject and object, is inherent in instrumental-rational thought once it is applied to social phenomena. This interest does not go away through being ignored, it merely

> recedes into the background so that it disappears from the consciousness of those participating in research. In this way, the appearance of pure theory can maintain itself in the self-understanding of the modern empirical sciences, too. In fact, the technological exploitability of scientistic research . . . is prefigured in the structure of statements, i.e. conditional predictions which follow the control of the success of actions inherent in the apparatus of social labour; the same applies to the pre-selection of fields of possible experience to which its assumptions refer and which provides their testing-ground. (Habermas, 1973a, p. 33, pp. 51-2)

The rise of a science of society 39

POSITIVIST SOCIOLOGY AND ITS METASCIENCE

When one considers Comte's contribution to the development of
scientism and scientistic sociology it becomes apparent that he
added little to the clarification of metascientific issues. His
significance rests, instead, in the programmatic formulation of
the new discipline of 'Sociology' and the definite social programme
it was devised to serve: the reorganization of post-revolutionary
French society.

Since Comte figures as the father of sociology, or at least as
the inventor of the term, it is necessary to provide an outline
of his epistemological tenets. Comte's empiricist doctrine was
stated by J.S. Mill in the following way:[2]

> We have no knowledge of anything but phenomena; and our
> knowledge of phenomena is relative, not absolute. We know not
> the essence, nor the real mode of production, of any fact, but
> only its relation to other facts in the way of succession or
> similitude. These relations are constant, that is, always the
> same in the same circumstances. The constant resemblences
> which unite them as antecedent and consequent, are termed
> their laws. The laws of phenomena are all we know respecting
> them. Their essential nature, and their ultimate causes, either
> efficient or final, are unknown and inscrutable to us.

It is apparent that Mill restricts the positive philosophy to
metascience - which provides an early indication of his rejection
of Comte's social programme while still wishing to adhere to his
philosophy of science. That Positivism is more than a particular
formulation of the empiricist conceptions of knowledge will, however become obvious in the course of considering Comte's social
philosophy.

Comte's point of departure is Hume's sensationalism and the
rejection of the value and validity of metaphysics and theology
as claims to knowledge. To this he contributed the view that the
latter were necessary stages in the process which ended in the
scientific view of the world. His one important contribution to
the development of scientism consists in the identification of
knowledge with science and the justification he gave for it in the
form of the 'Law of Three Stages'. This law, which was equally
applicable to the intellectual development of the individual and
that of humanity, provided Comte with a criterion for separating
real knowledge from religious belief and metaphysical speculation.
What characterizes the scientific, or 'positive', phase? It gains
knowledge through the study of facts and regularities in society
and the formulation of these regularities as laws. In opposition
to the pseudo-explanations of theology, which take recourse to
supernatural or divine powers in an anthropomorphic projection,
and metaphysics, which appeals to entities behind the phenomena
and constitutes only the de-personalization of theology, scientific

40   *The rise of a science of society*

explanations proceed by subsuming single events under general laws.

Science itself can be grouped hierarchically. Each of the six component sciences thereby presupposes the one below without being wholly reducible to it. A number of insights have been derived from this and today form a central part of the scientistic creed. The most important aspect of this model for my purposes consists, however, in the place Comte accords to sociology at the apex of the hierarchy of Science; the 'queen of science' represents the point of culmination of the best in human thought. In the context of the development of scientism it marks the point where the method that has proved its worth in the control of nature is harnessed to the creation of a society to be presided over by sociologists and bankers.

Comte's normative conception of science is further justified by reference to some outstanding characteristics of its methodology which have been identified as certainty, accuracy and usefulness.[3] Sense-certainty refers to the evidence of perception and is achieved through the observation of what is given; methodical certainty, in addition, stems from the unity of methods employed and rests on the reliability of its results. Accuracy of knowledge is achieved through the formal construction of theories which allows for the deduction of hypotheses, if the rules guiding the combination of general statements and of observation and theories are observed. Usefulness, finally, has long been associated with natural science; Comte merely applies this criterion to knowledge gained in the social sphere.

The prima facie plausibility of these considerations, which will be dealt with again when it is shown how scientistic sociology has 'internalized' a technocratic interest through the adoption of a methodology conforming largely to these postulates, should not distract from a circularity which is apparent in the justification of the cognitive monopoly of science. 'Knowledge' is identified with scientific knowledge and science is concerned with a particular segment of the whole of human existence; it is in regard to the applicability of its methodological rules that the objects of science are chosen, but these rules are themselves derived from empiricist tenets, where they represent the elements that characterize true knowledge. Knowledge in the sciences emerges, then, from the observance of rules which guarantee true knowledge and these rules are unchallengeable since they have been proven to be successful in providing an accurate description of - objectified - reality.

Comte's distinction between science and metaphysics remains abstract, however. The problems that formed the subject-matter of the latter are not even considered and are regarded as meaningless from the outset.

According to Caird, Comte was aware of Kant's work only through hearsay.[4] Whether his misinterpretation of Kant is due

The rise of a science of society   41

to faulty sources or an unwillingness to enter into Kant's universe of discourse cannot be decided. But it can be stated that if he had had a more adequate understanding of Kant's fundamental insights it would have made a great change to his theorizing considering that for him any transcendental inquiry had to be part of metaphysics. Earlier philosophers 'were metaphysical while he isn't; they made assumptions and substituted their own ideas for the teaching of experience, while he has simply made his mind into a mirror of nature, and stated the facts as they are' (Caird, 1893, p. 67).

By identifying metaphysics in the narrower sense as a transcendental science which goes beyond the presuppositions of ordinary consciousness in order to bring to light the principles upon which it rests with ungrounded speculation he is led to reject the former with the latter. In fact, it is only because of this stance that he can remain blind to the fact that he himself uses 'bad' metaphysical arguments in rejecting the necessity and legitimacy of self-reflection. This refusal to reflect lies at the heart of the abstract renunciation of the principles of thought that had prevailed in the two preceding 'stages' - while nevertheless claiming to have ushered in the third and last 'stage' which transcends these expressions of inadequate human existence.

Comte's contribution to the metascientific aspect of scientism is, in the end, not his most famous or influential. The methodological directives for the study of the new subject-matter, society, can be summed up in his postulate that this study should employ the methods of the exact sciences. Comte's significance for sociology resides, in fact, more in the use it was put to in drawing up a blueprint for his particular kind of Utopia. A comprehensive social programme requires, of course, an adequate view of its object which Comte provided in his conception of society as an organism.[5]

J.S. Mill
Only during his 'Coleridgean period' did Mill affirm the need for an adequate notion of society, which he felt was lacking among his contemporaries. By the time he came to write the 'Logic' he was once again 'back in the fold' and espoused something of a 'methodological individualism' with a concomitant rejection of 'historic' conceptions.

In questions concerning the origin and status of knowledge, Mill accepts Locke's sensationalism and Berkeley's phenomenalism as a matter of course. In particular, the objectivity of statements about physical objects is vouched for by their being testable in experience. This important statement of the positivist credo suffered no rejection even though 'test by experience' can only mean reference to the way things appear to me, i.e. to sensations which do not occur in exactly the same way in every person due to differing sensibilities - a point recognized by Mill and answered

42   *The rise of a science of society*

through the assertion of the existence of 'material objects' which guarantee the permanency of one's sensations. 'Experience' as the foundation of knowledge could continue to play its role so long as it remained identical to sense experience.

In common with Comte, Mill's knowledge of German philosophy was scarce and second-hand. Drawing on Locke, he rejected the idea of 'intuitive knowledge' and attempted to derive our knowledge of space from sense-experience in an argument that resembles Berkeley's postulate that all our concepts of properties of physical objects derive from ideas of sensations. Of greater consequence is Mill's further endeavour to derive mathematics from sense-experience, thereby abolishing the last bastion of Rationalism in even going beyond Hume, who still accorded a priori status to mathematics. The axioms of geometry, in his view, represent laws of nature which we get to know in the only possible way: through experience. Their realistic (in the naive epistemological sense) status in turn guarantees their success if applied to reality in empirical science. In addition to a priori synthetic statements Mill, then, also rejects the truth value of analytical judgments.[6]

Mill's theory of science revolves around the two concepts of induction and deduction which are both contained within the syllogism where, however, only the former represents a genuine inference and establishes new truth; the conclusion from a premise, on the other hand, is merely 'apparent inference', i.e. is tautological and as such a logic of mere consistency. A syllogism is not without a 'logic of truth', however, which is operative in the formulation of the premise and leads to general propositions concerning facts; it is on the 'logic of truth' that the successful inference from single events to generalizations rests.

Before considering Mill's celebrated 'logic of experience' as applied to empirical science, it may be useful to inquire briefly into the nature of logical truth. Mill's extreme empiricism shows itself here to be based on a psychologism that draws on common-sense beliefs for its principles. Like empirical knowledge, mathematics and logic, too, have to be based on experience and induction. Mill considers, as logical truths, the axioms of 'Contradiction' and 'Excluded Middle' (Mill, 1970, bk II, ch. 5). Concerning the former, he states his view in opposition to 'Sir William Hamilton and the Germans' by regarding it

> to be like all other axioms, one of our first and most familiar generalizations from experience. The original foundation of it I take to be, that Belief and Disbelief are two different mental states, excluding one another. This we know by the simplest observation of our own minds.

The law of the Excluded Middle is, equally, 'simply a generalization of the universal experience that some mental states are directly destructive of other states'.

The rise of a science of society 43

The axioms of logic derive their necessity from past experience from which they are, in fact, inferred. The psychological basis of Mill's doctrine receives further elaboration in the 'Examination of "Sir William Hamilton's Philosophy",'written twenty years after the 'Logic'. The proof of the logic of truth in terms of the limits of our imagination and the all-pervasive characterization of experience is startingly inadequate in its reliance on general prejudice. It is not difficult to feel the same sense of astonishment as Husserl considering that, at the very point where the last foundations of all science are in question, we have recourse to this naive empiricism with its blind mechanism of association' (Husserl, 1970b, I, p. 114).

Mill's outline of the methodology of science has never been used in actual practice even though it prepared the ground for the development of the analytical mode of inquiry in the social sciences. In Book III, 'On Induction', he states the principles for the establishment of causal relationships in nature in which he draws on Bacon's tables. Mill distinguishes 'Four Methods of Experimental Inquiry': Of Agreement, Difference Residues and Concomitant Variation. The application of these methods of inquiry was held to yield new truths in all fields of inquiry – and 'science' was identified by the use of the methods of induction. This logical underpinning of the scientistic belief in the 'unity of science' is of an importance that can hardly be over-emphasized and found its seminal formulation in the 'Introductory Remarks': 'the backward state of the Moral Sciences can only be remedied by applying to them the methods of Physical Science, duly extended and generalized' (Mill, 1970, VI, 1).

In opposition to the monocausal explanation of social facts by Bentham and his school they must be treated as an aggregate of forces – as is the case of mechanics. It is not enough merely to enumerate singular instances of human behaviour and thereby arrive at empirical laws. What is required is a more general law which allows deductive inference – just as astronomy has to refer to natural philosophy for its principles so 'the sciences called moral have to rely for their explanation on ethology, the science of the formation of character . . . [as the] . . . Exact Science of Human Nature; for its truths are not, like the empirical laws which depend on them, approximate to generalizations, but real laws' (VI, 5, § 4).

In addition to the science of individual man, Mill considers the 'science of man in society; of the actions of collective masses of mankind; and the various phenomena which constitute social life' (VI, 6,§1). Two methods for the study of these phenomena are excluded from the outset: the Baconian method, of which Macaulay was the representative, termed the 'Experimental or Chemical mode' and the 'Abstract or Geometrical mode'. Due to the complexity of the object, the four methods of inquiry referred to above, as well as the 'interest philosophy of the Bentham school' are inapplicable. The nature of social phenomena requires

44   *The rise of a science of society*

the use of the 'physical or concrete deductive method'. The
actions of the individual are no doubt governed by psychological
and ethological laws, but the existence of a number of external
forces impinging on him does not allow the prediction of effects
from given causes unless we are in possession of generalizations
from history; and even then it is possible to only predict
tendencies, since it is not likely that all factors influencing
actions are known at a given point in time. Laws of society are,
therefore, impossible to achieve but it is nevertheless possible
to establish a deductive science that will 'teach us how to frame
a proper theorem for the circumstances of any given case'
(VI, 9, § 2).

The data formed into empirical laws, which are to be employed
in the deductive science of society, are established through the
use of statistics – which, of course, restricts the status of these
'laws' to that of generalizations. This use of empirical generalizations in conjunction with 'eternal' laws of human nature should
lay to rest the myth of Mill the naive empiricist; it is in contrast
to Bacon's method that his version of social physics is established.

Mill finally distinguishes two forms of sociological inquiry: the
first investigates the possible effects of certain causes given
certain conditions and takes the form of deductive empiricism;
the second, for which he advocates the use of the 'inverse or
historical method', inquiries into the 'causes which produce, and
the phenomena which characterize, States of Society in general'
(VI, 10, § 1) – which, really, adds little to Comte's formulation
of Social Statics and Social Dynamics as part of a General
Science of Society.

Having considered the metascientific tenets of Comte and Mill
and their methodological formulations of sociology, it would be
apposite to discuss the practical implications of their findings.
This should provide a number of insights into the relationship
between scientistic conceptions of social science and the socio-
political practice characteristic of Positivism.

THE USE-CONTEXT OF POSITIVIST SOCIOLOGY

If it can be said that classical sociology emerged in response to
Marx, then it is equally possible to speak of Comte's philosophy
to be an argument against les philosophes. It is in reference to
these latter that Comte's work derives its cogency since their
'revolutionary metaphysics' are at the root of 'the crisis in which
France has been plunged since 1789. . . though destined to
terminate the Revolution which began, throughout the West, in
the fourteenth century . . . (it) has not yet a decisive character. . . . Yet the need for radically reconciling order and progress has been more and more felt for sixty years' (Comte,
1847, p. 27). Positivism was hoped to supersede intellectual and

The rise of a science of society   45

social anarchy without falling into the trap of reactionaries who,
like De Maistre, demanded the renewed subordination to the
medieval order of Church and State. Comte's social mission consisted in synthesizing the revolutionary and reactionary principles
of metaphysics and theology - which took the form of 'sociology'.

Critical thought is identified by Comte with metaphysics, the
historical significance of which lay in its attack on the theological
world-view. Ironically, it merely substituted anthropomorphic
explanations by 'substance' or 'entities' which were nothing more
than 'the disembodied ghosts, the negative reflexions, of the
gods whose place they took' (Caird, 1893, p. 11). Its intellectual
roots were to be found in the individualistic implications of
British Empiricism which came to fruition in the atomism of
Diderot and d'Holbach and their attack on the Catholic faith.
Rousseau's theory of the Social Contract which reduces the
state to a creation of the individual will represents the unwarranted application of the principles of individualism away
from a theory of knowledge to that of society so that the latter
acquired solely negative characteristics as the agency that
corrupted the pristine goodness of Natural Man.

Metaphysics was essentially interwoven with a social philosophy
that gave primacy to the individual over society and is characterized by its sole focus on Reason to the detriment of Feeling and
Activity. Theology, on the other hand, subjected the intellect
to the Heart and only in Positivism does it acquire its proper
place; not as the slave but as the servant of the Heart: 'it
teaches that while it is for the heart to suggest our problems,
it is for the intellect to solve them' (Comte, 1848, p. 13).
History up to the era of Positivism had been marked by a conflict between the metaphysical, i.e. individualistic, and the
religious, i.e. ordered, conceptions of social existence. But 'the
antagonism which, since the close of the Middle Ages, has arisen
between Reason and Feeling is now at an end' (p. 27). The
advent of the era of Positivism is characterized by the attributes
of the term 'positive': 'reality . . . usefulness . . . certainty . . .
precision . . . and a directly organic tendency' (p. 27). The
latter sets it off from the spirit of metaphysics which is incapable
of organizing; it can only criticize. By contrast, the objective
of Positivism is twofold: 'to generalise our scientific conceptions,
and to synthesise the art of social life' (p. 2).

Comte's urgency at uniting theory and practice by drawing on
the insights established in the 'System of Positive Philosophy'
and the 'System of Positive Polity' is the result of a growing
frustration at the sight of the aftermath of the French Revolution.
He senses that the crisis that has agitated Western society during the previous five centuries is now entering its second, or
positive, phase in which the basis for a new society has to be
established. The profound questioning of authority that prepared
the ground for the Revolution had one immensely valuable
aspect: the destruction of Catholic feudalism. The rocking and

46   *The rise of a science of society*

final overthrow of an order that seemed eternal raised the horizon of men's thinking as they found that they could take their fate into their own hands. It seemed, however, that their newly found freedom led the thinkers of the Enlightenment to disregard the element of continuity in social change and thereby played into the hands of the 'retrograde school' of de Maistre. Comte's 'new philosophy' was to incorporate the valuable elements of these two opposing strands and thereby represented a step ahead which his 'illustrious and unfortunate predecessor Condorcet' (p. 47) was unable to take.

It is, of course, easy to dismiss Comte's work as merely eclectic; his 'synthesis', nevertheless, provides a marvellously clear exposition of the correspondence of a particular conception of social science and the uses it can be put to. When Comte feels he has gone beyond Condorcet he is correct in the sense that it is in his 'system' that the latter's conception of a social science can truly come into its own. Positivism, then, denotes a syncretism of a particular kind: the formulation of a social science along scientistic lines for purposes that originated with theological conceptions of the world. The potential inherent in natural science was to be used for 'the final emancipation of Humanity' (p. 49). Not in the sense which Bacon, for example, had intended - i.e. as a means for providing the material preconditions - but as a means for organizing society itself. The unity of theory and practice in Positivism, which can be 'looked at as a philosophical system or as an instrument of social renovation' (p. 93) provided an alternative to 'plain empiricism' and its 'anarchic tendencies'. Outside the framework of moral purpose scientific notions can only lead to scepticism. For Comte, 'progress', itself an idea originating with Christianity, can in this context only mean the gradual emergence of order, i.e. a political system akin to the one that existed under theocratic rule and is now to be officiated over by the new priests, social scientists.

In contrast to this appeal to technocracy allied with traditionalism one remembers the verve of les philosophes. Their optimism is infectious and may be attributed to their staunch support of Reason as a valid and indispensable source of truth. In their hands the revolutionary impact of British Enlightenment ideas expressed itself in the unrelentless questioning of the origins of religion, the sanctions of the social order, the sources of state authority. Coupled with the Renaissance belief in the value of education, itself based on the perfectability of man, these constituted an impressive force that was intent on sweeping away any institution found to be unable to fulfil men's needs.

Just as Comte, so Mill, too, holds the view that to 'recommend the separation of practice from theory is, therefore, simply to recommend bad practice'.[7] To enable the 'application of science to human welfare' one had to draw on social science to provide a framework for the reorganization of society. Its method[8]

The rise of a science of society 47

is that by which the derivative laws of social order must be sought. By its aid we may hereafter succeed not only in looking far forward into the future history of the human race, but in determining what artificial means may be used, and to what extent, to accelerate the natural progress in so far as it is beneficial. (Mill, 1970, X, § 8)

FROM POSITIVIST TO SCIENTISTIC SOCIOLOGY

The transition from positivist to scientistic sociology has already been defined as the 'purification' of social science which accompanied the absorption of sociology into academia. Among the constraints that sociology faced in its attempt to make itself 'respectable' I would refer in particular to the dilemma of having to be seen to be useful while at the same time eschewing any definite commitment - especially to 'outside' forces which were perceived as a potential or actual threat to the academic and political status quo. In this respect Durkheim, and even more so Weber, can be considered as figures at the threshold of modern - academic - sociology.

With the eventual failure of the Positivist programme, sociology had demoted itself from its assumed status as the queen of the sciences to that of the handmaiden of the powers that be. Abandoning all grandiose plans, it settled down to picture society as accurately as possible, looking neither to the left nor the right of the socio-historical context in which it found itself; nor did it lose a sense of propriety that prevented it, on the whole, from asking really awkward questions.[9] Gouldner put it eloquently:

Academic sociology, in its Positivistic heritage, thus emerged from the failure of Comteanism as a practical social movement for cultural reconstruction. Viewed historically, in relation to the Positivists' own aspirations, modern 'value free' Sociology is the anomic adaptation of Sociological Positivism to political failure, an adaptation that commonly takes a ritualistic form in which pure knowledge or the methodology of map-making tends to become an end in itself. (Gouldner, 1971, p. 102)

The ostentatious renunciation of any practical 'bias' need not be taken at face value; rather, the gloss of apparent neutrality which lasted well into the 1960s provided the precondition for its integration into the technocratic machinery of government. Sociologists recognized that they could no longer serve the two gods of science and social transformation, abdicated responsibility for the use made of their work, and fitted meekly in with the needs of their changing masters - with the aim that they may be as useful, or even 'indispensable to Fascists, as to Communists and Democrats just as the services of physicians

48 The rise of a science of society

and physicists' (Lundberg, 1939, p. 53).

But the additional point that I am trying to make is that by assuming the mantle of neutral servants, sociologists merely strengthened the technocratic potential of the fruits of their labour which is inherently knowledge for control; and it can serve these purposes the better the more this knowledge is cleansed of any obvious practical interest. Lundberg may well have given a correct picture of the self-image and aspirations of the majority of sociologists. Yet the inherent link between scientistic methodology and practical use was spelled out a decade earlier by a member of the Vienna Circle who retained some of the Positivist desire for social change which he saw as being intimately linked with the establishing of scientific reason in the field of metascience.

Neurath was the person most concerned with the development of a truly scientific sociology among the founding fathers of Logical Empiricism. Reaffirming Mill's position, he developed his 'empirical sociology' as an alternative to Dilthey whom he regarded as having fostered a renewed upsurge of metaphysics in Germany:

> Empathic understanding [Verstehen] and the like may help the research worker, but they enter the totality of scientific statements as little as does a good cup of coffee which also furthers a scholar in his work. . . . He who keeps free from metaphysics, understanding [Verstehen] and similar strivings, can, as a sociologist, use only behavioristic phrases, as are proper to a discipline with a materialist foundation. (Neurath, 1973, p. 357).

Physicalism has discarded the dualism at the heart of the Geisteswissenschaften approach; it '. . . knows no "depth", everything is on the "surface"' (1973, p. 326). Concepts such as 'consciousness' should be discarded in favour of those depicting observable properties.

Neurath adds interestingly that 'To one who holds the scientific attitude, statements are only means to predictions; all statements lie in one single plane and they can be combined, like all parts from a workshop that supplies machine parts' (p. 326). This metaphor is not out of character with the rest of Neurath's thinking on this matter since one can very well 'speak of the physics of society in the same way as of the physics of a machine' (p. 390).

One could cite further examples which all go to evidence the close relationship of 'materialist', 'scientific', 'anti-metaphysical' sociology and the ideal science. Neurath considers his metascientific and socio-political stance as progressive - in fact, political radicalism and a scientistic attitude go hand-in-hand. He takes sides with the proletariat against the reactionary implications of bourgeois metaphysics. Marxism, the bearer of the

The rise of a science of society   49

new, scientific outlook, makes the most ample and successful use of sociology. This need not be surprising since 'A planned technology of society constantly requires sociological theories for its justification. . . . Hence we can compare large-scale practical political activity "in the grand style" with the experiments of the physicist. . . . The U.S.S.R. is full of planned conscious technology of society' (pp. 17-18).

Whereas Neurath feels himself a partisan of the progressive forces of history and considers sociology to be one of their main tools, a more recent observer is clearly 'opposed to making science the tail of any political kite whatsoever'.[10] Neurath is incorrect, both historically and logically, when he regards Soviet Marxism as the only fitting mast to fly the flag of sociology because:

> Such partisan commitment as may sensibly be imputed to this programme [i.e. that of scientistic sociology,] . . . . cuts across existing political camps. . [since] . . . No ideological gulfs between regimes seem to bear much relevance (freak historical variations notwithstanding) to their uniformly keen interest - sometimes recognized, but always 'objectively' present - in the kind of technical service so cogently exposed in Lundberg's programme. (Bauman, 1976, p. 37)

Methodological aspects

The critique of sociology in terms of its ideological use-context would be unlikely to have any great impact upon the self-understanding of its practitioners. If, however, it can be shown that the hermeneutic dimension cannot be by-passed or reduced to observable behaviour then such methodologically relevant issues as theory-formation and the identification of data for the statistical treatment of social phenomena can no longer be 'solved' by recurring to the tenets of scientistic metascience. In the next chapter I will attempt the formulation of a hermeneutic paradigm - in opposition to the positivist one - which recognizes the hermeneutic dimension between subject and object to be not only irreducible to, but also foundational of, the objectifying methods of scientistic sociology. But before entering on these discussions a brief reiteration of the relationship between the methodology and practice of scientistic sociology may be in order.

The focus on technically utilizable knowledge implies a conception of the relationship between subject and object as one between experts in the 'running of society' and the passive mass of the population. This monological relationship finds its mirror-image on the level of methodology. Here the subject conducting research is removed from the concerns and aspirations of those he studies so as to bar any unwarranted sentiments from the scientific process; this is best achieved through objectifying the object of study and through socializing the researcher into the mores of scientific research. This concern with maintaining at

50   *The rise of a science of society*

least a semblance of neutrality is linked with one further characteristic: the abhorrence shown to speculation which is seen to include the attempt to grasp social reality as a whole, thereby depriving empirical research of an explicit theoretical context within which its results could become meaningful. The price for the steadfast adherence to the canons of scientistic metascience at the expense of a hermeneutically informed approach is this: an arbitrary restriction of both the field of study and the methodology employed with the impoverishment of the sociological imagination as its result.

This is not to say that objectifying methods are logically inapplicable, but that the object of sociology is characterized by a class of 'facts' which can be comprehended fully only interpretively. The limitations of sociology which is conducted on an empiricist basis derive from the metascientific and methodological exclusion of 'meaning' as a central category in the study of social phenomena: as constitutive of the object, the researcher's relationship to it, and the socio-historical context in which both are located.

The scientistic self-understanding has been succinctly formulated by Johnson (1961, p. 1) when he defines sociology as empirical, i.e. based on analysis and reconstruction as opposed to revelation or speculation; it is theoretical, i.e. strives towards the formulation of observations into abstract and logically connected statements in order to make possible causal explanation; it is cumulative; it is value-free. This conception of sociology can accommodate both the inductive and hypothetic-deductive strands of empiricism.

This tradition in sociology can be traced to Mill and the work of Quetelet; more recent proponents would be Galton and Pearson. Here, scientific procedure centres on measurement and quantification with mathematical theory serving as an ideal. The emergence of computer techniques has provided a great impetus to the statistical analysis of social phenomena, especially through the use of such techniques as factor regression and path analysis, and has led to highly sophisticated forms of survey research.

Paralleling the development of the hypothetic-deductive model of explanation as the central plank in the quest for the unity of science there occurred during the 1950s a marked trend towards theory-construction and model-making in which propositions are formally and logically deduced from more general propositions and tested against empirical data.[11] This movement comprises such eminent figures as Homans and Blau and it is in their work that a stress on deductive argument is linked to a behaviourist approach in the study of social phenomena.[12] It may, in fact, be possible to consider a behaviourist approach[13] as the most representative strand of scientistic sociology. Its attraction for sociologists lies in the promise it holds for rendering the study of social phenomena objective through the elimination of any reference to subjective factors. Meaning, intentions are irrelevant in

The rise of a science of society 51

scientific analysis and only introduce empirically unverifiable assumptions into sociology. Yet, as I shall argue, social phenomena cannot be properly understood independently of their hermeneutic dimension. It is this refusal to consider the 'facts' that sociology investigates as symbolically structured that, for my purposes, defines scientistic sociology. For a hermeneutically informed sociology in contrast, 'a fact is like a sack which won't stand up when it is empty. In order that it may stand up, one has to put into it the reason and sentiment which caused it to exist'.[14]

3 THE DEVELOPMENT OF A NON-SCIENTISTIC SOCIOLOGY IN THE CONTEXT OF THE GEISTESWISSENSCHAFTEN AND IDEALIST PHILOSOPHY

Discussions so far have centred on the hermeneutic dimension in science and the methodological and practical implications of a conception of sociology that tries to eliminate it in its pursuit of a scientistic programme.

In the following chapters an alternative view is put forward in which the hermeneutic dimension is recognized and its implications for doing sociology are developed. This does not entail the view that the logic of inquiry is necessarily different, but that the object, itself meaningfully structured, can only be approached communicatively i.e. in the form of a participant who already has some pre-understanding of it, thereby rendering inappropriate the subject-object dichotomy characteristic of science and scientistic sociology on the level of both practice and methodology.

To formulate a critique and alternative to scientistic sociology it would be of benefit to examine, in outline at least, the contributions of Dilthey and Betti.

Their attempt at establishing a science of socio-historical phenomena is of interest for a number of reasons: the Geisteswissenschaften encompass sociology, and the problems encountered within them can but be of significance for a discussion of the nature and limits of sociological knowledge. Issues such as the scientific status of interpretive sociology and the historical dimension in the generalizing approaches of macrosociology have already occupied the thinking of both Dilthey and Betti. Finally, it can be argued that their ultimate failure to face the full implications of the hermeneutic dimension in the Geisteswissenschaften parallels a similar failure in contemporary conventional sociology. I shall argue, in later chapters, that the tradition which Dilthey represents, and also the two dominant sociological approaches to the study of social phenomena, remain within the orbit of objectivism. Objectivism, as I use the term, refers to the failure to take full account of the double hermeneutic.[1] It conceives of the relationship between subject and meaningfully structured object not in communicative terms, but monologically, i.e. as an object 'out there' confronting the scientist and being amenable to 'objective' investigation in which all traces of the scientist's socio-historical situatedness can be eliminated or at least neutralized. But despite these limitations, the standard of reflexivity in the work of Dilthey and Betti is of such a high degree as to be of great topical interest.

The development of a non-scientistic sociology 53

In relation to the Geisteswissenschaften hermeneutics acquires a more specialized sense as the methodology of the interpretive understanding of objectivations of mind. Dilthey's[2] thought evolved to the point where he considered its mode of comprehension as fundamental not only in the realm of fixed expressions of meaning, but all meaningful phenomena including, of course, socially relevant ones. As Ricoeur has argued:

> if there are specific problems which are raised by the interpretation of texts because they are texts and not spoken language, and if these problems are the ones which constitute hermeneutics as such, then the human sciences may be said to be hermeneutical (1) inasmuch as their *object* displays some of the features constitutive of a text as text, and (2) inasmuch as their *methodology* develops the same kind of procedures as those of Auslegung or text-interpretation. (Ricoeur, 1971, p. 529)

The view 'that there is an unavoidably "hermeneutical" component in the sciences of man' (Taylor, 1971, p. 3) forms the basis of the discussions that follow in which I will try and discuss its implications in relation to some major contemporary approaches to sociology. But before considering the contributions to this issue from within the Geisteswissenschaften it would be appropriate to set it in a wider context and consider the historical origin and practical dimension of the interpretive approach to sociology.

Knowledge acquired in contact with cultural tradition knowledge underlies the very possibility of successful social interaction and acts as a pointer towards alternative social arrangements. This 'practical knowledge' mediates social members and establishes a continuity between past and future thereby helping to establish individual and social identity. For this reason it is irreducible to instrumental knowledge and together with it provides the preconditions for the reproduction of society. Practical knowledge is distinguishable from the latter in that 'it is not directed at the comprehension of objectified reality but at the preservation of the intersubjectivity of understanding; it is only on its horizon that reality can appear as anything at all' (Habermas, 1968, p. 222).

It is this knowledge that mankind has of itself that is the object of the Geisteswissenschaften and within them, in particular, the historical sciences. The latter had the effect of fostering the relativization of tradition and at the same time arose in response to the up-rooting consequences of the process of industrialization; in this sense they are filling the void that opened up in the break with tradition and act as a scientific mediation of past and present.

In trying to account for the preoccupation with meaning so characteristic of German intellectual life one may refer to

54 *The development of a non-scientistic sociology*

economic and political factors. The delayed industrialization of
Germany - itself a consequence of the aftermath of the Thirty
Years War - engendered a more 'contemplative' attitude in contrast to the active, interventionist mode of conduct prevalent
in industrial and industrializing societies of the eighteenth and
nineteenth century. The political fragmentation of the German
states and principalities may also have led to an emphasis on the
one bond that united them: language - which came to be seen as
embodying the spirit of a people. The parallel emphasis on the
superiority of Geisteswissenschaften and freedom in the sphere
of thought over such mundane concerns as the active transformation of material and social conditions and the quest for individual political freedom may itself be seen as a surrogate for
political emancipation. Echoing Marx, Mannheim states that
'lacking a concrete socio-political focus for their thought and
action, the educated German middle class made their accommo-
dation to the bureaucratic state and spiritualized the idea of
freedom, to mean intellectual indeterminism' (Mannheim, 1958,
p. 31).

Mannheim goes on to note that 'this introverted concept of
freedom has become the keystone of the immanence theory and
one of the main academic barriers to a sociological approach
to history, thought, and politics' (pp. 31-2). This insight may
help to account for Dilthey's hostility towards the conception of
sociology developed by Comte and Mill. This hostility is also
apparent on the level of its use-context and his stress on
practical over instrumental knowledge.

He sees the Geisteswissenschaften as arising 'naturally from
the problems of life' (Dilthey, 1964-6, vol. VII, p. 70) and as
consisting of 'knowledge about facts, about general truths,
values, purposes, and rules' (vol. VII, p. 3); they find their
fulfilment in 'reacting back on life and society' (vol. VII, p.
138) through the provision of objective knowledge.

The process of industrialization, has in Dilthey's view, led
to the submerging of cultural values in the rise of instrumentally
guided forms of existence and the rule of capital, 'the beast
with a thousand eyes and ears and without conscience' (vol. II,
p. 245). Sociology, which both reflects and fosters these developments, is consequently 'unable to found the ideals that could
guide an age intent on reconstructing society' (vol. V, p. 361)
- but so, too, is the 'historical school' (e.g. Ranke's scientific-
objective study of history), which draws on the past in a merely
restorative, 'antiquarian' (Nietzsche) way. For Dilthey, it is the
Geisteswissenschaften alone which can provide practically effective knowledge since they recognize in their approach that 'the
present is filled with past elements and carries the future within
itself' (vol. VII, p. 232).

The development of a non-scientistic sociology   55

DILTHEY'S FOUNDING OF A HERMENEUTICALLY INFORMED SOCIAL SCIENCE

Dilthey's contribution centres on the direction he gave to the task of establishing a study of socio-cultural phenomena which takes full account of the hermeneutic dimension. In his view, it is ultimately not so much their specific object which distinguishes the human from the natural sciences, nor is it a unique method of investigation, but rather the relationship between the subject and his object. This 'basic relationship is, then, one of lived experience, expression and understanding. The researcher in the Geisteswissenschaften remains within this context. . . . His approach is fundamentally hermeneutic; he does not leave the sphere of understanding.[13]

Understanding as a relationship and mode of co-existence with the object rather than verstehen, by which I mean its methodically developed derivative, is the hallmark of the Geisteswissenschaften. It is itself grounded in that medium which envelopes both subject and object: in understanding, 'life meets life' (Dilthey).

Since, furthermore, the logic of inquiry in the Geisteswissenschaften does not differ fundamentally from the one apparent in the natural sciences,[4] it is the quality of the original relationship which deserves closer attention. In the Geisteswissenschaften we are dealing with the practical knowledge that man has of himself and which permeates his everyday activities and aspirations. When studying socio-cultural phenomena we are consequently not concerned with the control of objectified processes, but with trying to assimilate, and maybe expand, knowledge about how best to order our social and personal affairs.

At this point it becomes apparent that, given the fact that sociology, too, is concerned with the normative dimension of social reality - and is consequently dependent on a communicative relationship between subject and object -, Dilthey's work cannot but be of great interest. In the following account of the problems faced in the founding of the Geisteswissenschaften I shall pay particular attention to the issue as to whether these hermeneutically based sciences have successfully fused the study of meaningful phenomena with the quest for objective results.

The rise of the Geisteswissenschaften
The system of the Geisteswissenschaften has as its object the socio-historical existence of man which is investigated by its various branches. These individual sciences emerged in response to the need for reliable knowledge in the areas of history, politics, political economy, theology, literature and art. To arrive at a comprehensive picture of socio-historical reality it is, however, necessary to bring together the results of the individual Geisteswissenschaften. For this to be possible, Dilthey has to engage in some metatheoretical reflection to ascertain that the

56 *The development of a non-scientistic sociology*

latter share a common denominator which would make it possible and legitimate to draw them together to form a distinctive, yet internally cohesive, body of knowledge. This task can be undertaken through the explication of the term 'Geisteswissenschaften'.

Science is defined by Dilthey as a 'body of mental facts' which contains the following characteristics:

> concepts which are completely determined and constant and generally valid in a system of thought; connections which have been justified; and the combining of the parts to the whole for the purpose of communicating knowledge about a segment of reality or of guiding human activity through this combination of statements. (vol. I, pp. 4-5)

In contrast to this fairly straightforward conception of science - which is much in keeping with thought prevalent around the turn of the century - the crucial, *Geiste*swissenschaften' component is less easily definable.

Rothacker (1948, p. 7) traces the term Geisteswissenschaften to the translation of J.S. Mill's 'A System of Logic' by Schiel in 1849 who rendered the title of its sixth book 'On the logic of moral sciences' as 'Von der Logik der Geisteswissenschaften oder moralischen Wissenschaften' and who throughout uses 'Geisteswissenschaften' for 'moral sciences'. Mill's translator could draw on the terms Wissenschaft des Geistes, Geistwissenschaft, and Geisteslehre which were in use among Hegel's followers. By the time Erdmann noted that 'Hegel's system divided into Grund-Natur and Geisteswissenschaften as early as 1800', the plural form of the term introduced by Schiel was already widely accepted.

Dilthey himself refers to Mill's 'Logik der Geisteswissenschaften' but, in 1875, does not yet employ this term for the science which he, at this stage, calls 'moral-political' (vol. V, p. 31); not until 1883, in the 'Introduction to the Geisteswissenschaften' does he adopt it for those sciences 'that have as their object socio-historical reality' (vol. I, p. 3). He chooses the term Geisteswissenschaften with some reservation. Two points decided in its favour: the widespread influence of Mill's 'Logic' has contributed to its familiarity and, if compared with alternative terms, Geisteswissenschaften seems to be the least inappropriate one. 'Geisteswissenschaft' expresses the object of study adequately since, within it, 'the facts of mental life are not separated from the psycho-physical unity of human life' (vol. I, p. 6), other terms are too narrow in view of the object.

The identity of the Geisteswissenschaften vis-à-vis the natural sciences resides in man's self-awareness where, on a prescientific level, 'the sovereignty of will, the responsibility of action, the ability to subject everything to thought, demarcates an independently operative mental universe which derives its value and purpose from the creation of mental elements as the main aim of its activity.

The development of a non-scientistic sociology 57

In this way Dilthey distinguishes between the sphere of nature and that of history where

amidst the context of objective necessity, which we call nature, freedom appears in flashes at innumerable points; here, the active will actually does produce, through effort and sacrifice, something new in contrast to the mechanical process of changes in nature where the product is already contained at the inception. (vol. I, p. 6)

Turning to differences in the procedures between the natural sciences and the Geisteswissenschaften Dilthey emphasizes the importance of locating psychological and social phenomena within a context - which provides them with their resonating richness and significance. This fundamental point leads him to reject Mill's approach.

The latter is first of all applauded for two contributions to the foundation of the moral sciences: he rejected Comte's metaphysical speculations, especially in relation to the hierarchy of the sciences, and he attributed to psychology a status independent of the natural sciences and saw it as the basis for the moral and political sciences. The dismissive tone of Dilthey's opposition to Mill's empiricistic procedures, however, bears witness to the -fateful[5] - sense of superiority prevalent in German academic circles of the time in relation to West European culture which was seen as being permeated by a mechanistic conception of man and society and a materialistic, impoverished form of life - in contrast to the profound appreciation of truly human values and sentiments: 'only Germany can provide a truely empirical procedure in place of biased, dogmatic empiricism; Mill is dogmatic out of a lack of historical perspective'.[6]

Dilthey, in entering the task of founding a non-scientistic study of socio-historical phenomena, develops a 'historico-critical' approach in opposition to the one employed

recently and with increasing frequency by those who call themselves positivists who derive the content of the concept of science from a definition which grew out of their consideration of natural sciences and who use this definition to decide which intellectual activity may claim the name and status of science. (1964-6, vol. I, p. 5)

Dilthey, instead, proposes to proceed from actual studies undertaken within the various disciplines that constitute the Geisteswissenschaften to arrive at an appropriate method as well as the theoretical foundation of the latter. He appreciates Comte's endeavour, the constitution of a science of socio-historical reality, which was continued by Mill and Spencer who all placed the Geisteswissenschaften into the context of gaining valid knowledge through the construction of a comprehensive

58 *The development of a non-scientistic sociology*

scientific system. The fervour that accompanied their effort
blinded them, however, in regard to a vital necessity for the
elaboration of a systematic arrangement of the individual
sciences: 'the intimate feeling for historical reality that arises
only from long-term concern with it through research into
specific areas' (vol. I, p. 23). As a result, they constructed an
edifice that is founded on reckless speculation. The essence of
Dilthey's argument is that 'the Geisteswissenschaften do not
constitute a whole conceived in terms of a logical constitution
analogous to the ordering of knowledge gained from the natural
world, their interrelations have developed differently and need
to be considered historically' (p. 24).

But while rejecting any unfounded intrusion of methods
developed in the natural sciences, Dilthey acknowledges the
importance of empirical methods for the investigation of the
'psycho-physical unity of life' which is constituted by both mental and physical elements. Accordingly, we find two distinctly
different, but mutually irreducible, approaches which, if un-
mediated, are concerned with one part of the existence of man
only and which has been broken from its original whole through
abstraction. Man as a life-unit can be regarded as a complex of
mental realities if seen from the point of their inner perception,
or as a bodily whole which we know through sense-perception.
Both approaches are justified since 'inner awareness and outer
experience never occur in the same act' (vol. I, p. 15).

The task arises, therefore, of attributing to each approach a
legitimate sphere of activity after having recognized that there
exists a mutual relationship between physical and socio-historical
factors in the development of man.

The content of the Geisteswissenschaften
The material of the Geisteswissenschaften, socio-historical
reality, appears in the form of three classes of statements: those
referring to reality as it is given in perception; those developing
constant elements apparent in reality and constituting its theoretical component; and those expressing value-judgments and
prescribing rule-governed, practical action. 'Facts, theorems,
value-judgements and rules: these three classes of statements
constitute the Geisteswissenschaften' (vol. I, p. 26).

This reality the Geisteswissenschaften have made their object
with a view towards the comprehension of the individual and the
identification of uniformities. Among the various studies that are
concerned with the object the Geisteswissenschaften claim as
their legitimate field of activity, those dealing with the individual
are considered by Dilthey to take pride of place.

The descriptive science of psychology is of central importance
in the Geisteswissenschaften. It analyses the elementary unit of
socio-historical reality, the psycho-physical unity of man, and
deals with the process by which we gain knowledge of this
reality. The latter point is of particular relevance for the

The development of a non-scientistic sociology 59

Geisteswissenschaften since any knowledge of this object is here given immediately in the consciousness of the knowing subject – in distinction to the natural sciences which can arrive only at near-certainties through the gradual approximation of the content of knowledge gained through the senses to its external object; it has to remain necessarily hypothetical. While stressing the constitutive role of the individual, Dilthey hastens to sound a caveat: psychology only deals with a fraction of the content of the individual's mind and for this reason does not reflect all the realities that make up the object of the Geisteswissenschaften.

As a consequence it has been separated out through a process of abstraction and can be developed only in constant reference to the whole of socio-historical reality: the individual is a part of society and cannot be investigated in isolation; psychology is concerned with eliciting 'analytical knowledge of the general characteristics of man' (vol. I, p. 32). Its truths have to provide the basis for the construction of socio-historical reality. But since they represent only one part of it and acquire their relevance only in relation to it they cannot be used to determine the relationship of psychology to the Geisteswissenschaften and to this reality. This remains the task of epistemology. It is for this reason that Dilthey emphasizes the difference between the descriptive and the explanatory forms of psychology as the latter take it upon themselves to deduce the whole context of mental life from certain assumptions and so construct hypotheses on the basis of hypotheses which prevents the establishing of a sound foundation for this science.

In his further consideration of the different studies that make up the Geisteswissenschaften, Dilthey now mentions anthropology which has emerged from the descriptive efforts of historiography through the classification of similarities which led to the eventual formulation of a general human type and general laws concerning the life of psychological entities. Progressing from there we witness the emergence of ethnology, or comparative anthropology, which focuses on uniformities of a more restricted scope as they pertain to distinguishable groups of people: their common ancestry and racial and geographical differences. Common history leads to the formation of a people with a characteristic culture.

In order to determine what constitutes a people, nation, or the meaning of such entities as 'spirit or soul of a people' which are referred to when one tries to distinguish between nations, it is necessary to analyse the various sides of the life of a nation, as they are manifested in language, art, religion, the state, institutions, etc.

The social sciences are concerned with constant formations as they emerged from continuing relationships between individuals. For their investigation, Dilthey distinguishes analytically between systems of culture and formations of external organization. The former are based on anthropologically situated

60   *The development of a non-scientistic sociology*

purposes which express themselves in 'psychological acts' - thinking, feeling, willing - and lead to the formation of a purposive system (Zweckzusammenhang) while the latter bind together the wills of people and provide a framework for their ordered expressions.

In introducing the concept of 'system' Dilthey refers to the complexity of the lives of individuals. Although each individual possesses some characteristics uniquely his own, as the term itself implies, some components of his personality will be shared by his fellow human beings and provide the precondition for communal activity. Due to their complexity, individuals will find themselves at a point of intersection of a number of systems which take on a more and more specialized form as cultural activities progress.

Since each system is based on recurring traits within individuals these systems can persist even though its bearers play only a transitory role within them. 'The rootedness in human nature of the activities that make up these systems endow them with a massive objectivity - an external reality - that makes it possible to preserve in them a more lasting or recreative way and to mediate the impact made by quickly passing individuals' (1964-6, vol. I, p. 50).

It is as self-contained objectivities that the various systems that make up socio-historical reality appear to their members and to abstract science, e.g. religion and even science itself.

While an analysis of these systems may proceed by taking each one in turn, it is nevertheless impossible to investigate any of them without recurring to a different class of investigations which have as their object similarities existing between them. Each system develops within the totality of socio-historical reality because

> each is the product of a component of human nature and rooted in and deriving its specific activity from the purposive system of social life. . . . These systems are, to a varying degree, related to the external organization of society and it is this relationship that determines their more specific formation. More particularly, the study of the systems which constitute the practical activity of society cannot be separated from the study of the body politic since the will embedded in the latter influences any external activity of the individuals under its sway. (p. 52)

The two components of social reality: free independent social intercourse between individuals and the power exercised by an external source which binds them; free activity and regulation; independence and community, relate to each other dialectically and together realize the totality of purpose of human history. Considered separately - Dilthey refers to a pragmatic historian and Hegel, respectively - they represent the moments of the

The development of a non-scientistic sociology   61

truth residing in the totality of purpose in which the activities of people, spurred on by the desire to achieve some personal end, cannot fail to realize an ultimate, overarching purpose.

Following on the discussion of the science dealing with psycho-physical entities, Dilthey turns to a contrasting study, that which analyses socio-historical reality as a totality and which was given the name 'Sociology' in England and France. In his introduction to this branch of knowledge Dilthey focuses on two characteristic relationships: society-nature and society-individual.

The researcher attempting to investigate society is confronted by an object even more puzzling than our own organism. He finds himself among processes occurring around him and involving him in mutual relationships with others; he is part of something he has entered into but not created and he is aware of only a limited number of the rules that guide its further development. In short the possibilities for the comprehension of this mysterious machinery seem remote.

But, and here lies the crucial difference between society and nature, this reality is also our own world. Nature confronts us as an alien force, social processes we experience with the fullness of our being and become aware of as something that touches the nerve of our existence, evoking reactions that span the spectrum from love to hate as we get to know the conditions and forces underlying them. Nature, by contrast, is mute and for this reason can acquire a sense of serenity; any 'life' it may seem to contain has its source in our overflowing imagination. All this imparts certain differences to the study of society if compared with that of nature where we can rely upon uniformity and immutability. The dazzling array of interrelated processes in the social field is far less amenable to the establishing of law-like occurrences and here our desire for certainties will necessarily find less fulfilment.

> But all this is more than compensated for by the fact that the I, who can experience and know himself from within, am part of this social body and that the other elements are similar to me and can equally be known by me as they are inside. I understand the life of society. The individual is, on the one hand, an element in the interaction of society, a point of intersection of various systems of interaction, who reacts to these influences by consciously directing his will and his actions; he is, at the same time, the intelligent subject that observes and investigates all these processes. The interplay of blindly effective causes is here replaced by one between ideas, feelings and motivations. (p. 37)

The hermeneutic basis of sociology
From Dilthey's introduction to the Geisteswissenschaften it becomes apparent that we are dealing with an eminent sociological theorist

62 *The development of a non-scientistic sociology*

who anticipated and, to some extent shaped, sociology in its present forms.

In relation to the foundation of a non-scientistic sociology it would be at this stage appropriate to look more closely at the relationship between hermeneutics and sociology.

In the 'Introduction to the Geisteswissenschaften', completed in 1883, Dilthey considered 'descriptive psychology' as the basis for the Geisteswissenschaften. In contrast to analytic or explanatory psychology, which examines isolated aspects in the endeavour to establish causal accounts of human behaviour, it considers the individual in his 'living wholeness'. This leads Dilthey to stipulate that the activities of individuals have to be understood in relation to the 'vital unity' which they represent. A further implication of the view that the individual is the only real unit is that the conception of wholeness could be transposed onto complex, large-scale phenomena, such as society, only on a metaphoric basis.

In his later discussion of the status of biography, Dilthey came to see the individual as 'the point of intersection of cultural systems and organizations into which his existence is woven' (1964-6, vol. VII, p. 251). Consequently, the notion of totality could now be employed in the study of history and social life while interpretive understanding, which follows the movement from part to whole, would still have its central place.

On the other hand, it was now no longer possible to consider psychology as the fundamental science. Instead of the use of understanding in the psychologistic forms of empathy and reliving, Dilthey now associates it with the hermeneutic interpretation of objectivations of mind and considers this as the fundamental mode of getting to know the object.

As a result, it is the hermeneutical sciences on which now rest the whole edifice of the human and social sciences since it is here that their mode of cognition is most explicitly developed and employed.

This change in perspective is well expressed in the essay 'The rise of hermeneutics', written in 1900, which shows the influence Hegel - whom he had only recently re-introduced into German philosophy - and Husserl's critique of the psychologism of J.S. Mill's epistemology have had on his thinking.

The Geisteswissenschaften are now seen as being concerned with 'objectivations of Life' which the scientist stands in a 'living relationship' with. They overarch Hegel's 'objectivations of spirit, in two aspects: by including manifestations of 'absolute spirit' - i.e. art, religion and philosophy - and, since Life in its totality takes the place of Reason, 'lived experience, understanding, the historical context of Life, the power of the irrational' (vol. VII, p. 151), too have to be considered. This poses a new problem for the Geisteswissenschaften: since we can no longer accept Hegel's metaphysical construction and have to analyse what is given, we are now confronted with the task of

The development of a non-scientistic sociology   63

determining how 'universally valid knowledge of the historical world is possible' (vol. VII, p. 152).

The issue touched upon here is precisely the one that I wish to examine in terms of the double hermeneutic in sociology: how can we arrive at objective knowledge of meaningful phenomena once we accept that here subject and object stand in a communicative relationship?

In the context of Dilthey's founding of a study of social phenomena which centres on the recognition of this hermeneutic dimension, the problematic can be delineated in the following way: the hermeneutical sciences, which Dilthey also comprehends under the category of 'historical Geisteswissenschaften' not only constitute an independent branch of the system of Geisteswissenschaften but also, and more significantly, provide the basis for the 'systematic Geisteswissenschaften', such as sociology, which 'deduce from the objective comprehension of singular events general, lawlike relationships and comprehensive systems; as a consequence, the process of understanding and interpretation remains for them, too, a basic condition' (vol. V, p. 317).

If we accept this argument, as I am inclined to, then the question as to the implications of the double hermeneutic in relation to the objectivity of sociological knowledge pre-necessitates – or may even be co-extensive with – the problem of how hermeneutic interpretation of meaning can be made objective.

Dilthey himself was much preoccupied by this problem and the endeavour underlying his metatheoretical reflections is directed at the task 'to assert, in the face of the continued eruption of romantic arbitrariness and speculative subjectivism into the realm of history, the general validity of interpretation in a theoretic manner' (vol. V, p. 331). In order to arrive at a solution to this problem he engaged in a Critique of Historical Reason analogous, and complementary, to Kant's three 'Critiques'. Dilthey's conclusion is, briefly, based on the philosophy of Life and is the following: life, as the web supporting the reciprocal interpretations of social actors provides the intersubjective support for individual interpretations and the context within which they acquire their meaningfulness. What is shared by all must, further, be objective in the sense of transcending and encompassing the merely subjective as the private or idiosyncratic.[7] This position can, at the same time, co-exist with Dilthey's emphasis on the need to develop a 'historical consciousness', i.e. an awareness of the situatedness of all interpretations.

But this latter aspect need not be seen as a factor making for arbitrariness – if we accept the tenets of the philosophy of Life. What is more, Dilthey is able to extract positive insights from this condition: because interpretive knowledge is historic and never finite – man, too, is not at the mercy of determining historical forces but is free to make his own history.

64 *The development of a non-scientistic sociology*

VERSTEHEN BETWEEN SUBJECTIVISM AND OBJECTIVISM

Dilthey's contribution to the critique of scientistic sociology centres on his analysis of the hermeneutic dimension within the study of meaningful phenomena. Sociology, as a Geisteswissenschaft, it has been argued, is privileged in relation to the natural sciences since its 'data' and the researcher can, and always do, enter into a communicative relationship.

This privilege, however, carries with it certain responsibilities which are much easier to fulfil in the study of non-meaningful objects, in particular the attempt on the part of the researcher not to impose his own preconception on the object which would distort his account of it. The task facing the hermeneutic sciences, and by extension sociology, is to establish themselves between scientism and subjectivism.

The quest for objectivity in the study of meaningful objects is closely linked with the attempt to establish a methodology for the Geisteswissenschaften which would lead them, if not exactly on to the secure path of science, then at least to relatively objective results.

Dilthey did not concern himself with the formulation of a detailed methodology. I can, however, turn to the work of Betti (1967) for insights into the general theory of the objective understanding of meaning.[8]

Betti considers interpretive understanding as the inversion of the creative process and, with the mediation of 'meaning-full [sinnvolle] forms', to form a triadic scheme: spirit objectivates itself, and its content is reappropriated by the interpreter.

In this process, the meaning derived from expressions is that which the author had originally intended. The necessity to inquire into the author's intentions leads Betti to endorse a maxim proposed by his precursors: that author and interpreter should be of a similar intellectual and moral stature in order that full justice be done to the creation.

Just as creative activity does not take place out of nothing (creatio ex nihilo), but draws on an immense range of past achievements and present influences, so understanding in general too has to be envisaged as total perception that goes beyond abstractive consideration or atomistic observation. Given sufficient inner affinity, such an act can take place; in it interpretative activity only plays an ancillary role.

The existence of a relationship between author and interpreter not only provides the basis on which communication across time and place can occur - it also constitutes an obvious problem for the objectivity of the results of interpretation. It is to this problem of how to reconcile 'subjective conditions' and the 'objectivity of understanding' that Betti addresses himself in the final part of his epistemological considerations.

Betti stresses the requirement on the part of the interpreter to engage his whole sensibility. Under the rubric 'metatheoretical

The development of a non-scientistic sociology   65

conditions for the process of interpretation' he lists interest in understanding, attentiveness, open-mindedness, and self-effacement; a specific noetic interest in understanding determines the degree to which one engages in understanding, it is at its highest point when the desire to understand arises from an actual need. The existence of a gap between the interpreter and his object - which originally led to the application of interpretative procedures - necessitates a reflective approach which recognizes the 'otherness' of objectivations of mind and, at the same time, stimulates and trains the receptive apparatus of the investigator; this reflectivity appears as self-effacement and humility.

At the same time, Betti demands that a number of obstacles be removed in order that the 'other' be received in the right spirit. By indicating the major barriers to correct understanding it should be made apparent why Betti can attribute educational value to hermeneutical understanding, viz. the development of an attitude of tolerance which is helped by the recognition of one's own prejudices and shortcomings that only become apparent in the sincere attempt to understand an Other and which have to be overcome before successful understanding can take place. Among these obstacles are: (a) the conscious or unconscious resentment towards ideas and positions which differ from the more common ones, and especially from those held by the observer; which leads (b) to their denigration and distortion; (c) the attitude of self-righteousness which sees issues in terms of black and white and unaware of the dialectic between good and bad; (d) the conformism towards dominant conceptions and the pharisaic acceptance of 'conventional bias' in judging others; (e) the lack of interest in other cultures, as well as intellectual and moral narrowness or laziness - which shows itself in the growing tendency to shirk from sincere theoretical discussions and an open exchange of opinion in general. Betti here makes the interesting remark that 'the intolerance of political and cultural propaganda tries everything to suppress and suffocate the critical spirit' (p. 202, and note 18).[9]

All these barriers to correct understanding 'stem from the totality of prepossessions and selfish concerns which can be traced back to a shared form of preconceived intellectual attitudes.[10]

But the fact that the highest subjectivity of the interpreter, i.e. his receptivity, sensitivity, sensibility and open-ness represent a precondition for successful interpretation should not lead to the confusion of interpretation with speculation in general and the problem of 'self-understanding' in particular. Betti traces this, the confusion characteristic of existentialism, back to Dilthey who had conceived of a necessary relationship between verstehen and erleben. The result:

Dilthey is finally led to confuse the process of *verstehen* with the 'inner lived experience' itself; he thereby loses out

66 The development of a non-scientistic sociology

of sight the clear distinction between verstehen and causal explanation and also regards verstehen as the elementary position of experiencing any kind of objectivity, thereby moving it closely towards the status of a pre-understanding. (p. 166)

It is, of course, Heidegger who attributes central significance to the role of a pre-understanding which has always already taken place when we make a conscious attempt at verstehen. In the formulation of the 'hermeneutic circle' this conception will be more extensively dealt with in the next chapter. At this stage I shall only indicate the bone of contention between Betti and the Protestant theologian Bultmann whose 'demythologization' is greatly indebted to Heidegger's existential interpretation of existence.

Two implications of this conception attract Betti's great displeasure. The first one is expressed in Jaspers's view of verstehen as 'mere understanding of what is already understood': it is only concerned with correct results; it is the hallmark of this kind of cognition that it becomes less effective the more neutral, 'value-free', it is. Only 'fundamental understanding' can distinguish between good and bad, true and false, beautiful and ugly. The second implication not only relegates methodical understanding to the 'antiquarian' reproduction of the past, but even denies the possibility of objective historical knowledge. The work of Bultmann provides Betti with an exposition of what he considers to be a 'subjectivist and relativist conception'. The postulation of pre-understanding as the condition for understanding eliminates the distinction between interpretive understanding and 'lived experience' and insists on the necessity of an existential relationship between interpreter and object (text) in which the latter addresses the former and discloses new possible ways of existence. The underlying relationship determines not only the questions that will be put to the object, but the whole position of the interpreter vis-à-vis his object and the standards applicable for evaluating the result of this encounter. Interpretation, in the narrow sense, only plays the ancillary role of testing and developing a pre-understanding. Betti regards this topic as closed by referring back to his distinction between objective and speculative interpretation; since existential interpretation fails to follow the maxim that 'meaning has to be derived from the text and not inferred into it', it has excluded itself from the prospectus of valid interpretation.

In conjunction with his rejection of the subjectivism and relativism introduced into hermeneutics by existentialist philosophers, Betti set out to reaffirm the possibility of, at least, relative objectivity of the results of interpretation. Objectivity is possible in principle owing to the autonomy, the existence-in-themselves, of objectivations of spirit; but their objectivity can never be absolute owing to the distance between written or spoken speech and its addressee - a factor that pertains even

The development of a non-scientistic sociology   67

to communication here and now. A more important factor intruding into the objective reconstruction of human artefact is, in fact, apparent in any process of cognition: the antinomy between the objectivity of the meaning under investigation and the subjectivity of any understanding, i.e. the spontaneity and 'actuality' of the knower.

In hermeneutical activity we have to be aware of its 'axiological moment': the interpreter has to participate in the values he finds in his object, it is 'the recognition of noetic value, an appropriation and adaption' (p. 210). But, as Betti stresses, following Husserl, 'meaning' as the recognition of something that is valued, important, i.e. meaning as an act, need not be confused with meaning-in-itself, as unchangeable, i.e. 'meaning as the ideal unity of the manifold of possible acts'. The former, the meaning-activity, is a prerequisite for the understanding of the meaning-content of an object and is, therefore, axiological since it guides the recognition of something as something. But this form of participation with the object - while making for subjective fluctuations - does not lead to a collapsing of the difference between subject and object since 'the evaluative position-taking is directed at objectivity insofar as the subject negates himself' (p. 210). The 'anthropocentrism' of the existentialists would, from this perspective, appear as self-indulgent 'intellectual egotism'.

It is this dialectic between subjectivity and objectivity, the actuality of the subject and the otherness of the object, that has, in the course of hermeneutical practice, given rise to the formulation of a methodology which, it is hoped, will guarantee correct results.

Betti outlines four canons which can be subdivided into two groups of two which pertain (a) to the object, and (b) to the subject of interpretation:

a_1 the canon of the hermeneutical autonomy of the object and immanence of the hermeneutical standard;
a_2 the canon of totality and coherence of hermeneutical evaluation;
b_1 the canon of the actuality of understanding;
b_2 the canon of the harmonization of understanding: hermeneutical correspondence and agreement.

Among these canons the same difficulty is reproduced that initially led to their formulation, i.e. that of reconciling unavoidable subjectivity and required objectivity, and which here emerges as the 'intersection of the canon of autonomy (a_1) with that of the actuality of understanding (b_1).

Betti is able to put the apparent dichotomy to good methodological use. The tension between objectivity and subjectivity is a precondition for the perception of a personal or cultural 'style' in which continued 'tendencies' and an 'inner coherence' are apparent.

68 The development of a non-scientistic sociology

Referring to Schleiermacher's emphasis on the need for a total commitment of the interpreter's inner experiences and intellectual and aesthetic capabilities, Betti reaffirms the importance of the actuality of understanding. When it comes to evidencing the precise, necessary, and justifiable subjective moment in interpretation Betti follows, among others, Simmel who had argued against the possibility of a 'direct' contact between subject and object; the interpreter can commence his activity only on the basis of the use of categories of thought - or rather, these categories have already been 'put to work' when he approaches anything.

Summing up it can be stated that any interpretative act is a triadic process in which meaning-full forms mediate between the spirit objectivated in them and the spirit of the interpreter. These forms confront the interpreter as something 'other'. The crucial difference between the process of interpretation and that of any other process of cognition in which subject and object are confronted lies in the fact that here the 'object' consists of objectivations of mind and it is the task of the interpreter to re-cognize or re-construct the ideas, message, intentions, manifested in them; it is a process of internalization in which the content of these forms is transposed into an 'other', different subjectivity.

In this way, elementary understanding occurs through the mediation of language: the speech of an other subject represents an appeal, a call on us to understand, which we follow by reconstructing its meaning with the help of our categories of thought and by fitting together the various pieces of evidence in order to reconstruct an author's intended meaning.

Adequate understanding can, however, only develop on the basis of correct knowledge. Betti has remained sufficiently close to the neo-Kantian tradition of the Kulturwissenschaften to insist on a firmly conducted analysis of the phenomena under consideration - without allowing it to become an end in itself: the ultimate aim of hermeneutical investigation is the explication of their meaning, leading to a better understanding of self and others.

4 TOWARDS A HERMENEUTIC PARADIGM FOR SOCIOLOGY

In the course of being considered as a project, the natural sciences appeared as the analysis of objectifiable processes in the interest of control. The limitations of this approach, if transposed on to social phenomena, derive from its strengths. Monologically based investigations, which allow the technological/ technocratic mastery of the object, cannot account for the metatheoretical conditions underlying it: the subject of science cannot itself be completely objectified, and nor can the object of the social sciences.

The hermeneutically oriented disciplines, by contrast, do not form a system of logically connected statements which makes possible the explanation and prediction of events, but they help to extend a communicative space; they are not concerned with 'data' but with 'dantia', not given facts or instances of natural laws but human creations: words, texts, actions, which bear witness to the intentions, hopes, fears and suffering of individuals, and where something general is manifest in the particular.

Seen in the context of the fundamental difference between nature and culture, the Geisteswissenschaften remained peculiarly ambivalent both in relation to social practice and, linked to it, methodology.

In Dilthey's view the 'relatively recent' emergence of a systematic study of socio-historical reality has its roots in the shockwaves which the French Revolution had sent across Europe and they owe their blossoming to developments since that event. Arguing in a similar vein to Comte, the task of post-revolutionary social thought was to serve the stabilization of the system that emerged. An adequate understanding of social processes has become a precondition for the survival of social order. In this context the Geisteswissenschaften represent the culmination of a development in which the practical needs of society were catered for by investigations into history, politics, political economy, theology, literature and art.

The increase in the complexity of societies and the concomitant need for trained personnel supervising social development led to the birth of the specialist. The various empirical disciplines which make up the Geisteswissenschaften could serve the purpose of acquainting those concerned with the steering of society with the rules and mechanisms that maintain that awesomely complex apparatus, society.

70 *Towards a hermeneutic paradigm for sociology*

Dilthey's uncertain position in relation to the use-context of sociological knowledge, in which both technocratic and liberative themes are apparent, is mirrored on the level of methodology. In my view, both Dilthey and Betti, to a different extent, fail to give a satisfactory account of the double hermeneutic and its implications.

By turning to the seminal work of Gadamer, 'Truth and Method', I hope to arrive at the outline of a hermeneutic paradigm for sociology in which the communicative relationship between subject and object is given full recognition. Gadamer's hermeneutic reflections represent a move from methodological to philosophical concerns which is to say that before giving an answer to the question whether verstehen can be an objective method we have to examine the conditions of the possibility of verstehen itself.

It is by now apparent that the search for sociological procedures which take as their starting-point the recognition of the hermeneutic dimension is tied to, or rather an expression of, a projected approach to social knowledge in which the 'object' is regarded as an equal, a co-subject - with all this entails for the conduct of research and the use of its results.

THE HERMENEUTIC CONCEPTION OF UNDERSTANDING

The place of understanding in the Geisteswissenschaften is dealt with by Gadamer in terms of the 'hermeneutic circle' with the aim of raising their philosophical self-awareness. Gadamer builds on both Heidegger's exposition of the forestructure of understanding and Bultmann's stress on pre-understanding in that the former is concretized and the latter is widened into the conception of 'prejudices' which constitute a given 'horizon of understanding'. All understanding is 'prejudicial', says Gadamer, and invests a great deal of thought into the rehabilitation of a concept that acquired its negative connotation with the Enlightenment.

From its claim to autonomy Reason could consider prejudices only as remnants of an unenlightened mentality which impedes rational self-determination. This view also entered the thinking of some romanticists and consequently shaped the formulation of the doctrine of historism. In their rejection of prejudices, the Enlightenment and the historistic Geisteswissenschaften of the nineteenth century enter into an unholy alliance which finds its common denominator in the quest for objective knowledge which they hope to achieve by following a system of rules and methodological principles and in the 'conquest of mythos by logos' (pp. 257, 242.[1])

Gadamer sees in this, however, the loss of the continuity of tradition which nevertheless underlies both approaches. In addition to prejudices and tradition, authority, too, has been

Towards a hermeneutic paradigm for sociology 71

rejected by the Enlightenment as anathema to the use of one's faculty of Reason. As the demand for blind obedience it certainly deserved this fate but this does not capture the essence of true authority which can only be maintained through the consent of those affected by it: it has to be acquired and continually re-affirmed through their consent. In fact, 'authority has nothing to do with blind obedience but rather with knowledge' (pp. 264, 248).

The idea of absolute Reason overlooks the fact that Reason can only actualize itself in historical conditions. Even the most neutral application of the methods of science is guided by an anticipation of moments of tradition in the selection of the topic of research, the suggestion of new questions and the wakening of interest in new knowledge. It is therefore the task of a philosophical hermeneutic to evidence the historic moment in the comprehension of the world and to determine its hermeneutic productivity. In this sense, the hermeneutic problem underlies all knowledge. The natural sciences derive the direction of their development from the laws of their object, but reference to the element of tradition that affects them is not sufficient for grasping the systematic influence of historic factors on the Geisteswissenschaften: their object does not remain the same but is constituted ever anew by different questions directed towards it. The Geisteswissenschaften can only be freed from their obsessive identification with the procedures exemplified by the natural sciences if the historic character of their object is acknowledged as a positive moment rather than as an impediment to objectivity.

Gadamer's radical reappraisal of the situation of the interpreter is apparent when he evaluates the existence of prejudices. Lest he be misunderstood from the outset, Gadamer sounds a caveat:

a person trying to understand a text is prepared for it to tell him something. That is why a hermeneutically trained mind must be, from the start, sensitive to the text's newness. But this kind of sensitivity involves neither 'neutrality' in the matter of the object nor the extinction of one's self but the conscious assimilation of one's own fore-meanings and prejudices. The important thing is to be aware of one's own bias so that the text may present itself in all its newness and thus be able to assert its own truth against one's own fore-meanings. (pp. 254-4, 238)

And so Gadamer rehabilitates authority and tradition and negates their opposition to Reason by referring to 'legitimate prejudices'. How are we able to separate legitimate from arbitrary prejudices, and what are their foundation?

Heidegger's temporal interpretation of Dasein points at time as the ground in which the present finds its roots. When historism insisted on a gap between the present and the past, which

72 *Towards a hermeneutic paradigm for sociology*

issued in the methodological postulate to re-cognize past events
in the concepts employed at the time so as to arrive at objective
results, hermeneutic philosophy regarded this 'distance' as con-
tinuous, i.e. bridged by tradition, which provides the interpreter with cognitive potential. Hermeneutical theory, we
remember, focused on understanding as an activity of the
interpreter's subjectivity which was best conducted on the level
of two congenial minds. Betti's methodology, for example, laid
great store by the spontaneity of the subject - without acknowledging the overarching integration of the act of understanding
into historic processes. Gadamer therefore states that 'Understanding is not to be thought of so much as an action of one's
subjectivity, but as the placing of oneself within a tradition, in
which past and present are constantly fused' (pp. 274-5, 258).
It is this insight that obsessive concern with method has
obscured.

One prejudice which Gadamer examines is that of 'perfection'
in which formal and material elements fuse in the understanding
of the content of a text - which we antecedently assume to be
unified under one meaning and to be telling the truth. We are,
evidently, concerned with the content of a text and not with the
opinion of the author as such. Methodological hermeneutics objectified the original reader and replaced him with the interpreter.
By placing himself within his tradition, however, the interpreter
brings into play his own prejudices in the attempt to do justice
to the text's claim to truth thereby superseding his initial isolated standpoint and his concern with the author's individuality.
The interpreter is always embedded in a context of tradition
which can now be regarded as the sharing of basic and support-
ive prejudices. It would be presumptuous to imagine that the
whole range of prejudices which make possible and guide understanding can be brought to awareness and be employed at will;
outside the process of understanding it remains impossible even
to separate misleading from productive prejudices. The filtering
out of the 'legitimate' prejudices occurs in the dialectic between
otherness and familiarity, between object and tradition, that is
initiated by the temporal distance: 'It not only lets those prejudices that are of a particular and limited nature die away, but
causes those that bring about genuine understanding to emerge
clearly as such' (pp. 282, 263-4).

By bringing his own conceptions to bear on the text, the
interpreter does not, of course, aim at reproducing it in its
pristine state; not only does the text, at all times, represent
more than the author intended, it is also read differently in
different circumstances and understanding is, therefore, a productive endeavour. In this process our prejudices will have
either to prove adequate to the subject-matter or be modified,
and it is in this trial and error approach that the truth-claim
of the text can come to the fore. The relevance which historism
places upon methodical certainty leads it to neglect this historic

Towards a hermeneutic paradigm for sociology   73

element in understanding and to chase after the phantom of a
historical object that can be comprehended progressively. In
opposition to this view, Gadamer uses the Hegelian formula of
the unity of identity and difference to describe the process of
understanding as one in which the 'object' is part of the self
and in which both develop in the course of cognition.

Gadamer deals with this aspect under the title 'Wirkungsge-
schichte' (effective-history) and outlines the emergence and
content of the consciousness of it. This term eludes short
definitions but Gadamer, in a brilliant analysis, evidences its
structural elements: awareness of one's hermeneutic situation
and the 'horizon' that is characteristic of it; the dialogical
relationship between interpreter and text; the dialectic between
question and answer; openness for tradition. The awareness of
effective-history Gadamer also identifies with 'hermeneutic consciousness' as one that overarches both historical and historic
consciousness.

Effective-history represents the positive and productive
possibility of understanding. In its context, the interpreter
finds himself in his own 'situation' from where he has to understand tradition by means of the prejudices he derives from
within it. Any cognition of historical phenomena is, therefore,
always guided by the results of effective-history which determine in advance what is to be regarded as worth knowing. This
force can either be ignored in the objectivist reliance on methods
of interpretation – only that it will not go away as a result but
makes itself felt 'behind the back' of the naive observer; but it
could equally be harnessed for arriving at the truth which is
attainable to us despite all the limitations imposed upon us by
the finitude of our understanding.

To become conscious of the fundamental preconditions of our
understanding of the effects of effective-history remains a
necessary demand for truly scientific work. This would involve
an awareness of the hermeneutic situation, i.e. the situation in
which we find ourselves vis-à-vis the tradition we wish to
understand. Like all reflection, this one, too, has to remain
within the limits imposed by our historicality: 'to exist historically means that knowledge of oneself can never be complete.
All self-knowledge proceeds from what is historically pre-given'
(pp. 285-6, 269). For this reason, any historical situation contains its own horizon. Historical consciousness recognizes
different epochs which have to be understood in their own terms
by attempting to enter into the position occupied by the original
addressees of an author's intended meaning. But, paradoxically,
the desire to reconstruct past situations for the purposes of
objective knowledge aims straight past the real task: to find
out the valid and comprehensible truth embodied in tradition it
turns a means into an end. The hermeneutic consciousness, by
contrast, regards the conception of unitary epochs with a
closed horizon as an abstraction: 'The historic movement that is

74 *Towards a hermeneutic paradigm for sociology*

human Dasein is characterized by the fact that it is not determined by any definite situation and therefore does not possess a truly closed horizon. An horizon is, rather, something into which we wander and that moves with us' (p. 288). Both the interpreter and the part of tradition in which he is interested contain their own horizon; the task consists, however, not in placing oneself within the latter, but in widening one's own horizon so that it can integrate the other.

Gadamer terms the elevation of one's own particularity and that of the 'object' on to a higher generality the 'fusion of horizons'; this is what occurs whenever understanding takes place, i.e. our horizon is in a process of continued formation through the testing of our prejudices in the encounter with the past and the attempt to understand parts of our tradition. It is, therefore, inadequate to conceive of an isolated horizon of the present since it has already been formed through the contact with the past. This awareness of effective-history is to assist us in the controlled fusion of horizons.

Gadamer can, in this way, integrate Bultmann's pre-understanding,[2] as the questioning approach, with Heidegger's projective conceptual Vorgriff in the concept of 'horizon'.[3] The interpreter is, therefore, first aware of a distance between the text and his own horizon which leads in the process of understanding to a new, comprehensive horizon transcending the initial question and prejudices. The experience he makes in the course that leads to a new understanding is a hermeneutic one and essentially different from the experience that underlies the formulation of scientific methods. The objectivity of science has, since Bacon, been based on the possibility of constant, i.e. repeatable, experience which guarantees the intersubjectivity of findings. This approach is intent on eliminating all historic elements, as is exemplified by the experimental method in natural science. Husserl's analysis of the 'life-world' was directed against the monopoly of the experience gained within the 'world of science' - but with him experience, even in the pre-scientific sphere, carries a characteristic of the latter: it is directed at tangible phenomena.

The element of historicality in knowing has found its most emphatic acknowledgment with Hegel. Experience, as dialectical, feeds on determinate negation, and that indicates the fact that a new experience does not merely imply the overthrow of an earlier one, but represents a new and higher stage of knowledge which comprehends both the new insight and an awareness of what had wrongly been regarded as a matter of fact previously: we now not only know more, but we know better. Dialectical experience does not capture the specifically hermeneutic element in the fusion of horizons, however. It is part of a scheme that finds its completion in absolute knowledge, the total identity of object and knowledge. What is presumed - the system of total self-knowledge - precisely contravenes the central hermeneutic

Towards a hermeneutic paradigm for sociology   75

insight that self-knowledge can never be complete. Hermeneutic
experience does not imply a desire for knowing everything, but
being open to new experiences; it 'has its own fulfilment not in
definite knowledge but in that openness to experience that is
encouraged by experience itself . . . it refers to experience as
a whole' (pp. 338, 319).

The experience we are concerned with here is one of human
finitude; it does not mean merely to recognize what is just at
this moment there in front of us, but to have insight into the
limitations within which the future is still open to expectation.
Thus, true experience is that of one's own historicality.

Understanding as a dialogical process
Hermeneutic experience is neither monological as is science, nor
is it dialectical as is Hegel's universal history. Since Gadamer
explicates it on the model of human discourse I shall refer to it
as 'dialogical' rather than 'dialectical'.

A dialogue can be treated analogous to the interpretation of a
text in that in both cases we experience a fusion of horizons;

> both are concerned with an object that is placed before them.
> Just as one person seeks to reach agreement with his partner
> concerning an object, so the interpreter understands the
> object of which the text speaks . . . in successful conversation
> they both come under the influence of the truth of the object
> and are thus bound to one another in a new community . . .
> [it is] a transformation into a communion in which we do not
> remain what we were. (pp. 360, 341)

The central task of the interpreter is to find the question to
which a text presents the answer; to understand a text is to
understand the question. At the same time, a text only becomes
an object of interpretation by presenting the interpreter with
a question. In this logic of question and answer a text is drawn
into an event by being actualized in understanding - which itself
represents a historic possibility. The horizon of meaning is
consequently unlimited and the openness of both text and interpreter constitutes a structural element in the fusion of horizons.
In this dialogical understanding the concepts used by the Other,
be it a text or a thou, are regained by being contained within
the interpreter's comprehension. In understanding the question
posed by the text, we have already posed questions ourselves
and, therefore, opened up possibilities of meaning.

The linguisticality of understanding
The fusion of horizons is, however, inconceivable without the
medium of language. It has already been pointed out that understanding has to be seen as an interpretation and that interpretation is the explicit form of understanding. This insight is
connected with the fact that the language used in interpretation

76 Towards a hermeneutic paradigm for sociology

represents a structural moment of interpretation - something that Bultmann had completely failed to take into account.

For Gadamer, the problem of language presents the central issue of hermeneutic philosophy. His concern with language even marks the point where he transcends the concerns of existential hermeneutic; it also provides a way out from Hegel's 'speculative chain of a philosophy of world history' (pp. 343, 323). Instead of a total mediation of universal history, and in the light of the awareness that a mediation is required in the fusion of horizons, Gadamer develops a theory of the universality of language. Linguisticality as the mediation of past and present has the additional advantage of providing a powerful argument against the ideal of objectivity advanced by the Geisteswissenschaften.

In his discussion of the linguisticality of all understanding Gadamer gathers the insights so far accumulated in his book and provides them with a sharpened edge. The 'ontological turn of hermeneutics under the guidance of language' acquires its penetrative capacity through the incorporation of the work which Heidegger produced after his own famous 'turn', which is best reflected in the single statement that 'language is the house of Being' (Heidegger, 1967, p. 145).

Heidegger's thought is now 'on the way to language', as a title of his work suggests. Hermeneutic philosophy is now no longer seen as a theory but as the means of interpretation itself the focus of which is not given in terms of an understanding of existence but in terms of understanding language or, rather, to understand existence itself in terms of a language that addresses us from inside it. Language can, therefore, not be conceived of as an objectivation, but is itself that which speaks to us. A text, consequently, should not be examined in respect of the author's intention but in view of the subject matter contained within it which addresses itself to us and to which we respond with our words. Man's nature itself has to be defined as being linguistic: he exists by ant-worten, re-sponding with words, to the claims of Being. In 'Identity and Difference' the term 'hermeneutic ' even refers back to its original meaning, as the message of the gods transmitted by Hermes. Gadamer develops the theme of Being 'being brought to language . . . , [it] comes to language by opening itself up' (Gadamer, 1967, p. 192) through determining the task of hermeneutic reflection in respect of language as the medium, the means, ground, and 'middle' in and through which dialogue takes place. It cannot be used as a tool, as is the case in language considered as a system of signs; it already brings a situation, or the subject matter of a text, to disclosure. It discloses our 'world', the space enclosing and uniting the participants of a 'game' in which they gamble with their prejudices. 'From language's relation to the world there follows its specific factuality. Matters of fact come into language' (pp. 421, 403). There is no world outside language:

Towards a hermeneutic paradigm for sociology 77

the linguistic analysis of our experience of the world is prior, as contrasted with everything that is recognized and addressed as beings. The fundamental relation of language and world does not, then, mean that the world becomes the object of language. Rather, the object of knowledge and of statements is already enclosed within the world-horizon of language. The linguistic nature of the human experience of the world does not include making the world into an object. (pp. 426, 408)

The circularity apparent is again evaluated positively - it is impossible to observe linguistic existence for 'we cannot see a linguistic world from above in this way; there is no point of view outside the experience of the world in language from which it could itself become an object' (pp. 429, 410).

This line of argumentation is founded on the connection between language and understanding. Language does not produce a formulation of something we might have already understood pre-linguistically, but it is the mode of Being qua meaningful understanding as such. Its universal aspect consists in this: 'it is not the reflection of something given but the coming into language of a totality of meaning - . . . . Being that can be understood is language' (pp. 450, 431-2). All understanding is linguistic and 'the linguisticality of understanding is the concretion of effective historical conscience' (pp. 367, 351); the agreement emerging from a dialogue or in the interpretation of a text, i.e. on a subject matter, takes place in the medium of language. The fusion of horizons can now be seen as 'the full realization of conversation in which something is expressed that is not only mine or my author's, but common' (pp. 366, 350). The interpreter's horizon merges into the meaning of a text, or a partner's position, and is in this sense determining - without, however, assuming a fixed standpoint; it is, rather, an opinion and possibility that is open to change when encountering those of an other 'object'. Only in this way can a subject matter come to light.

SCIENCE AND LANGUAGE

In the experience we gain through our involvement with art, philosophy, and history Gadamer evidenced the possibility of truths that cannot be verified with the methodical means of science. The attempt to question their legitimacy involved a reflection upon the process of understanding and, with it, the hermeneutic problem exemplified by the circularity of understanding. Heidegger had already considered understanding as a mode of Being which underlies and guides all methodic scientific investigations - an insight Husserl expressed in reference to the pre-scientific 'life-world'. The experiences in that sphere Gadamer calls 'Welterfahrung' (experience of the world) and they

78 Towards a hermeneutic paradigm for sociology

do not consist of the calculation and measuring of what is present-at-hand, but in becoming aware of the meaning of beings. This fundamental understanding represents the field of universal hermeneutic and takes the form of a dialectic between question and answer operating on the basis provided by language, as is apparent when the participants in a dialogue come to an agreement about a subject matter. Another way of putting it would be to point at linguistic games in which the subjectivity of players is drawn into and subordinated to the game played by language itself which addresses them, suggests questions, questions us, lets itself be questioned by us. As in the 'language games' Wittgenstein referred to,[4] it would be absurd to try and transpose one that is being played out in science on to experiences of the life-world, or to legislate for either. When we understand, we do so by letting a subject matter address us; it is an event in which something meaningful occurs to us. It also takes place within a context to which both listener and subject matter belong: belongingness of recipient and message, of interpreter and text, characterizes the intimate relationship existing in this context - which now shows itself to be formed by 'tradition' and language.

Gadamer extends this insight in terms of the universality of the hermeneutic dimension to science as well. The hermeneutic reflection on the place of language in science centres on the recognition that 'Being that can be understood is language.' In Gadamer's development of Heidegger's existential analysis truth as disclosure is possible in and through language. Our experience of the world is always preformed by language, that is, interpreted in advance of being consciously appropriated through, for example, the employment of scientific methods. 'The linguistic experience is "absolute" . . . in contrast to it the presence of things, which science investigates and through which it acquires its objectivity, is part of those relative aspects which are comprehended by language's reference to the world' (p. 426).

Consequently,

> the world which appears in language and which is linguistically constituted is not in-itself in the same sense and not relative in the same sense as is the object of science. It is not in-itself in so far as it has not in the least the character of an object and insofar as the encompassing whole, which it is, can never be given in experience. (p. 428)

Hermeneutic reflections is concerned with the conditions of truth which are not a subject of the logic of science but which precede it. In relation to our primordial understanding of the world the objectifying approach of the sciences is the result of an abstraction; scientistic thought in this light 'forgets' the process of objectification which precedes scientific inquiry and it denounces the conception of truth as disclosure in its sole

Towards a hermeneutic paradigm for sociology 79

concern with its derivative: truth as empirically verifiable knowledge.

All scientific activity is, consequently, guided by some pre-knowledge embedded in our language. It makes itself felt not only in the formulation - of the aims of science, which necessitates normative discussions, but also in the communication between scientists concerning the criteria for a successful testing of hypotheses and, notably, in the formulation of scientific findings in everyday language - which is a precondition for their being put to use by 'outsiders'. The understanding taking place in science represents only one segment of the basic understanding that underlies all our activities and which contains conditions of truth preceding those of the logic of science. Can one derive from this an argument for the inadequacy of scientific methods to arrive at objective results?

Gadamer is at pains to dispel such a misleading view. His hermeneutic reflection brought to light the limitations of any striving for objectivity posed by the structural elements of understanding: all knowledge emerges from a historic situation in which the influence of tradition makes itself felt - even in science, e.g. in the form of preferred directions of research. But the recognition of this fact cannot be extrapolated into a questioning of the scientificity of its results. Science follows the laws of its subject matter and can only be judged in relation to that. When it transgresses its legitimate sphere of activity - that of objectifiable objects - and when it usurps the role of purveyor of all truth, hermeneutic consciousness will assert the legitimacy of a discipline of questioning and inquiry in which the methods of science cannot take hold; and it will re-affirm the fact that method can not guarantee truth, but only secure degrees of certainty about controllable processes.

As a final insight emerging from the linguistic basis of all - scientific - thought, the time-honoured distinction between the natural and human sciences gains a more plausible basis when considered in terms of the role that the pre-understanding of the object plays in both: the linguisticality of experience of the world enters the objectifying sciences in the form of inevitable preconceptions and preferences which can partly be rendered ineffective through the adherence to a quantificatory methodology and terminology. But judgments and propositions are only a special form of linguistic activity and remain embedded within the totality of existence from where the human sciences derive their sphere of investigation; here, the role of prejudices is a positive one in that they open up possible fields of meaning in the object.

80 *Towards a hermeneutic paradigm for sociology*

OBJECTIVITY AND OBJECTIVISM IN THE GEISTESWISSENSCHAFTEN

Hermeneutical theory, for which Betti may stand as a representative, is concerned with the formulation of a methodology of the Geisteswissenschaften; it thereby continues Dilthey's endeavour to provide an objective account of meaningful phenomena.

Objectivity is, within this tradition, conceived in relation to the ideal of objectivity associated with the natural sciences and, therefore, predicated on the clear separability of subject and object. Despite Betti's qualificatory reference to the relative objectivity attainable in the Geisteswissenschaften, it can be stated that hermeneutical theory does not take full account of the double hermeneutic - which Dilthey himself recognized when he stated that 'the first condition for the possibility of a science of history consists in the fact that I myself am a historical being; that he who researches into history is the same as he who makes it' (Dilthey, 1964-6, VII, vol. p. 278).

Yet, the antinomies of hermeneutical theory are already apparent in Dilthey's work.

He considered himself to be a 'stubborn empiricist' and it is in this light that his quest for objectivity in the Geisteswissenschaften had best be considered. The stipulation that the Geisteswissenschaften be of use for social-political activity necessitates that, in Dilthey's thinking, their results aspire to the degree of certainty and generality normally attributed to the natural sciences. Gadamer (1975, pp. 61-2) and Habermas (1968a, pp. 226-8) have retraced the line of argument that leads Dilthey onto scientistic territory.

Empiricistically, he focuses on something 'given'; the ultimate unit of experience which in the sphere of hermeneutics is the 'lived experience'. Equally, 'reliving' - a concept from which Dilthey never seemed able to free himself - functions as the equivalent to observation: 'both fulfil on the empirical level the criterion for a copy theory of truth; they guarantee, it seems, the reproduction of something immediate within an isolated consciousness that is free of any subjective elements' (Habermas, 1968, p. 226).

By dealing with the problem of objectivity in such terms, Dilthey seems to have fallen behind his own intentions - to establish the Geisteswissenschaften as a non-objectivist study of man - and high standard of reflection.

By regarding historical objectivations as 'givens' that could be deciphered with the help of hermeneutical techniques, Dilthey failed to do justice to his characterization of the relationship of interpreter and text as one of subject/subject and stylized it into the familiar subject/object one. The price for securing a degree of objectivity in the study of expressions of an other mind: the inability to take the step from 'historical consciousness'

Towards a hermeneutic paradigm for sociology   81

to 'historical experience' or to 'hermeneutic consciousness'; that
is to say, Dilthey was too concerned with emphasizing the need
and value of taking a critical stance towards the past and also
trying to secure an objective status for this undertaking. This
posture shows Dilthey as a child of the Enlightenment and as
following in the Cartesian tradition; but it leads him to overlook
the challenge a historical object may make on the interpreter's
conceptions and values, and to remain blind to the need for
self-reflection in which the subject realizes his indebtedness to
tradition and language as the bases and media of thinking.
Accounts of Dilthey's sliding into objectivism differ slightly.
Gadamer (1975, p. 226) refers to a conflict between the philosophy
of Life and a scientistic conception of knowledge with Dilthey
finally taking the side of the latter. Habermas (1968, p. 230),
in contrast, sees such a development as being inherent in the
philosophy of Life itself which seems to allow for the transposition
of the ideal of objectivity from the natural sciences to the
Geisteswissenschaften.

Turning now to Betti's hermeneutical theory, we find that the
Rationalist background to his conception is not only apparent in
his emphasis on method and demonstrable knowledge, or the
setting of the whole problematic of hermeneutics within the
subject-object scheme, but also underlies his, ultimate, failure
to provide a consistent account of the role of the subject. 'Subjectivity' is subdivided by Betti into subjective and intersubjective moments which he equates with normative and theoretical
approaches to the subject matter. Betti follows Neo-Kantianism
when he affirms the primacy of the theoretical and exemplifies
this point by referring to the investigation of values. These
represent the ideal being-in-itself for value-oriented interpretation; in opposition to mere feeling or empathy it is that which
is able to become the content of an articulated and conscious
'judgment', i.e. something that claims 'validity'.

Betti's metascience cannot escape objectivism. Despite his
affirmations and copious quotations, which indicate his close
affinity with idealist thought and his roots in the humanist
tradition, he remains within the orbit of the mode of knowledge-
acquisition characteristic of the natural sciences. It is only from
this perspective that he is able to reduce the interpreter's
historic situatedness, which fuses understanding-of-others and
self-understanding into a dialectical unity, to a factor making
only for subjectivism and relativism. Betti's methodology is thus
trapped by the same constraints that had already been limiting
Dilthey's systematic contribution to the epistemology of the
Geisteswissenschaften. But it is with the latter that we find
some signposts pointing in the direction in which an answer to
the questions so far left unanswered may be found; as Betti
himself has remarked, Dilthey fuses 'understanding' and 'lived
experience': both take place on the basis of a shared experience.
Betti strongly disapproved of this conception, sensing that it

82 Towards a hermeneutic paradigm for sociology

implied the transformation of the subject-object relationship in which the former questions the latter into one pertaining between two subjects of a communicative interaction. It is not that Betti has failed to recognize the moment of self-development in the process of understanding; in his epistemological 'prolegomena' he provides a cogent defence of it:

> by discovering the cosmos of values a thinking being develops in the course of a process of communication that takes place among various subjects. . . . The axiological judgement is, just as is cognition, in a continuous state of development . . . so that the continuous development of one point necessarily brings to light new aspects in the other. (pp. 20-1)

This statement comes close to a recognition of the hermeneutic circle, but Betti immediately slips away from its relativistic implications and seeks refuge with objectivist tenets. It will be remembered that Betti saw his chief task in clarifying the relationship between understanding and interpretation and in defending the objectivity of the latter. Gadamer's hermeneutic philosophy, on the other hand, has provided us with insight into the structure of understanding that profoundly challenges the objectivist remnants not only in Betti's work, but at the same time, those in sociological approaches which take their starting point in Neo-Kantian philosophy – all of which fail to give an adequate account of the historicality of knowledge which Gadamer has explicated in terms of the consciousness of effective-history, which seeks to reflect upon its own prejudices and to control its pre-understanding.

Hermeneutic philosophy focuses not on the methodology of the Geisteswissenschaften but on their relationship to the whole of our experience of the world; by evidencing understanding as a fundamental characteristic of existence, it does not intend to restrict the disciplined and skilled understanding of texts, but only hopes to free it from a false self-understanding.

As is immediately apparent, the interpreter who is concerned with historical rather than ontic phenomena is himself part of tradition when he approaches segments of it; the subject-object dichotomy existing between the res cognitans and res extensa (Descartes) is therefore not applicable. Understanding is part of a game that is being played around him, an event which represents nothing less than the precondition for his scientific activity.

From his hermeneutic situation the interpreter, or social scientist, derives a comprehensive pre-understanding which guides the questions he formulates within a framework of societal norms. His standpoint is initially determining and it is only after reflecting upon his immediate preconceptions that he can exclude the more direct influence of his own environment. Understanding is not a construct from principles, but the development of know-

Towards a hermeneutic paradigm for sociology   83

ledge we have gained of a wider context and which is determined by the language we use. The fact that the interpreter's technical concepts have to mediate between those apparent in the 'object' and his own puts the onus on him to subject the latter to continued reflection. He should avoid conceptions that may be current in his time and which express class or ethnic bias and should allow himself to keep his own concepts open to correction in the course of his close acquaintance with the subject matter.

The historicality of understanding so far outlined refers to three aspects: the socio-historic mediation of pre-understanding; its constitution of possible objects; and the value decisions formed by social praxis. Betti and Hirsch (1967) have attacked this notion and fear the unwarranted intrusion of subjective elements into what could be objective interpretation. Their views seem to rest, however, on a misconception of the role of pre-understanding in particular, and of philosophical hermeneutic in general. By failing to recognize that the latter does not attempt to meddle into the skilled interpretation of texts but only tries to show what happens in all understanding, both these authors have simply missed the point; in fact, the adequate conduct of hermeneutical research ought to be aware of both the 'negative' and 'positive' aspects of the role of pre-understanding.

The interpreter's thoughts have already fused with the subject matter when he tries to arrive at the meaning of a text - but this initial function of his standpoint does not, of course, imply that he will stubbornly try and maintain his pre-notions in the face of unfolding textual meaning. As the description of the fusion of horizons and the concept of a 'game' indicates, understanding can be successful only in the constant revision of one's standpoint which allows the subject matter to emerge. The prejudices held by the interpreter, therefore, play the important part of opening an horizon of possible questions and it is the hallmark of a truly scientific endeavour that it tries to bring them to consciousness.

Betti is, on the other hand, justified in fearing for the 'canon of the autonomy of the text'. The fixedness of the meaning of a text as the author intended it has already been recognized by Dilthey as the precondition for the objective interpretation of meaning. With Schleiermacher a similar conception led to the principle of an 'affinity of minds' that would do justice to the intellectual stature of the author. Hermeneutics has, therefore, always been tied to this specific conception of meaning as the author's intention that could be arrived at through the inversion of the process of creation. Closely connected with this view was the maxim that the author could be understood better than he had understood himself - which betrays the roots historism has in the Enlightenment and its conviction of the superiority of the present in the development towards the self-determination of Reason - thereby failing to recognize that the interpreter 'is enveloped by changing horizons and changes with them' (p. 506).

84 Towards a hermeneutic paradigm for sociology

In other words, there can be no 'one correct' interpretation.
As Gadamer exemplified in reference to understanding as a
dialogical event, such communication occurs only in the form of
a mediation of past and present, the fusion of the horizons of a
text and of its interpreter. Once completed, a work of art can
no longer be tied to its creator but has to be seen as assuming
an existence of its own which may embody insights which the
author may have been unaware of. In opposition to inverting
the process of creation, understanding will try to shell-out the
subject matter contained in the text and bring it to expression.
The interpreter's activity follows the logic of question and
answer and provides the 'object' with the possibility of resonating with new and widened meaning. The context of tradition
thereby comes to life again – not in the form of a repetition of
the experience the original perceiver may have gained from it,
but in a new way: something emerges that had not been there
before. The conception of an existence-in-itself of a text is,
therefore, quite incorrect and exhibits an element of dogmatism.
This is what Gadamer means when he talks about the 'speculative' character of interpretations which are not restricted to
the methodical approach. The words used by the interpreter
have their origin in the context of language that comes to form
an aura of meanings which are quite unique. The appropriation
of textual meaning, consequently, has to be regarded not so
much as a duplicative effort but as a genuine creation itself;
each appropriation is different and equally valid. From here
Gadamer can go on to suggest that to understand literature
implies not a referring back to past events, but a participating
here and now in what is being said, the sharing of a message,
the disclosure of a world.

What relevant insights can be derived from Gadamer's hermeneutic philosophy concerning Betti's other canons?

The need to participate in the event of understanding seems,
on first sight, to be covered by the 'canon of the actuality of
understanding'. A closer look will, however, evidence the
crucial point that Betti cannot give a systematic account of the
subject's historicality. While requiring his active interest in the
author and his work – following hereby the hermeneutical maxim
that one can only understand, and consequently should only
attempt to interpret and translate, a which work one is, at least
potentially, in agreement with – Betti does not situate the subject historically as a participant in a tradition, universe of discourse, etc., and can, therefore, conceive of the concepts he
employs initially only as instrumental, and potentially detrimental,
to the objectivity of interpretation; in any case, it is the historicality of understanding that Betti sees negatively as one
factor allowing only 'relative objectivity'. Paradoxically, Betti
considers the process of interpretation in terms of a scheme that
is apparent in all forms of cognition – just as Gadamer did; only
that Betti cannot escape from the subject-object relationship

Towards a hermeneutic paradigm for sociology   85

even where an other mind addresses us. The consideration of the process of interpretive understanding, as involving the re-cognition and re-construction of an author's intention and creational process, consequently remains within a psychologistic conception that dismantles and then reassembles human expressions in an almost mechanical way. The paradox referred to resides, consequently, in the fact that despite his profoundly humanist stance, Betti remains unable to regard the Other as another subject with equally strong demands to be recognized, listened to, and agreed with; in the process of understanding subject and 'object' are irredeemably tied together.

To conclude this chapter it may be worth asking what insights Gadamer's investigation into interpretation yield for a better conception of the process of understanding – remembering that Betti considered this question to be the rationale for his own work. The latter, put in a nutshell, found that both interpretation and understanding develop in a triadic process involving an author and a perceiving subject who both are mediated by meaning-full forms; (objective) interpretation, in relation to understanding, serves as a means to an end.

How does Gadamer see it? In fact, he draws Betti's wrath by not only collapsing interpretation and understanding into one another but even introducing 'application' as the third moment of what is, essentially, a unitary phenomenon.

Gadamer sets out to legitimate the truth-claims of knowledge derived from extra-scientific spheres of experience via reflections upon the phenomena of understanding; he does so in the light of his view that science, both social and natural, is today, in the shape of the 'expert', filling the vacuum left by the disintegration of religious interpretations of human existence and the demise of tradition as a source of orientation. That is to say, the successful completion of his task would equally stake a claim for prudence and ensuing praxis in opposition to ever-encroaching technical knowledge and instrumental practice. It is obvious that the field of hermeneutics represents the proving-ground – or last bastion – for non-scientistic debates concerning values and norms. The sphere of interpretation acquires its significance for social development because it is here that communicative understanding about the aims and purpose of social existence is achieved.

The historistic Geisteswissenschaften have been characterized by their attempt at assimilating the research process in the field of objectivations of mind, especially in history, to the standards of the natural sciences. Betti has argued forcefully against a misconception in this view which fails to take account of the specificity of the object of the Geisteswissenschaften – which requires an internal recognition and reconstruction and is, therefore, dependent on the spontaneity of the perceiving subject. In this sense, Betti could reject the overtly objectivist nature of the 'historical school' around Ranke. But it can be

86 *Towards a hermeneutic paradigm for sociology*

argued that his concern with salvaging at least 'relative objectivity' through the employment of a set of canons represents a residual of the scientistic approach to the non-natural sphere. Gadamer has rightly linked science with method - a development originating with Galileo - and its introduction into the hermeneutical process can only lead to the objectification of the 'object' and the subject's mastery over it; at the same time, it provides the basis for approaches that are 'value-free' in respect of their treatment of the subject matter, and 'neutral' in regard to the use of its result, rendering the results open for re-examination by other interested parties who can ascertain their correctness by following the same routes of inquiry. In the theory of interpretation this conception gave rise to the distinction between interpretation and application.

In contrast, the unity of understanding, interpretation, and application can also be argued for and shown briefly.

Intellegere and explicare find their unity in the fusion of horizons that characterizes any true understanding. This event implies that, for example, a text is created anew in an interpretation which is guided by a horizon of understanding that itself changes in the course of its activity; put in another way, the linguisticality of understanding renders interpretation speculative in that the content of an aspect of tradition is given voice and is empowered to communicate to us its truth in terms intelligible to us and consonant with our life experiences. Understanding tradition can not be limited to the acquisition of knowledge concerning a specific text but finds its fulfilment in the recognition of truths and insights; it is directed at, and based upon, effective-history and is, therefore, part of its object in such a way that the past is constantly reinterpreted or, what is the same, understood differently.

The distinction between normative application, re-cognitive and re-constructive interpretation, and reproduction is equally rejected by Gadamer. Reproduction he considers to be, initially, interpretation aiming at a correct view and is, therefore, also a form of understanding - it does not constitute a recreation but rather allows a work of art to come into its own. Since understanding always contains interpretation there can be no difference, in principle, between the interpretation of a musical and philological text: it is in both cases undertaken in the medium of language and merges into the immediacy of truth.

In the case of normative application, Betti seems to stand on firm ground when he states that interpretation in jurisdiction and theology proceeds from a dogmatic point of view which requires the application of an objective meaning-context to a particular situation. Gadamer argues that it is impossible clearly to distinguish between dogmatic and historical interpretation since, in the case of jurisdicial hermeneutics, a historian of law and a jurist approach a legal text from the standpoint of the present legal situation and consider its relevance from this per-

Towards a hermeneutic paradigm for sociology 87

spective; they both mediate between past and present: the former can not exclude the contemporary effects of a law, the history of which he is tracing, whilst the jurist has to determine the original intention of the law-maker before he can draw conclusions for the present. Equally, a theologian's sermon represents the concretion of the Good News in that it explicates a received truth. 'Application' as the mediation of past and present appears as the third moment of the unity of understanding, interpretation and application constituting the hermeneutic effort: adequate understanding of a text, which corresponds to its claim and message, changes with the concrete situation from which it takes place; it is always already an application.

That understanding and application are interwoven Gadamer further clarifies by reference to Aristotle's description of the opposition between phronesis on the one side, and épistémé and techne on the other. Phronesis (prudence) as practical knowledge is internalized knowledge and cannot be forgotten even if it is not needed at the moment nor can it develop without a 'prejudice'. As action-oriented knowledge, it is not directed at particular aims, as is technical know-how; maxims of action have to be applied to changing situations whereby the original knowledge is itself further developed. This relationship between phronesis and applicative understanding underlies the work of the interpreter concerned with tradition; its unity is guaranteed by the dependency of understanding on the structure of prejudices.

Gadamer's hermeneutic philosophy obviously represents a gigantic re-orientation of hermeneutics by freeing it from the constraints it imposed upon itself in its narrow striving for methodically secured objectivity. At the same time, it provides a perspective for viewing scientific progress in general in terms of the universality of the hermeneutic aspect which was expounded on parallel lines by Kuhn's paradigm-oriented conception of scientific revolutions. Hermeneutic reflection upon the effective-history underlying all thought represents not only a critique of the objectivism of historism, but also of the physicalism underlying the ideal of a unity of science - without for a moment impinging upon the scientific character of the result achieved under the auspices of historism and Positivist Logic of Science.

5 OBJECTIVE INTERPRETATION IN MACRO-SOCIOLOGY AND THE HERMENEUTIC DIMENSION

Sociology, as developed within the framework of behaviourism and its empiricistic metascience, cannot concern itself legitimately with social phenomena that are irreducible to the behaviour of individual actors. One such phenomenon is, of course, society, but even 'the social' as a category is here in danger of losing its independent character leaving sociology without a distinctive subject matter. From the aspect of methodology, it has to be added that the imposition of a specific set of procedural norms for the study of meaningful action can only be carried through if the practitioners of this discipline refuse to engage in any critical reflection concerning the appropriateness of this particular mode of investigation.

The price to be paid for trying to emulate the 'hard' sciences is a kind of intellectual sclerosis that manifests itself in narrowly conceived research programmes with often utterly trivial results and the tendency to misperceive the object. It is my view that this undesirable condition is intimately linked with the failure to come to grips with the meaning-dimension that exists both within the object and between it and the researcher, or, to put it differently, there is more to social phenomena than meets the eye.

Non-scientistic sociology can, therefore, be defined by its recognition of the meaningfulness of social phenomena. Yet within this alternative approach to sociology there exists a major cleavage in relation to how this 'meaning' is to be conceived and studied. Macro-sociology focuses on objective meaning, thereby paralleling Dilthey's systematic Geisteswissenschaften, whereas micro-sociology considers subjectively intended meaning as the object of sociology which gives rise to a problematic similar to the one that emerged in the discussion of the historical Geisteswissenschaften and hermeneutical theory.

Both these contemporary strands can claim Weber as their ancestor - given certain modifications which they consider to be required.

Weber's methodology shares to some extent Dilthey's concern when it is stated that the 'cultural sciences . . . analyse the phenomenon of life in terms of cultural significance' (Weber, 1949, p. 75). Human creations cannot adequately be studied within the framework of the natural sciences, which can only capture quantitative aspects, since they 'are concerned with psychological and intellectual phenomena'; it follows that here

Objective interpretation in sociology 89

'empathic understanding is naturally a problem' (Weber, 1949, p. 74).

Historical phenomena are characterized by the fact that they embody cultural values which, through being meaningful, attract the historian's interest: they are constituted by a 'value-orientation'. The relationship that emerges between the historian and his object is a form of understanding, 'value-interpretation', in which the meaning of objectivations is explicated.[1]

The problem that confronts the study of meaningful phenomena is to render it objective. In relation to this hermeneutic problem, Weber's scheme, which tries to bring together the interpretive understanding of meaningful phenomena with a concern for scientific canons, centres on the requirement that sociological accounts be adequate on both the levels of meaning and cause. That is to say that sociologically relevant interpretations have to be supplemented by a causal explanation of action in terms of its underlying motives. Hypotheses arrived at in the course of interpretation have to be tested in relation to 'typical courses of action', 'tendencies', states of 'normality'.[2]

It is on account of having incorporated the duality of interpretive and explanatory accounts within his scheme that Weber could provide the stepping-stones for a general theory of social action and interpretive sociology.

In this chapter I shall deal with the former offshoot of Weber's work, Parsons's general theory of action, and with a related attempt at objective interpretations of meaningful phenomena: structuralism.

PARSONS'S FRAMEWORK FOR THE STUDY OF THE OBJECTIVE MEANING OF ACTION

Weber's device for providing causally adequate accounts of subjectively meaningful action is that of the 'ideal type'. The centrality of this analytical tool bears witness to the formalistic tendency in Weber's work which he shares with sociology in Germany at his time, dominated, as it was, by Neo-Kantian thinking. In accordance with the 'principle of subjectivity', which states that the subjective meaning of social phenomena is to be apprehended, this is achieved through the employment of formal categories which benefit from being logically unambiguous.

In view of the further course of objective understanding the ideal type of purposive-rational action is of particular interest. An external observer can, given that he knows the actor's goals and purposes, assess the rationality of the choice of means employed.

Parsons's early work, 'The Structure of Social Action', incorporated the principle of subjectivity into a projected voluntaristic theory of action. The voluntaristic element in the action framework, which itself was from the outset conceived in opposition

90 Objective interpretation in sociology

to the behaviouristic reduction of sociology to social psychology, centres on the ability of an actor to choose what he considers to be the appropriate means for achieving certain ends within a given situation.

But this choice, Parsons emphasizes, is not random. For one thing, the 'situation' in which actions take place exerts a conditioning and delimiting influence. More important, though, is 'the influence of an independent, determinate selection factor, a knowledge which is necessary to the understanding of the concrete course of action. What is essential to the concept of action is that there should be a normative orientation' (1968, pp. 44-5).

The development of Parsons's work towards, at times, a near-behaviourist position in relation to the study of action may be rooted in his concern with the normative orientation of action and a general theory of action in which the spontaneity of individual actors is all but obliterated. The shift towards Durkheimian themes is apparent in Parsons's treatment of the 'problem of order': action is guided by values and norms which are themselves part of the 'institutionalized normative culture'.

As, at about the same time, Parsons incorporated Freudian insights into his theorizing the interpretive aspect of his initial scheme could now altogether be jettisoned. The mechanism of 'internalization' of socio-cultural norms - which resembles Durkheim's conception of social control through moral authority - made it possible to by-pass introspective accounts of the intentions guiding social action.[3]

From 'The General Theory of Action' onwards, voluntarism in social action was replaced by a model of the actor who participates in social intercourse in order to satisfy his needs; this requires him to have internalized a pre-given pattern of behaviour which is institutionalized in patterns of culture. As a concomitant to rendering redundant the task of choosing an authentic course-of-action, the individual himself need no longer be at the centre of analysis: 'the social system is composed of relationships of individual actors and only of such relationships. . . . For most analytical purposes, the most significant unit of social structure is not the person but the role' (Parsons, 1951, p. 23).

In this way, the meaning of social action can be ascertained objectively, i.e. without direct reference to the intentions of the actor. Social analysis can consequently abandon the hermeneutic access to its object in favour of a structural analysis of the conditions of action: 'It consists now of exploring the de-subjectivating factors; mechanisms and pressures which prevent actors' choices from being random in defiance of systematization and predictability' (Bauman, 1978, p. 144).

The movement from the actual intentions of concrete actors to the analytical level in which possible motives are located within the web of societal needs was seen by Parsons as a remedy to Weber's failure to carry through a systematic functional analysis. Sociology can, and has to be, regarded as a science. Weber

Objective interpretation in sociology 91

provided the foundation by bringing together the ethos of science and the art of interpreting individual and cultural meaning; but he had ultimately failed to establish sociology as a general theory of action.[4] In Parsons's remedy, objective understanding of meaning takes place in the context of a systems theory in which 'pattern variables of value-orientation' are linked to the functions of systems of action.

The general theory of action seems to solve the hermeneutic problem at a stroke - through by-passing it: the intentionality of action is reduced to needs of a given system and then substituted by reference to the internalization of socially approved cultural values; the explanation of action consequently refers to objective-institutional rather than subjective-motivational factors: the 'value-relation' is, finally, relegated to the pre-scientific sphere in keeping with the scientistic separation of the contexts of discovery and verification.

The question, therefore, is whether general theories of action can circumvent the hermeneutic dimension. I shall attempt an answer by examining the issue of whether the categorical framework employed in the objective interpretation of meaningful phenomena can avoid all traces of its historic context. Here I can follow Habermas's argument (1973a, pp. 164-84) that this is not the case and that the concepts formulated and employed in general theories of action bear traces of their socio-historic origin.

As far as the analysis of systems of roles is concerned, it appears that the social scientist remains within the hermeneutic dimension. The action-orienting meaning at the basis of a role derives from cultural tradition which, consequently, introduces hermeneutic interpretation into the objective analysis of action. Institutionalized values, which provide their meaning-content, have to be seen in relation to an overarching whole, i.e. their socio-historic context, by an observer who does not stand apart but who participates in the same, or a similar, system and who therefore brings into his work his own experiences which have sedimented to form his pre-understanding of the object: the family, society, the state, etc.

Parsons conceived of patterns of value-orientation as universal features of social existence and could thus see them as transcending specific historical situations. They represent a constant set of elementary units which can be actualized in a number of combinations. Yet the set of values which Parsons considered may not, after all, be exhaustive and the link which he establishes between value-orientations and necessary functions for the maintenance of social systems is at best plausible but has, in any case, to remain arbitrary. Aron contributes the following query concerning Parsons's aim at providing a[5]

conceptual vocabulary useful for the understanding of any society. It claims to be independent both of modern society

92 *Objective interpretation in sociology*

and of the philosophy that inspired Max Weber. Has the reference to the present really disappeared from the Parsonian conceptualization or more generally from the conceptualization proper to modern sociology? (Aron, 1971, pp. 251-2)

Following this line of argument, Habermas notes a further link with the present when he asks whether existing control values which maintain a social system in a state of equilibrium may not themselves be historically specific - and therefore open to challenge and change. It may be the case that given institutionalized values do not accord with objective possibilities for freeing needs that remain repressed in a given system of roles.

Extending this argument on to the level of the use-context of knowledge produced by general theories of action, Dreitzel has argued that they have 'a tendency to obscure relations of production and their historical context. Understood in this way, it functions as an ideology which today contributes to establishing and maintaining the technocratic consciousness of the educated middle classes' (Dreitzel, 1972, p. 169).

On this point, Habermas is even more emphatic. In the context of his debate with Luhmann he states that 'a systems theory represents, as it were, the highest form of a technocratic consciousness which makes it possible that practical questions are in advance defined as technical ones and thereby excluded from public, unrestricted debate' (Habermas and Luhmann, 1975, p. 145).

THE STRUCTURAL(IST) ANALYSIS OF MEANINGFUL PHENOMENA

At this point of my consideration of the double hermeneutic in macro-sociology, I would like to move on to another formal approach to the study of meaningful phenomena which equally relies on a classificatory scheme built up through progressive dichotomizations: structuralism. Linguistics as a model for sociology? Structuralist thought is not entirely free from scientistic tendencies which, for example, are apparent in the attempt to establish the unity of science in which, again, one particular branch of science is to serve as the model for the social sciences.

Logical Empiricism extended the methodology of (macro)-physics to all other areas of scientific activity, regardless of the constitution of the object. The driving force behind this imperialism derived from an unshakeable belief in empiricist dogma, especially the assumption that knowledge is acquired only through the faithful duplication in mind of objects existing independently of the observer. Once the rationalist critique evidenced its untenability, a different approach to the unity of science was required: the social sciences could be put on

Objective interpretation in sociology   93

equal footing with the natural sciences not by aping the approach
of physicists but by modelling themselves on a science that
emerged from within their own conspectus. This science is
linguistics. It is held to (a) represent a body of genuinely scientific knowledge, and (b) explicit features which are apparent in
all social phenomena. By approximating linguistics, in respect
of both its methods of analysis and the features of the modes of
existence of its objects it selects, it is hoped that the recalcitrant element in the social sciences that has so far prevented
them from reaching the status of mature sciences, i.e. socio-
historical relativism, may be overcome.

It is not necessary here to recount the history of structural
linguistics, apart from stating its two most central insights: one,
the division of language as an object of study into language
seen as a system ('langue') and as practice, i.e. speech ('parole')
originating with de Saussure.[6] La langue stands for the system
of rules and relations shared by a speech community whereas
la parole, the spoken word, refers to the use of formal elements
in order to express a thought or a feeling. Individual use of
language is in this view seen as being based on the uncon-
sciously operating constitutive rules of an underlying code.

Two, the distinction between unconscious structure and its
manifestation in speech was further developed in Trubetzkoj's
phonological method where language is treated as a system in
which phonemes from a 'morphological structure' and are defined
not in reference to their acoustic quality, but their position in
a system; the most prominent relationship between phonemes
being one of - binary - opposition.

This model has proved fruitful in the investigation of socio-
cultural phenomena apart from language. As informing the science
of signs, semiology,[7] it has proved its potential for decoding
signs such as rites, customs, myths, gestures which all play an
important part in regulating social processes. As the name of
this new science indicates, its objects are investigated in view
of their signalling function, as signifying something, i.e. the
signified.[8] Barthes, who is generally considered as one, if not
the, great master of this approach to literature, is not forgetful
of the limitations of this formal science.[9] As far as I am aware,
Barthes does also not employ the efficacy of the semiological
approach for the study of significations to 'browbeat' the rest of
the social sciences into falling in line with this approach. It
seems to me, however, that both these points are treated differently by Lévi-Strauss. His eagerness to impose a structuralist
methodology on the social sciences leads him to elevate the purely
formal, and thereby a-historical, aspect of this science into its
greatest asset when he gives formal arrangements the logical,
methodological and, at times even, ontological priority over their
semantic and pragmatic significance.

My discussion of the unity of science as proposed from within
the structuralist tradition consequently comes to focus on the

94 *Objective interpretation in sociology*

question: in what sense can linguistics be considered as a model for sociology?

Lévi-Strauss's work contains the perhaps most ambitious and wide-ranging application of semiological methods. He outlines this approach in the following way:

> First, structural linguistics shifts from the study of conscious linguistic phenomena to their unconscious infrastructure; second, it does not treat terms as independent entities, taking instead as the basis of analysis the relations between terms; third, it introduces the concept of system . . . ; finally, structural linguistics aims at discovering general laws. (1968, p. 33)

Lévi-Strauss's famous treatment of kinship systems, myths, and other cultural phenomena in analogy to language, that is as codes, is based on a number of methodological premises:[10] structural methodology is non-empiricist in that it conceives of structures as the unconscious infrastructure of perceived events and as the syntax of transformations which generates empirical phenomena. This ontological commitment also implies that these structures have to be evidenced by scientific reason after all relevant empirical data have been gathered. Such a method is also anti- rather than non-historicist and, furthermore, reductionist, since all human creations are seen as solutions to general problems which are embedded in the universal laws of the human mind.

The limitations of this method are inseparable from its strengths. The focus on the syntactical dimension of the phenomena under study excludes consideration of the pragmatic intention that informed their creation and their continuing, if changing, re-appropriation. Theorists arguing from a hermeneutic position would stress that the acquisition of traditioned meaning takes place through the conscious re-acquisition of a symbolic content by an interpreter who enters directly into the semantic field of an object which he wishes to understand and thereby finds himself involved in the hermeneutic circle.

To what extent, then, has the 'structuralist promise' been fulfilled? It derives from the possibility that 'in search of the necessary general laws governing human culture we can now descend to the unconscious system which precedes and conditions all specific empirically approachable, socio-cultural choices' (Bauman, 1973a, pp. 71-2).

The transference of the structuralist approach to other, non-linguistic, cultural aspects is circumscribed, however, and encounters two principal constraints.

First, 'no single and qualitatively homogeneous model can account for all empirical phenomena of culture' because in addition to its informative function a cultural system 'also shapes the world of concrete beings' (p. 74).

Objective interpretation in sociology 95

Second, the exclusive concern with semiotic functions also underlies the tendency to overlook items

> which in the course of time grew out of their meaning and having not found any new semiotic function linger on as an inexplicable and meaningless relic of the past. . . . Once again, what may be said on a culture from the point of view of its actual semiotic function does not exhaust the richness of its empirical existence. (p. 76)

Structuralist dogma and the study of society
The linguistic analogy, like any other, can be fruitfully employed - as long as one remains conscious of its limitations and is aware of the danger of moving from the heuristic to the ontological level. It appears to me that the move from structuralist methodology to structuralism is an instance of the unwarranted extrapolation from scientific method to a Weltanschauung[11] with strongly scientistic underpinnings.

Chomsky employed mathematical methods for the investigation of the syntax of language - as did Lévi-Strauss in his anthropological work. Yet it seems that the latter's brilliant success in his study of the 'savage mind' may have led him into succumbing to the doctrine associated with structuralism.

One can, initially, agree with Lévi-Strauss when he states that 'structuralism uncovers a unity and coherence within things which could not be revealed by simple description of the facts somehow scattered and disorganized before the eyes of knowledge' (1977, p. ix). It is this conception which, however, also serves to legitimate structuralism, i.e. a particular view of reality in which structures are given pre-eminence, and change, history or the subject are considered as secondary, if not dispensable.

In the work of Foucault,[12] for example, socio-historical processes are conceived as manifestations of a concealed logic. The 'a priori historique' and the 'épistémé' of an epoch are here hypostatized into the unfathomable roots of historical appearances such as the laws of economic exchange or various classificatory schemes. At the same time, we are confronted with the celebration of the end of the era of man, humanism, and Reason.

To what extent can society be analysed in relation to unconscious structures? Or, to put it differently, can social phenomena be investigated in terms of the code/message dichotomy deriving from linguistics?

Chomsky has indicated his support of this proposition when he stated that:

> As a linguist I am interested in the fact that English and Japanese are rather minor modifications of a basic pattern. . . . A serious study of morals or of social systems would attempt

96   *Objective interpretation in sociology*

the same thing. It would ask itself what kinds of social system
are conceivable. Then it would ask itself what kinds have
actually been realized in history and it would ask how these
came into existence, given the range of possibilities that exist
at some moment of economic and cultural development.
(Chomsky, 1969b, p. 32)

One important contribution to this programme is the result of
a structuralist reading of Marx and it is to theorists falling into
this category that I would like to turn for further insights.

Lévi-Strauss states that his Savage Mind is, in fact, focusing
on 'ideology and the superstructure'. He accepts, by and large,
Engels's conception of the relationship between economic base
and superstructure as one of reciprocal influence but with the
economic moment being the determining factor in the last instance; in addition to this view, he aims at uncovering the laws
behind the transformation of natural into cultural phenomena.
This perspective is more explicitly developed in the structuralist
analyses of society produced by Althusser[13] and Godelier.

For Althusser, 'In different social structures the economy is
determinant in that it determines which of the instances of the
social structure occupies the determinant place. Not a simple
relation, but rather a relation between relations, not a transi-
tive causality, but rather a structural causality' (Althusser and
Balibar, 1975, p. 310). Society, a 'structured social whole',
has a complex structure in which a number of elements are interrelated rather than being effective in a causal way. In opposition
to 'vulgar Marxists', Althusser stresses that social institutions,
for example, cannot be seen as direct expression of the economic
base but are characterized by 'an autonomy within a structured
whole where one aspect is dominant . . . in the last analysis the
economy' (p. 313). Social processes are consequently no longer
viewed as the phenomenal forms of an underlying essence - as
Hegelian Marxists[14] have done - nor is there any place for a
recognizable 'subject' within this 'totality'.[15] 'L'homme est fini'
(Foucault). The agent of history, whether seen as the solitary
individual or consciously co-acting members of collectivities, is
obsolete. Tied into the web of interrelated structures, subjects
are not self-initiating entities, but mere occupants of points of
intersections in a given configuration. To view their place in
history differently is to remain enveloped in a 'humanistic
ideology' which has to be dispelled in favour of the view that

the structure of the relations of production determines the
places and *functions* occupied and adopted by the agents of
production, who are never anything more than the occupants
of these places, insofar as they are the 'supports' (Träger) of
these functions. The true 'subjects' are . . . the definition
and distribution of these places and functions . . . : the
relations of production. (Althusser and Balibar, 1975, p. 180)

Objective interpretation in sociology 97

How, then, are we to account for social development, given
that conscious, choosing, willing actors are hardly more than
mythological figures? Godelier provides a clear suggestion as to
how this vexing problem - which for Marxists is of crucial
theoretical and practical import - could be dealt with. Taking
his cue from Lévi-Strauss, Godelier accepts both the possibility
of a structuralist study of social phenomena and the compatibility
of Marxism and structuralism. If we regard Marx's critique of
political economy as the 'anatomy of civil society' (Korsch), then
a structuralist account of Marxian theory would be the prolegomena to a structuralist theory of contemporary society and social
evolution.
'Capital', according to Godelier, 'is a theory of capital, that
is of the relationship between structures within the capitalist
system' (1966, p. 181). Methodologically, it anticipates the
approach of structuralist linguistics in postponing 'the examination of history by subordinating it to the discovery of structures . . . that is . . . by affirming the priority of the synchronic over the diachronic' (Godelier, 1966, p. 181).
The similarity in approach of both Marx and structuralist
thinkers extends well beyond the mere identification of objective
structures to an ontological commitment which differentiates
between apparent and real, visible and invisible, inversed and
true structures. In Godelier's words, 'A theory of the structures
of the capitalist system is necessary because the practical conceptions manifesting it are contradictory to the real structures'
(Godelier, 1966, p. 187).
The close fit between structuralist tenets and social reality
seems guaranteed with the existence of contradictory structures
within capitalist society, that is the basic contradiction between
the 'structure of productive forces and the structure of relations
of production' (p. 183). Godelier stresses the implications of
the structuralist conception of 'contradiction' in this context,
in particular the point that 'it denotes unintentional dimensions
of social reality' (p. 183).
If these theoretical elaborations are accepted in full, then a
structuralist reading of Marx would commit us to a number of
propositions: firstly, that the direction of social development
arises out of the interrelations between structures; secondly,
that the superiority of one social system over another can be
ascertained scientifically in that socialism is that state of
arrangements in which there exists full harmony between all
relevant structures, in other words, it is now possible to arrive
at value statements scientifically; thirdly, that 'this Marxist
theory of contradiction brings the human sciences in close
relation to the natural sciences. . . . If a structure is an invariant, its relation to another structure is viable within knowable
limits. The discovery of these limits is nothing other than the
discovery of laws' (Godelier, 1966, p. 186). That last point is
expanded upon in a later essay where Godelier states that:

98 *Objective interpretation in sociology*

A scientific study of social structures (kinship, politics, religion, economics, etc.) is, then, nothing other than the study of the functions, forms, influence, and place occupied by each of these structures within different types of social and economic formations and their transformations. But this *relationship* of each social structure to all the others constitutes the basic *structure* of the society. It is the causal source of each of its social structures and of their reciprocal *correspondence*. But this correspondence exists only in certain *limiting* cases which definitely reveal the objective and historical content of each structure. (Godelier, 1972, pp. 168-9)

The structuralist interpretation of Marx, and co-extensive with it the structuralist approach to the study of society, has met with strong opposition from other Marxist theoreticians. Sève considers Marxism and structuralism to be 'diametrically opposed' (Sève, 1972, p. 312). His central criticism of Godelier's reformulation of Historical Materialism concerns the displacement of the class-struggle in favour of a cybernetic, technological vision of the path towards socialism. While the emphasis on structural contradiction is certainly in line with Marx's view, the mechanism whereby these get translated into revolutionary action remains unclarified – or is seen as some form of cybernetic process. In any case, structuralists are led to demote the role of consciousness – of how needs are perceived, formulated, realized in the context of a given historical situation – and consequently consider class-struggle as a derivative phenomenon. As a result, Marxist theory is not only deprived of an adequate account of how social transformations come to be effected, but also of the recognition of the influence the powerful vision of a better, more humane, form of social organization can exert upon conscious human actors whose spontaneity cannot be contained and accounted for within a technological conception of social change.

The debate within Marxism about the status of consciousness, humanism and the 'motor role of class-struggle' (Sève) has evidenced the limitations of a structuralist perspective on social phenomena. If socio-historical processes cannot be seen solely as the result of the workings of – unconscious – structures, but are fundamentally shaped by the conscious action of individuals, then this point does not require us to reject structuralist methods out of hand – as, for example, Sève suggests we should do on account of their 'ideological' implications. If seen as enabling and delimiting factors in human action – and not as determining ones – then knowledge of structural relationships may provide us with important insights into moments of the social totality which are outside the (present) scope of socio-historical praxis.

Objective interpretation in sociology 99

SYSTEM, STRUCTURE, AND MEANING

The scientistic and structuralist programmes differ markedly as a consequence of their conflicting metascientific stance: the former tries to universalize a scientific methodology that is based on the hypothetico-deductive schema for which macro-physics provides the model; structuralism lays great store by structuralist linguistics which, among the human sciences, most adequately conforms to the ideal of a generalizing science that establishes the fundamental structure of its object. The rationalistic underpinning of the latter approach has one important advantage as far as sociology is concerned: its active support for model-building prevents it from dismantling the independent status of sociology – as happens with the reductionist approach of a behaviourist sociology. On the other hand, its a-historical tenor inevitably brings structuralism the charge of formalism, as the models it establishes seem to lack the openness and reflexive self-relativization of other systematic accounts of 'hidden' aspects.

On the other hand, both scientistic and structuralist perspectives engender a definite break between theory and practice. That this should be linked with approaches to metascience which rest on the science/metaphysics or science/ideology dichotomy has been well perceived by Sève who, in answering Godelier, makes the point that

> by his far too simple dichotomy between lived experience – identified in fact with pure ideological misrepresentation – and scientific knowledge it seems to me that Godelier has gravely underestimated this element of working-class spontaneity and has presented us with a distorted, *theoreticist* version of Marxism. Is it merely a coincidence that just this theoreticist conception of science is also a typical trait of the structuralism of Lèvi-Strauss? (Sève, 1972, p. 305)

This rhetorical question provides a lead into scientistic aspects of structuralist metascience and methodology. Lèvi-Strauss considers the social and human sciences to be positioned some distance away from true science and he makes the interesting distinction between them according to which the human sciences are further advanced than the social sciences. Between these two fledgling disciplines and hard science Lévi-Strauss locates the behavioural sciences which 'bring together all the human problems which permit or demand a close collaboration with biology, physics and mathematics' (1977, p. 305).

Yet, why should the human sciences show greater maturity than the social sciences? This question can best be answered by reference to the status of linguistics within Lèvi-Strauss's scheme where it can, 'of all the social and human sciences . . . be put on an equal footing with the hard sciences' (1977, p. 299).

100 *Objective interpretation in sociology*

Lévi-Strauss's scientism is an 'indirect' one: he does not try to push the social sciences into copying the empiricistically conceived methodology of the natural sciences, but tempts them with a model approach that is both thoroughly mathematized and related to their subject matter. In linguistics the structural method proved highly successful because here it encounters:

> a) a universal subject, articulated language, which no human group is lacking; b) its method is homogeneous (in other words, it remains the same whatever the particular language to which it is applied, modern or archaic, 'primitive' or civilized); and c) this method is based on some fundamental principles, the validity of which is unanimously recognized by the specialists in spite of some minor divergences. (1977, p. 299)

It is because their subject matter lends itself to being objectified that

> very traditional branches of the classical humanities . . . can be said to be attaining the level of exact sciences. In the race to scientific exactness, we must reserve the rights of numerous outsiders. One would indeed be greatly mistaken in thinking that the sciences called 'social' benefit at the start from advantage over some of the sciences more simply called 'human'. (1977, p. 300)

The focus on universal features in meaningful objects may, however, have led Lévi-Strauss into misconstruing empirical evidence[16] about myths and kinship systems. In addition, the primacy given to the explanation of myths over the hermeneutic interpretation of their meaning-content overlooks differences between myths and leads to an impoverished, one-dimensional account of these. In Lévi-Strauss's 'The Savage Mind' the preoccupation with the internal logic of meaningful objects is particularly prominent and has provoked Ricoeur's criticism.[17]

The mind of the 'savage' is an object amenable to structuralist procedures by constituting an unconscious order, a system of differences which can be studied in independence of the observer. Again, 'understanding' is not directed at existing intentions of meaning in the attempt to incorporate them into a different tradition - and thereby give them a new life; it is, instead, directed at the rationality embedded in a code of transformative rules which underlies the homologies between structural arrangements as they are apparent on the various levels of social reality.

While acknowledging the efficacy of this approach, especially its highlighting of the importance of arrangements, Ricoeur nevertheless voices a number of misgivings.

He notes a lack of reflectivity, which is already evident in

Objective interpretation in sociology 101

earlier writings, concerning the conditions of the validity of
one's findings and the price that has to be paid in opting for
syntax rather than semantics. The lack of reflectivity permits
the formulation of generalizations concerning the minds of
savages - and the step from structuralist science to structuralist
philosphizing which constitutes a transgression of its self-
imposed limits.

The selection of totemism may have provided Lévi-Strauss with
an unrepresentative form of myth and one that is favourable to
his kind of investigation since, in 'totemistic illusion', the
arrangement of myths assumes greater importance than their
content and the thought contained in them can indeed be characterized as bricolage, i.e. the handling of heterogeneous elements
of meaning.

When Ricoeur counterposes the treasure of myths in the
Semitic, Hellenistic, and Indo-Germanic spheres he does so not
in order to suggest that here the structural approach is inappropriate, but only in order to question whether these myths are
completely exhaustible by it. The price to be paid for the use of
the structural method is here higher than in totemism where the
content is in any case nowhere near as productive as the
arrangement so that it provides the most nearly ideal object for
such methods. In the case of the Jewish kerygma, however, the
interpretation of the activity of Yahweh provided Israel with a
historical interpretation of itself. It enabled its people to form
an identity by re-incorporating accounts of a unified people
that had initially been projected into tradition. Israel's history
became the object of belief and of believed accounts. It is, therefore, possible to detect an element of historicality in the interpretation of the kerygma which necessitates an excess of meaning
that could be appropriated differently over time.

The symbols with which the interpreter is here concerned are
characterized by containing a 'temporal energy' ('charge tem-
porelle') and a meaning-surplus; because, as expressions of
'objective spirit', they always contain more meaning then they
express verbally, they give rise to a continued production of
new statements and therefore necessitate an interpretative endeavour which is directed at the existential, spiritual meaning
underlying their literal, profane sense. Their historicality marks
them off from myths which represent a narrative of events that
occurred 'long ago' and, in addition, vails the 'temporal potential'
of symbols to a certain extent - a consequence of the integral
place they occupy in the social structure of a society.

This characteristic underlies the peculiar ineffectiveness of
structural analysis in the case of true and effective tradition.

Because here the semantic relation emerges from the excess of
potential of meaning over its use and function within a given
synchronic system, the hidden time of symbols can convey the
historicality of tradition, which passes on and sediments tra-

102 *Objective interpretation in sociology*

dition alive and renews it. (1974, p. 64)

For this reason, Ricoeur is justified in considering totemistic myths and the kerygma as occupying the extreme ends of the spectrum of myths - which also represents the gradual diminution of the efficacy of structural analysis.

At this point Ricoeur addresses himself to the question of how structural analysis and hermeneutic appropriation are related to one another. He briefly summarizes their characteristics (p. 72): structural explanation refers to (a) an unconscious system, (b) constituted by differences and opposites, that is (c) independent of the observer; the interpretation of traditioned meaning occurs as (a) the re-appropriation of (b) an over-determined wealth of symbols through (c) an interpreter who proceeds under the conditions of the hermeneutic circle.

Myths can, to a large extent, be considered in respect of their inner logic (langue), thereby suspending the referential aspect, the thing they talk about. The distinction which Frege made within 'meaning' between Sinn and Bedeutung, sense and reference, is clearly pertinent here. For one, myths cannot merely be regarded as an algebra of constitutive units; even Lévi-Strauss's 'mythemes' have to be expressed as sentences which contain sense and reference. The oppositions with which one is dealing, furthermore, derive their significance from the fact that they do refer to something; if they did not, structural analysis would merely reproduce and arbitrarily combine meaningless elements of discourse. But because myths contain a subject matter, because they talk about birth and death, etc., we are able to interpret them, i.e. allow their world-decoding potential to address us. Structural analysis may wish to relegate the hermeneutic pre-understanding underlying the typology of, for example, 'high' and 'low' as a residual element - residual it may be to varying degrees, but the pre-understanding of the meaning-potential of 'high' and 'low' which the anthropologist has inherited from his own culture can never be 'meaningless'. 'There can be no structural analysis . . . without a hermeneutically enlightened comprehension of the transfer of meaning (without "metaphor", without translatio), without this indirect meaning-attribution, which constitutes the semantic field, from which one then distils structural homologies' (1974, p. 79).

But while stressing the hermeneutic preconditions for the objective analysis of meaning, Ricoeur is also aware that 'there can be no re-acquisition of meaning without a minimum of structural understanding' (1974, p. 76). Symbols, myths, texts, words, i.e. elements of discourse, are characteristically polysemic. 'Fire', for example, warms, purifies, renews, destroys - and can symbolize the Holy Spirit. Structural analysis, through its considerations of differentiated elements within a whole, brings into play an economy and order that sets limits to polysemic meaning and, at the same time, allows symbolism to achieve

Objective interpretation in sociology 103

its significant character: 'symbols can only symbolize within the framework of a whole that limits and articulates their meaning' (1974, p. 79).

This account of structural analysis forms a necessary, mediating link between naive understanding that accepts symbols in their surface-meaning and hermeneutic understanding proper. Only in mediating the objectivity of sense and the historicality of personal decision does Ricoeur see a possibility for the interpretation of the kerygma that remains faithful to the origin of Judaic-Christian belief and, at the same time, can address contemporary man. The case involving belief can be extrapolated to cover all understanding of texts in which both 'sense' and 'event' are joined in mutually enhancing harmony.[18]

Both structural-functionalism and structuralism aim at providing objective accounts of meaningful phenomena, thereby overcoming subjectivist and relativist barriers to the integration of sociology into the fold of science – however the latter may be defined in their respective metasciences. At the same time, they provide a plausible alternative to scientistic approaches.

Their promise is, however, linked to their limitations. Focusing on relations between units within a system at the expense of intentional actors, they can generate insights into the mechanisms which sustain complex supra-individual entities. The meaning of relations and sets of relations can be explicated by reference to either the function they fulfil in the maintenance of a system or the place they occupy in a social 'syntax'.

Referring to this joint approach as 'objective' interpretation consequently links the non-subjective, 'scientific', study of social phenomena to a focus on supra-individual configurations, i.e. the a-subjective structure of self-regulating systems of action and the mentalistic constitution of individuals and society, respectively. The double hermeneutic is here replaced by a double objectivism. I have tried to bring to light two related aspects of the latter: one, the hermeneutic situatedness of the observer is ineradicable and imparts conceptual schemes with traces of the socio-historical context in which they have been formulated; two, the methodologically rooted relegation of human agency is connected with a peculiarly static conception of the meaning of social and cultural phenomena.

The price exacted for disregarding the process of meaning-creation and the sterile handling of its results – in which the question as to their continuing significance for object and subject is not and cannot be, legitimately, asked – is an impoverished depiction of what is, potentially, a rich and resonant object.

The problems attaching to theories of action provide a clue to the irreducibility of the double hermeneutic even in formal approaches to meaningful phenomena. Classificatory schemes, the formulation of types, hypothetical constructs, etc., cannot obliterate the traces of their historic context. Or, to put the same point in more positive terms: the social sciences can only

104   *Objective interpretation in sociology*

proceed on the basis of a hermeneutic clarification of the meaning of the object. The implications of the double hermeneutic can be defined away or simply overlooked - and the more easily so the closer subject and object are to each other. The more familiar the subject is with taken-for-granted aspects, i.e. the more he shares in an existing consensus about the meaning that is to be assigned to given words, actions, patterns, the less urgent a hermeneutic self-reflection can appear. In structuralist thought the tendency to disregard the hermeneutic situatedness of sociology, and with it the epistemological problematic surrounding the subject of science, is supported by the elimination of history as the context of human practice.

6 THE DILEMMA OF INTERPRETIVE SOCIOLOGY

Contemporary approaches to interpetive sociology have also
been shaped by Weber's work - but they have taken the opposite
route from the one pursued by Parsons. In a sense they provide
a reverse image of the latter as now the requirement of adequacy
on the level of cause is either eroded or consciously rejected -
as had been the fate with the requirement of adequacy on the
level of meaning in macro-sociology. Interpretive sociology consequently provides both a critique of, and alternative to,
scientistic and macro-sociology.

The common denominator of the various branches of interpretive
sociology is provided by a defiant re-affirmation of humanist
orientations - which is clearly apparent in its conceptualization.
Whereas the schemes outlined in the previous chapter see 'action'
in terms of an endeavour to conform to given norms, or as a
manifestation of forces located 'below' the intentions of the actor,
interpretive sociology sees it in relation to human agency which
is historically situated; that is to say, action is an intentional
mode of interacting in socio-historical reality which is both
changed and reproduced through it. Actors are consequently
not passive recipients of existing demands and constraints but
conscious, willing agents who create themselves and their environment in an ongoing process.

One immediate methodological consequence of this conception
of the nature of the 'object' is the necessity to find out the point
of an action, to interpret its intended meaning, rather than to
reduce it to quasi-causal mechanisms.

Weber's 'principle of subjectivity' is the most well-known formulation of this consequence in that it requires the researcher to
consider the actor's subjectively intended meaning of social
action. Whether this conception of 'meaning' is an appropriate
one will be the subject of discussions during this and the next
chapter.

It appears, therefore, that we are again confronted with a
problematic that had already emerged in Dilthey's work,
especially in the relationship between the systematic and the
historical Geisteswissenschaften where the former are based on
the latter - in the same way as social systems are sustained by
the intentional, meaning-creative activity of socialized individuals.
Locating interpretive sociology in this way brings to light its
affinities with the historical Geisteswissenschaften - and the
problems that were discussed above in relation to hermeneutical

106 *The dilemma of interpretive sociology*

theory: how to study the meaning of social phenomena objectively. As the title of this chapter suggests, I do not consider this issue to have been solved in a satisfactory way and to present something of a dilemma[1] which itself stems from the project of interpretive sociology in which the implications of the double hermeneutic are not fully recognized.

SYMBOLIC INTERACTIONISM

One of the approaches to sociology most commonly associated with the basic assumptions of interpretive sociology as outlined above is 'symbolic interactionism', which provided a methodological and substantive reorientation within Anglo-Saxon sociology towards the 'principle of subjectivity'.

This principle is formulated in the following way by Blumer: 'social acts, whether individual or collective, are constructed through a process in which the actors note, interpret, and assess the situations confronting them' (Blumer, 1969, p. 50). I shall first indicate the theoretical perspective connected with this principle before considering its methodological elaboration in the light of the hermeneutic paradigm.

Theoretical perspective
The symbolic interactionist perspective considers individuals as 'selves', i.e. as organisms who are able to respond to situations in terms of their perception of them - rather than as mere media situated between initiating factors such as motives, norms or structural constraints and - predictable - reactions. According to G.H. Mead, one of the progenitors of symbolic interactionism, successful social intercourse requires the ability on the part of individuals to 'take the attitude' of others and to direct their actions accordingly. Social interaction consequently presupposes self-interaction which Mead depicts as the dialectic between the 'I' and the 'me' within the 'Self'. Here the 'I' is the immediate, conscious, acting, willing self engaged in a dialogue with the 'me', which represents the repository of experiences and memories in which the attitudes of others towards the self are stored: 'The "I" is the response of the organism to the attitudes of the others; the "me" is the organized set of attitudes of others which himself assumes. The attitudes of the others constitute the organized "me", and then one reacts toward that as an "I"' (Mead, 1934, p. 175).

The irreducibly subjective element in social action and the sense of freedom and initiative which is associated with it, and which defies attempts to force it into the Procrustean bed provided by the stimulus-response scheme, can be accounted for by reference to the 'I'; the response to given situations is uncertain since 'there is a moral necessity but no mechanical necessity for the act' (1934, p. 178).

The dilemma of interpretive sociology 107

In developing the sociological implications of Mead's conception of the self and of the social act Blumer differentiates within social interaction between non-symbolic interaction, which takes the form of direct responses to gestures or actions, and symbolic interaction which involves the processes of interpreting the meaning of actions and definition or 'conveying indications to another person as to how he is to act'. In both the latter cases, action takes place 'on the basis of the meaning yielded by the interpretation' (Blumer, 1969, 2, p. 66).

Projected on to the level of social analysis, this conception of the social act leads Blumer to consider society itself as symbolic interaction, i.e. as the ensemble of individual and collective actions which are all characterized by the fact that they involve a process of interpretation: 'social action is lodged in acting individuals who fit their respective lines of action to one another through a process of interpretation; group action is the collective action of such individuals' (Blumer, 1969, 3, p.84).

It is clear from this strategy that symbolic interactionism aims at providing a coherent account of micro - and macro - social processes. As far as the latter are concerned, such phenomena as institutions, large-scale organizations, systems of social stratification are seen as 'arrangements of people who are inter-linked in their respective actions' (1969, 2, p. 58). Symbolic interactionism therefore avoids the tendency to reify social processes apparent in structural approaches in which 'the participants in the given unit of societal organization are logically merely media for the play . . . of the system itself' (1969, 2, p. 57). Symbolic interactionism then, does not deny the importance of 'objective', structural features in social reality; but it denies that they exert any determining influence over actions since the latter issue from interpretations which generally vary between actors and contexts.

For an illustration of this point I would like to refer to the reformulation of role-theory that emerged from within the symbolic interactionist tradition.

Role-theory as developed in structural-functionalist sociology conceives of actions as the resultant of a parallelogram of forces depicted as dispositions - which owe their origin to psychological processes - and sanctioned expectations. The latter, in the form of role-expectations, serve to channel dispositionally oriented interaction into socially approved, normative behaviour. In accordance with the requirement of predictability associated with this role-model, socialization consists of the internalization of the role-expectations operative in a given society in relation to given sets of roles.

As my reference to Mead's dialogical view of the development of a 'self' made clear, such a mechanistic account allows little room for 'moral necessity' - and it is a concern with the unpredictable, spontaneous, purposive and deliberating moment in action, and a concern for the fate of individuals confronted by

108   *The dilemma of interpretive sociology*

overpowering social forces, that led to the approach which
strives to give the 'inside view' of actions. The fruits of this
labour can be found in such concepts as 'role-taking', 'role-
making', 'role-distance', 'role-performance', all of which bear
witness to the processual character or role-guided action. The
perspective on social interaction entailed by the stress on the
situatedness of role-enactment does not lead to the denial of
social behaviour that conforms to normative role-theory; but
it would consider such behaviour to be occupying one extreme
on a spectrum which might range from role-identification, as in
the case of highly explicit, formalized actions, to actions which
have self-expression as their aim. To indicate the place assigned
to the twin pillars of role-theory, i.e. disposition and role-
expectations (which themselves eventually merge with need-
dispositions), I quote Blumer again: 'Factors of psychological
equipment and social organization are not substitutes for the
interpretative process; they are admissible only in terms of
how they are handled in the interpretative process. Symbolic
interaction has to be seen and studied in its own right' (1959,
2, p. 66).

Methodological aspects
Blumer's methodological considerations can be summarized by the
'simple injunction: respect the nature of the empirical world and
organize a methodological stance to reflect that respect' (Blumer,
1969, 1, p. 60) - an exhortation which is hermeneutic in its
concern with methods which are appropriate to the object.
  Its immediate consequence is a reaffirmation of the principle
of subjectivity which is expressed in various ways at numerous
occasions, but most clearly perhaps in this quote which states
that:

> since action is forged by the actor out of what he perceives,
> interprets, and judges, one would have to see the operating
> situation as the actor sees it, perceive objects as the actor
> perceives them, ascertain their meaning in terms of the mean-
> ing they have for the actor, and follow the actor's line of
> conduct as the actor organizes it - in short, we have to take
> the role of the actor and see his world from his standpoint.
> (1969, 2, pp. 73-4)

His commitment to a faithful account of the object leads Blumer
into an attack on some central conceptions within sociological
analysis and to the adumbration of a counter-methodology.
  Methodological issues in sociology are too frequently resolved
with reference to the standard repertoire of statistical and
quantitative techniques in social science. Blumer notes here
a glaring discrepancy between the sophistication of the research
apparatus and the quality of its results. The limitation of a
methodology unreflexively imposed on to social phenomena resides

The dilemma of interpretive sociology 109

in the primacy given here to method over the 'obdurate character of the empirical world' (1969, 1, p. 27) and the likely failure to actually engage with the latter. In this context, adherence to a standardized scientific protocol may act to blind the researcher as to the inadequacy of his approach and to provide him with illusory self-assurance as to the scientific character of his work.

In Blumer's view, the deductive approach of macro-sociology is equally fraught with difficulty. It commences with a pre-conceived scheme concerning the area under study and then proceeds to formulate hypotheses and subjects the latter to empirical tests. His objections are here not as principled as in the case of scientistic sociology but act, rather, as a reminder that all too often the initial 'as if' underlying the conceptual framework is eventually mistaken to present an actual depiction of reality.

Blumer's critique of much of contemporary sociology therefore amounts to this: 'Theoretical positions are held tenaciously, the concept and beliefs in one's field are gratuitously accepted as inherently true, and the canons of scientific procedure are sacrosanct' (1969, 1, p. 37).

As regards the employment of certain research methods, Blumer has mounted a strong attack on the survey methods favoured by, for example, structural-functionalists and most ably represented by the work of Stouffer (1949) - whose monu-mental study of the American soldier acted as a catalyst in the upsurge of empirical research since its publication. This study is famous for exhibiting the limitations of common-sense concep-tions, but at the same time has attracted a good deal of criticism. Some observers note a discrepancy between the amount of time and money lavished on the project and the comparative triviality of its findings which can be summarized on half a page. Clearly, there is no obvious correlation between statistical and sociological significance. The discrepancy between input and insight tends to become more marked in the case of less able researchers investigating even more narrowly defined issues. It would con-sequently appear that the data gathered are only as telling as the hermeneutically derived framework within which they are interpreted.

The employment of survey methods is in danger of failing to conform to the central tenet of symbolic interactionism: to acquire a first-hand knowledge of the object. It often does not bridge the gap which Blumer sees as separating the researcher and his object - a drawback which is accentuated by the fact that not only may the researcher himself have no direct knowledge of the object, but he is likely to be employing helpers, such as inter-viewers, who may have less interest in the project itself and in the concerns of the people under study. The results derived from survey methods are therefore likely to be inaccurate due to both a failure to engage with the object and the mechanical acquisition and processing of data.

110 *The dilemma of interpretive sociology*

Blumer makes a further observation concerning the 'democratic' assumption underlying methods such as random survey: responses elicited from a randomly chosen population may not carry equal weight. But even in matters of private opinion the differential distribution of power will make some responses more authoritative - if for no other reason than the one that we may be dealing with an 'opinion-leader', or even opinion-maker, whose views may soon become the property of the mass of other respondents. The existence of manipulation and repression in society has also another important consequence: respondents may actually be unable to given an adequate account of themselves and their situation.

Following on his not very incisive critique of conventional research methods, Blumer re-emphasizes his stress on first-hand knowledge and commences to draw some conclusions which serve as guide-lines for a 'naturalistic examination of the empirical world' (1969, 1, p. 40).

The latter revolves around two central parts: 'exploration' and 'inspection'.

The use of exploration frees sociologists from the fetters of canonized research procedures and encourages them to be eclectic. Flexibility in approaching reality is, therefore, the key word and it allows the researcher to remain attuned to an ever-changing object through changing his methods or revising his concepts whenever required to do so.

This procedure, which introduces openness and an element of common-sense into methodology, is supplemented by 'inspection', i.e. the careful scrutiny of the object of study. The latter is hereby considered from all possible perspectives with a view to discovering relations between variables and their explanation through the use of theory.

The formulation of theory which provides an adequate account of empirical reality is seen as an inductive process in which generic propositions are abstracted from observed situations. For this purpose, 'sensitizing concepts' are given a high priority in contrast to defining ones employed in a deductive system which may act as a straitjacket on scientific investigation. The former can alert the researcher to nuances in his object and can provide valuable heuristic insights into the contextual determination of meaning.[2]

The 'dilemma' within symbolic interactionism
The symbolic-interactionist approach to sociology developed in an ongoing debate with scientistic and macro-conceptions of sociology. Arguing against the imposition of a pre-established methodology on to the object, it raised the fundamental issue of the adequacy of the methods employed. Blumer's reflections on this point parallel hermeneutic concerns in that they evidence the structure of the object before suggesting methods appropriate to its study. Here he was not led into a dogmatic anti-scientific

The dilemma of interpretive sociology 111

stance, but engaged scientistic conceptions on their own ground, showing how such central aspects of their methodology as the operationalization of concepts, the method of deduction, etc., meet with unavoidable difficulties in the sphere of meaningful objects.

Yet Blumer by no means gives a coherent, never mind full, account of the double hermeneutic. In common with other symbolic interactionists, he gives little consideration to the relationship between subject and object - or conceives of it in objectivist terms.

Blumer is concerned with refuting 'two pernicious tendencies in current methodology . . . the stress that is placed on being objective, which all too frequently merely means seeing things from the position of the detached outside observer' (1969, 1, p. 51). The reason for Blumer's concern here is that 'the objective approach holds the danger of the observer substituting his view of the field of action for the view held by the actor' (2, p. 74).

At other points in his discussion he employs hermeneutic arguments. This is the case in his review of 'The Polish Peasant in Europe and America' by Thomas and Znaniecki, a study which relied to a large extent on the interpretation of 'human documents' in the endeavour of 'preparing the ground for the determination of really exact general laws of human behaviour'.[3] His main aim was to demonstrate the logical impossibility of arriving at general statements about human behaviour through the use of inductive procedures. He goes on to examine how the authors actually proceeded, how they managed to produce a coherent account of the lives and experiences of a group of people entering a different culture. He notes, for example, that 'while there can be no question but that much of the theoretical conceptions of the authors came from handling the documents, it is also true that a large part of it did not' (1969, 6, p. 121).

This recognition leads Blumer to state that the understanding of meaning draws on knowledge which the interpreter brings with him and which 'makes the materials more significant than they were'. The results obtained, furthermore, 'depend markedly on the competence and the theoretical framework with which the document is studied. As these factors vary, so will vary the interpretation' (p. 123).

The hermeneutic tone of this argument is, however, misleading. Blumer sees the hermeneutic dimension not as enriching, but as leading to

> something in the nature of a dilemma. On the one hand, the study of social life seems to require the understanding of the factor of human experience. . . . Yet the identification of the human experience or subjective factor, seemingly, is not made at present in ways which permit one to test crucially the interpretation. (6, p. 125)

112   *The dilemma of interpretive sociology*

Blumer, then, deplores the fact that we cannot decide whether 'the interpretation is either true or not, even though it is distinctly plausible' (1, pp. 74-5). Consequently, human documents can only yield 'insights, questions suitable for reflection, new perspectives, and new understandings.' (6, p. 122) so that, as a consequence, 'documents become suspect as a scientific instrument'.

Seen in relation to the hermeneutic paradigm, three definite objectivist features emerge from Blumer's methodological discussions: one, the interpretation of 'human documents' is merely a heuristic device and cannot achieve results which are even only 'relatively objective' to use Betti's term; two, interpretive accounts of social phenomena which provide general statements do not follow the logic of induction, yet the imaginative leap required for such interpretations is non-scientific and therefore, in Blumer's view, unacceptable; three, the status of sociological interpretations is judged in relation to the scientistic model of verification of theory.

Blumer's insistence that in sociology 'methodological principles have to meet the fundamental requirements of empirical science' (1969, 1, p. 21) is supported by his - objectivist - conception of the subject-object relationship. The object, 'empirical reality' can 'resist' our conceptions by 'not bending to' them. 'It is this obdurate character of the empirical world - its ability to resist and talk back - that both calls for and justifies empirical science' (1, p. 22). But this reference to 'talking back' is obviously a metaphorical use of language since Blumer does not allow for such a hermeneutic dimension between the researcher and an object which *stands over against* the scientific observer' (1, p. 21).[4]

The dilemma of symbolic interactionism resides in the fact that while stopping short of a full recognition of the double hermeneutic, it cannot satisfy the canons of science either, as is apparent in Huber's reference to ambiguities in the 'logico-theoretic component' of symbolic interactionism: 'often such words as theory, hypothesis, concept have meanings which are quite different from those they have when used by conventional methodologists' (Huber, 1978a, p. 116).

The ambiguities within Blumer's work become more pronounced if we consider two sub-schools within the perspective which he helped to establish.

Becker (1967), following the Chicago tradition, advocates a complete identification with the object. His siding with the 'underdog' is justified by the logical non-sequitur that, since all research is permeated by values, we may as well employ them openly and for a deserving cause. His work on outsiders demonstrates both the insight which commitment can yield and the limitations of such an approach.

On the issue of establishing sociology as the voice of the underdog, Gouldner's (1968) opposition to such a partisan view sounds

The dilemma of interpretive sociology   113

a warning against what he perceives as another form of a retreat from commitment; a retreat, that is, from a sociology that, in Blumer's words, 'respects empirical reality' and for this reason tries to take a wider range of views into consideration and considers isolated phenomena within their socio-historical context - which may bring to light inadequacies in the perspective of the underdog.

In contrast to Becker's free-ranging interpretations, sociologists associated with the Iowa school have tried to approximate the standards of canonized research procedures, in particular the use of definite concepts, deductive argument and a stress on quantification. Douglas (1971, p. 17) distinguishes, therefore, between 'phenomenological' and 'behaviourist' interactionism. In relation to the latter, Blumer himself considered such endeavours as to 'operationalize the "self" or devise an appropriate scale to measure the interpretation of gestures . . . or use statistical procedures in analyzing the formation of new social objects' as 'non-sensical', as the imposition of 'alien criteria of an irrelevant methodology' (Blumer, 1969, 1, p. 49).

This unequivocal rejection of scientistic methodology would include attempts made by sociologists such as Denzin to bring into fruitful union the two opposing strands of symbolic interactionism within a 'logic of naturalistic inquiry'. Here, 'a sensitizing framework for organizing naturalistic studies is presented (and) special attention is given to the problems of sampling, measurement and causal analysis' (Denzin, 1971, p. 166, 'Abstract'). Denzin also promises to give 'control weight . . . to *introspective* [my emphasis] investigator accounts of social processes' (ibid). But hopes for some hermeneutically relevant insight soon fade. Sociologists are, yet again, 'obliged to enter people's minds'; what they will find there is a 'major data *source* [my emphasis]' (1971, p. 181). Denzin's subjectivist view of the meaningfulness of the object is paralleled by his monadic conception of the researcher when he states that 'significant sociological studies begin from the attempt to understand *personal* [my emphasis] problems' (1971, p. 180). The limitations of Denzin's approach in relation to the hermeneutic paradigm are those of symbolic interactionism in general: an incoherent and impoverished account of the meaning of the object and the dialogical access to it.

Turning, finally, to the approach of the 'discovery of grounded theory' outlined by Glaser and Strauss (1977), some observations have to be made relating to the conception of theory and its relationship to research within symbolic interactionism. Grounded theory, in contrast to logico-deductive 'Grand' theory, is formulated in constant reference to 'data'. The strongly objectivist tenor of their argument in its favour is most apparent in their criticism of Znaniecki's rejoinder to Blumer's review. Here, the former refers to 'the inadequacy of that general conceptual framework with which we approached our data'. This, essentially

114 *The dilemma of interpretive sociology*

hermeneutic, recognition of the role of pre-understanding in the process of interpretation and the need to be prepared to adjust it in its course, is used by the authors as evidence of an inadequate view: 'He was still thinking of the generation of theory largely in terms of a pre-existent conceptualization' (Glaser and Strauss, 1977, p. 15). Unfortunately, the authors leave us unenlightened about the possibility of a 'theory based on data' (p. 4) which is completely free from preconceptions. In addition, they fail to recognize the hermeneutic situatedness of grand theory, too, in that they regard the latter to be a - prioristic - thereby accepting at face-value the objectivist self-misunderstanding of this approach. As a last point it should be mentioned that their insistence that theory is 'to enable prediction and explanation of behaviour . . . and to be usable in practical applications . . . to give the practitioner under-standing and some control of situations' (p. 3) owes more to the Columbia tradition (represented by Merton and Lazarsfeld) than to Chicago and it leaves us with yet another failed attempt at facing, never mind solving, the dilemma of interpretive sociology in the course of yet another attempted synthesis.

'PHENOMENOLOGICAL' SOCIOLOGY AND THE ANALYSIS OF THE LIFE-WORLD

My outline of symbolic interactionism did not contain any account of either the symbolic or interactionist aspects of this approach to interpretive sociology[5] - and it thereby reflected an absence within this perspective itself. That is to say, Blumer and his followers take for granted the possibility that members co-ordinate their actions in such a way as to produce mutually recognizable conduct. Reference to the fact that this involves the actors in the mutual interpretation of their respective inten-tions merely restates the issue that has still not found an ade-quate answer.

It appears that the symbolic aspect of interaction serves only to differentiate between behaviour that involves the interpretation of gestures and that which does not. Yet the problem of how gestures come to be perceived in the intended way, i.e. how meaning comes to be shared, is not considered fully enough. It is, therefore, not surprising that symbolic interactionism also fails to take into account the dimension which binds subject and object given that such a communicative relationship is not recognized in the object either. I therefore turn to phenomeno-logical and linguistic analyses of the social world in the hope of gaining clarification of the place of the double hermeneutic and of uncovering elements of a sociological approach which is in accordance with the hermeneutic paradigm.

The dilemma of interpretive sociology 115

Schutz and the critique of sociology
When tracing the development of Schutz's analysis two major
figures are usually referred to: Husserl and Weber.

Husserl is of interest in relation to the hermeneutic paradigm
for a number of reasons. His critique of 'objectivism' provided
a formidable refutation of the applicability of the methods of
the natural sciences to the study of meaningful phenomena. In
his later work he established a new field of investigation: the
life-world - which is itself the ground of all methodical investigation.

Schutz's programme includes an analysis of the structures of
the life-world and methodological reflections which take as their
starting-point Husserl's reservations against Dilthey's project
of launching the Geisteswissenschaften on the 'secure path of
science', and some problems Weber failed to resolve in his
formulation of the 'principle of subjectivity'.

Schutz proposes a social science which no longer takes for
granted such processes as interaction and intercommunication
or the possibility of a scientific approach in which the meaning
of social phenomena is objectively ascertained - thereby promising a more adequate account of the double hermeneutic than was
offered by scientistic, macro, Weberian, and symbolic-
interactionist sociology.

Schutz stresses that the social world can be studied under a
subjective and objective frame of reference, which is to say
that the meaning of social phenomena can be determined in
relation to what they mean to the actors involved and to the
scientific observer respectively. It is this duality within the
social sciences which, I think, underlies Schutz's cautious
rendering of the 'principle of subjectivity' that 'has to be understood in the sense that all scientific explanations of the social
world *can*, and for certain purposes *must*, refer to the subjective
meaning of the actions of human beings from which social reality
originates' (Schutz, 1962, p. 64).

It is recognized here that a study of phenomena such as social
institutions can be 'performed without entering into the problem
of subjectivity' (1962, p. 6). The price exacted for such an
approach is a certain formalism and a concomitant remoteness
from the 'social life-world'. Consequently, Schutz emphasizes
that in 'objectively-oriented studies, the reference to the subjective point of view always can and should be performed'.

It appears that Schutz has reservations against a certain mode
of analysis 'accepted by the majority of social scientists'.
The structural-functional approach, in particular, is beset by
two tendencies: one, the misplaced identification of theoretical
constructs with reality, and two, the hypostatization of social
processes in its reference 'to the socially distributed constructs
of patterns of typical motives, goals, attitudes, personalities,
which are supposed to be invariant and are then interpreted as
the function or structure of the social system itself' (1962, p. 63).

116   *The dilemma of interpretive sociology*

In functional and structural analysis, objectivist tendencies can remain latent; a scientistic-behaviourist approach, in contrast, is characterized by the 'most radical' objectivism since here the researcher is tied to 'the description of the overt behaviour and of admitting the behaviourist tenet of the inaccessibility of the actor's intelligence' (p. 5). In a train of thought similar to the one developed in Blumer's work, Schutz states that 'the fallacy of this theory consists in the substitution of a fictional world for social reality by promulgating methodological principles as appropriate for the social sciences which, though proved true in other fields, prove a failure in the realm of intersubjectivity'.

Schutz provides a concise account of the implications of the 'monopolistic imperialism' apparent in the imposition of alien methods on to the study of the social world in his examination of the relevant work of Nagel and Hempel where he notices a number of inadequacies in relation to their own approach and in their conception of interpretive sociology. In their 'identification of experience with sensory observation in general, and of the experience of overt action in particular' (p. 53), centrally important dimensions are methodically excluded from inquiry. For example, the meaning of a form of overt behaviour may differ if seen from the perspective of the actor and the observer; as 'Thomas's postulate' stresses, beliefs defined as real are real in their consequences and a large segment of social reality consists of processes and relationships not observable in the atomistic approach which can only take cognizance of overt face-to-face interaction.

A further very important aspect relates to the fact that everything can be objectified - apart from the subject himself: behaviourism may be able to explain the behaviour it chooses to observe but not that of the behaviourist himself. The latter proceeds on the basis of 'a mutual understanding existing among scientists which allows them to control and verify the observational findings of a scientist and the conclusion drawn by him' (1962, p. 53).

Schutz's affirmation of the hermeneutic dimension underlying all scientific activity leads him to an important restatement of the process of verstehen - and to rebuff scientistic misconceptions of it. He stresses the necessity 'to distinguish clearly between verstehen 1) as the experiential form of common-sense knowledge of human affairs, 2) as an epistemological problem, and 3) as a method peculiar to the social sciences' (1962, p. 55). Since (3) is commonly associated with introspection and the subjectivist account of what goes on in someone else's mind, it can safely be discarded - along with the scientistic misconception of verstehen which conceives of it in this way. This leaves (2) - which I shall discuss presently in the context of Schutz's elaboration of an alternative account of the method of interpretive sociology - and (1) which he, in a hermeneutic manner

The dilemma of interpretive sociology 117

that indicates Heidegger's influence on his later thinking, describes as 'the particular experiential form in which common-sense thinking takes cognizance of the socio-cultural world' (1962, p. 54).

Objectivistically inclined social scientists fail to take account of their own acculturation into a given 'natural world' and proceed in a common-sensical, i.e. unreflexive, way to take concepts acquired in this sphere as given an unproblematic. Yet, it is precisely knowledge based on these which sustains the practices of both scientists and laymen and which Schutz considers to be the object of interpretive sociology.

Once this view is accepted we are led back to the subjective frame of reference mentioned earlier on which, in contrast to and preceding 'any idealizations and formalizations of the social world', does not accept the latter as 'ready-made' and meaningful beyond question. Instead, a hermeneutically informed analysis 'undertakes to study the process of idealizing and formalizing as such, the genesis of the meaning which social phenomena have for us as well as for the actors, the mechanism of the activity by which human beings understand one another and themselves (p. 7).

For an interpretive approach to the social world, which for Schutz takes the form of a 'theory of action, the subjective point of view must be retained in its fullest strength' (p. 8).

Sociology as the objective understanding of subjective meaning
In his endeavour to establish a non-scientistic social science, i.e. one which allows interpretive access in the objective study of – subjectively – meaningful phenomena, Schutz proceeds hermeneutically in that he proffers methodological suggestions in the light of his phenomenological description of the object. He presents this programme as the attempt 'to base Weber's epistemology of the social sciences on Husserl's phenomenology' (Schutz, 1962, p. 140).

Despite important changes in his later writings in relation to Husserl's phenomenology, especially the problem of how it is possible to account for intersubjectivity from within the ego-logical perspective, this quote serves well to describe the direction of Schutz's work. I shall discuss its two component elements in turn.

On the problem of intersubjectivity, Schutz has recourse to the notion of a taken-for-granted, common-sensical world in which both laymen and sociologists find themselves prior to any reflexive analysis. This primordial sphere, 'our environment', is characterized by the 'we-relationship': 'it is only from the face-to-face interaction, from the common lived experience of the world in the We, that the intersubjective world can be constituted' (Schutz, 1972, p. 171). Intersubjectivity here stands for mutual understanding achieved through ongoing reciprocal interpretations of the actions of the other.

118   *The dilemma of interpretive sociology*

In his account of the social world, Schutz introduces Heidegger's insight into the structure of Dasein - and for this reason also appears to be closely linked to the analysis of the life-world offered by Husserl. Schutz's earlier work, 'The Phenomenology of the Social World', still adheres to Husserl's unsuccessful attempt to 'solve the problem of the constitution of the transcendental intersubjectivity within the reduced egological sphere' (Schutz, 1962, p. 149), while later he comes to the conclusion that the problem of intersubjectivity has to be sought within the life-world, which itself is an ontological category of human existence. From this perspective intersubjectivity emerges as a common-sense assumption which is examined only once it has failed to materialize. It also provides the object of social analysis as the inquiry into the conditions of its possibility.

Schutz commences his analysis of the structures of the social world with the subject's biographical situation and his specific stock of knowledge accumulated in his experiences of his immediate and more distant surrounding. From this result both his unique and his socially shared characteristics: he is tied to a network of relationships extending backward and forward in time and across social space which will shape his outlook on self and others; since we all occupy different points at which the various cross-currents intersect we can never be the same as the next person. Yet, in social intercourse we learn to partake in the body of shared knowledge which stipulates what is to be regarded as desirable or socially approved action and from which we derive reciprocally recognizable intentions. Consequently, the individual's stock of knowledge allows him to make sense of his own behaviour retrospectively and also to understand the behaviour of others. The possibility and successful interpretation of each other's action is a condition and defining characteristic of the object of social science: '"I know he knows that I know". The everyday life-world is therefore fundamentally intersubjective; it is a social world' (Schutz, 1974, p. 16).

Having evidenced the meaningful structure of the object of social science, Schutz proceeds to formulate a methodology appropriate to it. His argumentation here is hermeneutic in that he does not impose a pre-established approach but advocates procedures which are employed by the actors within the life-world - which is in keeping with the insight that in the social sciences the subject is part of the object and has no privileged access to the latter. The 'method' employed by both subject and object as they make sense of social reality is the use of typifications.

As ordinary members of the life-world we typify others who exist outside the face-to-face interactions in which we engage in our We-relationships. Contemporaries, as opposed to consociates, predecessors and successors are 'understood' in

The dilemma of interpretive sociology   119

relation to ideal-types which differ in their degree of abstractness, related to the relative anonymity of the object, and which can be grouped into personal and course-of-action types. Personal ideal-types may be characterological, habitual, or of greater anonymity, such as 'the state' or 'the nation'. These two kinds of types allow the individual to build up a picture of the world from the intimacy of the We-relationship to the total anonymity of his successors.

In relation to Schutz's account, Weber's treatment of the 'principle of subjectivity' and the 'ideal-type method' is relatively crude. For Schutz, Weber's account suffers from two unclarified aspects: the problem of intersubjectivity and the concept of 'motive'. As to the latter, Schutz discerns a failure to distinguish between the meaning of an action as perceived by the agent and by the observer. Consequently, Weber is led into treating action as a given rather than problematizing it prior to its incorporation into a theoretical scheme. Schutz's solution here is to draw on the temporal grounding of the meaning of action and to distinguish between the orientation of action in view of a project, i.e. 'in-order-to' motives, and the reference to a past experience, i.e. the 'because-of' motive. It is on the basis of this phenomenological deepening of Weber's methodology that the dilemma of interpretive sociology can be overcome in the establishing of 'objective meaning-contexts of subjective meaning-contexts' (Schutz, 1974, p. 241).

Objectivist remnants
For Schutz, the question of 'how it is possible to form objective concepts and an objectively verifiable theory of subjective meaning-structures . . . is the most serious question which the methodology of the social sciences has to answer' (Schutz, 1962, p. 60). I would suggest that both the ways in which the problem is posed and answered do not allow Schutz to arrive at a fully adequate account of the double hermeneutic and evidences objectivist remnants in his thinking.

The social scientist, in common with ordinary members of society, employs ideal-types in his attempt to render social reality intelligible. Yet there exists a difference in that the types that he employs are 'constructs of the constructs'; they are, according to Schutz, 'objective ideal types' of a second degree which supersede first degree, common-sense ones.

The social world, as it is reflected in the social sciences, is consequently not populated by concrete human beings but by 'puppets' or 'homunculi' to which are ascribed typical purposes and goals. Schutz pre-empts the obvious point of how we can be sure that objective ideal types provide us with an accurate description of reality by insisting that they are 'subject to the postulate of logical consistency and to the postulate of adequacy . . . which warrant . . . the objective validity of the thought objects constructed by the social scientist . . . and . . . their

120 *The dilemma of interpretive sociology*

compatibility with the constructs of everyday life' (Schutz, 1962, p. 65).

Central to the completion of the task of the social scientist is the need and possibility of the observer to enter into a 'scientific situation' which represents something of a plateau that is reached after having left behind an interest in the common-sense world of the object and that offers a clearer sight of it. 'To become a social scientist the observer must make up his mind to step out of the social world, to drop any practical interest in it, and to restrict his in-order-to motive to the honest description and explanation of the social world which he observes' (Schutz, 1962, p. 17).

Schutz's failure to overcome objectivist elements in Weber's methodology and to recognize fully the hermeneutic dimension binding subject and object is apparent in his discussion of 'the manner in which the data of the social sciences are established. . . . In the face-to-face relationship the Thou-orientation is *reciprocal* between two partners. In direct social observation, however, it is *one-sided*' (Schutz, 1972, p. 173).

For Schutz, then, the split between subject and object is a precondition for social science. He has to assume a privileged vantage-point for the 'neutral'[16] observer who himself is in full control of his cognitive processes and who can master, on his own, the complexities of everyday life. It may be that Schutz's adherence to the subject-object dichotomy is linked to the still unresolved problem of how to overcome the dilemma of interpretive sociology - i.e. the danger of succumbing to the temptation to introduce externally derived conceptions of objectivity into the argument.

As I mentioned, Schutz's methodologically relevant reflections ran parallel to the epistemological and ontological analysis of the possibility of intersubjectivity within the social world. In fact, Schutz considers it the scandal of the philosophy of social science 'that so far the problem of our knowledge of other minds . . . - the question: "How is understanding possible?" . . . and in connection therewith, of the intersubjectivity of our experience of the natural as well as socio-cultural world, has not found a satisfactory solution' (Schutz, 1962, p. 57). The reason for the continuation of this scandal after Schutz may lie in the realization that he, as a disciple of Husserl, still attempted to secure certainty and intersubjectivity in the course of an analysis of the constitutive consciousness.

In an important later essay Schutz deals with 'The Problem of Transcendental Intersubjectivity in Husserl', where he concludes that:

> Husserl's attempt to account for the constitution of transcendental intersubjectivity in terms of operations of the consciousness of the transcendental ego has not succeeded. It is to be surmised that intersubjectivity . . . is a datum of the life-

The dilemma of interpretive sociology 121

world. It is the fundamental ontological category of human existence. (Schutz, 1966, p. 82)

Yet, as some theorists would maintain, Schutz, too, remained tied to transcendental subjectivism and, despite his recognition of the shortcomings of Husserl's scheme, failed to clarify the relationship of consciousness and intersubjectivity. Giddens states that 'having adopted the starting-point of a phenomenological reduction Schutz is unable to reconstitute social reality as an object-world' (Giddens, 1976, p. 31). The monological conception of the constitution of intersubjectivity which commences with the self-reflexive subject is pin-pointed by Bauman (1978, p. 182) in his explication of the phenomenological programme in reference to Kant's 'transcendental analytical logic'; this would allow us to trace the shared failure of Husserl and Schutz to their aprioristic starting point and their consequent inability to supersede transcendental subjectivism towards a hermeneutic of facticity.[7]

It appears that phenomenological descriptions of the life-world inevitably lead to the generalization of the phenomenologist's own experience. Habermas[8] consequently draws the conclusion that any reflection on the possibility of intersubjectivity has to recognize the hermeneutic dimension within the object and between subject and object. Preceding any analysis, lived-in system of communication provided for a shared life-world encompassing subject and object. Intersubjectivity, in its double articulation in the context of sociology, should therefore be seen as pivoted on the transcendental rules of processes of communication.

WINCH AND THE LINGUISTIC CONCEPTION OF INTERPRETIVE SOCIOLOGY

Two strands in Schutz's thought may be indicative of his failure to give a full account of the double hermeneutic. The first, his notion of objectivity, derives from the natural sciences and the subject-object dichotomy characteristic in them[9] - despite his own warnings 'not to forget that with the change in the scheme all terms in the formally used scheme necessarily undergo a shift of meaning. To preserve the consistency of your thought you have to see to it that the subscript of all terms and concepts you use is the same!' (Schutz, 1962, p. 8). Second, despite statements to the contrary, Schutz conceives of understanding in terms of hermeneutical theory i.e. as introspection, stressing that 'I cannot understand a social thing without reducing it to the human activity which has created it and, beyond it, without referring this human activity to the motives out of which it springs' (p. 10).

Concerning the object of social science, Schutz, here again

122 *The dilemma of interpretive sociology*

paralleling Dilthey's view, considers it to be that communicatively established ground which practising (social) scientists take for granted. But while recognizing the hermeneutic dimension existing both within the subject of science and, in the case of the social sciences within the object and between subject and object, both theorists have been unconvincing in their account of it. In this respect they share the Cartesian presuppositions which still characterize thinking on this matter and which are manifest in an individualized view of social processes and a monological-objectivist conception of their study.[10]

Winch, in contrast, employs the communicative relationship existing between scientists as a pointer to the one existing between subject and object,[11] which leads him to claim a special status for the 'social studies'. Furthermore, the hermeneutic dimension is recognized in full as the shared, rather than reciprocally exchangeable, aspect of the life-world; it is based on the medium and ground of social life: language.

More precisely, in Winch's scheme the possibility both of intersubjectivity and of understanding social phenomena is predicated on the 'following of a rule', i.e. the grammatical rules of language-games.

Intersubjectivity is always already presupposed in the use of language. If the question: 'what is it for a word to have a meaning?' is answered in terms of knowing which rules were followed in uttering it, the following reasoning can be employed: When one asks 'What is it for someone to follow a rule?' (Winch, 1973, p. 28) then the answer to this question is linked to the claim that 'the notion of following a rule is logically inseparable from the notion of making a mistake' (p. 32) - which itself presupposes shared criteria for judging whether a rule has been followed correctly or not. Action or speech[12] is meaningful qua being communicative, i.e. based on, and understood through, a shared knowledge of the rules that have been followed or broken.

As a further consequence, members and sociologists can understand social phenomena only on the basis of being able to participate in the 'form of life' which is circumscribed by the rules operative in a speech community. 'To give an account of the meaning of a word is to describe how it is used to describe the social intercourse into which it enters' (1973, p. 123).

Winch, indeed, seems to be in a position to establish a study of social phenomena which recognizes the double hermeneutic and its implications.

Critique of sociology
Winch's view that 'social relations between men exist only in and through ideas' (1973, p. 123) provided a radical alternative to scientistic and macro-sociology.

Meaningful behaviour implies rule-governed forms of life, norms, linguistic prescriptions; it derives its meaningfulness

The dilemma of interpretive sociology   123

from within the context of human practices and has to be interpreted in relation to them. Consequently, Weber's characterization of meaning as subjectively intended, as the motive of action, should not lead us to assume the necessity to introspect. Motives are not private and unique, but are themselves formed in communicative processes and can therefore be explicated on the level of language. That is to say, 'the concepts in terms of which we understand our own mental processes and behaviour have to be learned and must therefore, be *socially* established, just as much as the concepts in terms of which we come to understand the behaviour of other people' (1973, p. 119).

Considering the scientistic call for causal explanation, Winch states that reference to psycho-physiological factors is misplaced in the social studies since human action is logically different from animal behaviour. The latter can successfully be studied in stimulus-response terms because any 'learning' involved here does not involve the reflexive ability to employ criteria for deciding what is similar and for judging what is right or wrong. Since meaningful behaviour is rule-governed and not dispositionally caused, social norms can also be broken - which obviously rules out the predictability of action.

Even in non-scientistic studies of large-scale social phenomena generalizations are precarious and are only possible if the sociologist has an adequate knowledge of the norms followed by the actors involved. The 'principle of subjectivity' can therefore be reformulated in the following way: if the concepts used in the defining of situations and if the intentions which orient actions are not known then anything has to be expected within certain parameters. It is this insight which underlies Winch's rejection of Weber's call for explanations to be adequate on the level of cause since 'if a proffered interpretation is wrong, statistics, though they may suggest that this is so, are not the decisive and ultimate court of appeal for the validity of sociological interpretations in the way Weber suggests. What is then needed is a better interpretation, not something different in kind' (p. 13).

Having given a brief outline of Winch's critique, it would be appropriate to indicate some of his positive recommendations for the study of social phenomena.

Paralleling Schutz's work here, Winch emphasizes that the concepts employed by the 'reflexive student of society' are dependent on those used by the 'object': 'reflexive understanding must necessarily presuppose, if it is to count as genuine understanding at all, the participant's unreflective understanding' (1973, p. 89). The relationship between the concepts used by both parties is a logical one: that is, scientific concepts presuppose an understanding of the activity they refer to. This means that concept-formation in sociology requires the 'tracing of internal relations' of ideas rather than the 'application of generalizations and theories to particular instances' (p. 133).

124 *The dilemma of interpretive sociology*

The linguistic approach to sociology and the problem of objectivism

From a hermeneutic position, Winch's conception of a social study seems to hold great promise. As Winch put it, 'any worthwhile study of society must be philosophical in character and any worthwhile philosophy must be concerned with the nature of human society' (p. 3).

His critics, on the other hand, share their dislike of the relativistic implications of this programme. But it can also be asked how well it conforms to the hermeneutic paradigm.

Apel (1973) and Habermas (1973a) discern an objectivist residue in Winch's conception. Despite his recognition that subject and object are bound together in a communicative relationship, Winch can conceive of it only in monological terms; that is to say, the observer enters into a language-game and participates in its accompanying form of life so as to gain an inside view of social phenomena - relinquishing, it seems, his own habits of thinking, personal concerns, social conditioning.

Habermas aptly refers to this view as a 'linguistic version of Dilthey. From a free-floating position the researcher can enter into the grammar of any language-game and reconstruct it without being in any way tied to the dogmatism of his own language-game which is related to his linguistic analysis' (Habermas, 1973, pp. 243-4).

Reference to Dilthey's historistic-objectivist scheme is fruitful if one considers the way it was superseded in the formulation of a hermeneutic paradigm where understanding different language-games was seen as a translation, i.e. a mediation of two language-games.

Winch's account of the double hermeneutic remains incomplete. While providing us with a highly reflexive insight into the meaningfully structured object of sociology in terms of the intersubjective ground and medium of language, his conception of the relationship between subject and object has not fully transcended the limitations characteristic of other approaches to interpretive sociology considered so far - nor can it account for systematic distortions in the following of societal 'rules'.

7 BETWEEN INTERPRETIVE AND HERMENEUTIC SOCIOLOGY: THE CASE OF ETHNOMETHODOLOGY

The approaches grouped together under the term interpretive sociology remain in a state of ambivalence as they aim to provide an objective account of meaningful social phenomena. They seem unable to do full justice to either: their mode of procedure cannot satisfy scientific requirements, and even where the latter are rejected as inappropriate to their subject matter the double hermeneutic is reduced to the monological appropriation of the - subject - meaning of action.

At this point it is therefore worth asking whether the hermeneutic paradigm can in fact generate a positive approach - rather than being employed as a yardstick no actually existing sociological practice seems to be able to measure up to. I shall, in this chapter, consider ethnomethdology as the radicalization of interpretive sociology and as a hermeneutically informed study of social phenomena. Since its 'radical' aspect derives from an uncompromising and self-critical questioning approach this discussion should also provide some insight into the possibility and limitations of sociology in general.

ETHNOMETHODOLOGY AS THE RADICALIZATION OF INTERPRETIVE SOCIOLOGY

Schutz's work centred on the reality underlying, yet taken for granted, by scientistic as well as Weberian sociology with particular attention being paid to the problem of intersubjectivity. His solution to the latter involved a reference to the ontological features of the life-world such as the reciprocity of perspectives and typifications and an analysis of the constitutive acts of members which made possible a shared conception of the world.

Ethnomethodology takes Schutz's phenomenology of the life-world as the starting-point for empirical investigations in a truly radical manner since it is now asked how members manage to establish a sense of intersubjectivity. So when, for Schutz, it can 'be said with certainty that only such an ontology of the life-world can clarify that essential relationship of intersubjectivity which is the basis of all social science even though, as a rule, it is taken-for-granted and accepted without question as a simple' (Schutz, 1966, p. 82), then ethnomethodology takes the next step and asks what rules members employ in producing a sense of intersubjectivity and of 'objective' structures in general.

126 *Between interpretive and hermeneutic sociology*

Consequently, aspects of the life-world employed by interpretive sociology as a resource, for example norms or intersubjectivity, are made the topics of ethnomethodological research. This central point is put forcefully by Zimmerman and Wieder (1971, p. 293):

> The distinction between the account or description and the thing accounted for or described is an essentially unexamined resource for laymen and sociologists, for on this distinction rests the 'orderly structure' of the social world. Once brought under scrutiny, the 'orderly structure' of the social world is no longer available as a topic in its own right (that is, as something to be described and explained) but instead becomes an accomplishment of the accounting practices under investigation as phenomena in their own right without presupposing the independence of the domain made observable via their use that constitutes the radical character of the ethnomethodological enterprise.

ETHNOMETHODOLOGY AS A HERMENEUTICALLY ORIENTED SOCIOLOGY

In their analysis of the procedures employed by members as they produce for themselves a sense of meaningfulness, some ethnomethodologists draw on the study of everyday language[1] and the notion of 'rule-following' which parallels the hermeneutic approach. In fact, Garfinkel's answer to 'What is Ethnomethodology?' abounds with hermeneutic concepts: common understanding, communality of practical action, shared agreement, etc., which give an indication of his focus on the linguistically mediated relationship within and between the subject and object of social research.

Members' 'practical accomplishments', in which a shared sense of the phenomenon in question is achieved, are made possible on the basis of a preceding, but partial, consensus which has to be affirmed, widened and secured – at least for the duration of an encounter in any social setting. They hereby draw on the method of 'documentary interpretation' which follows the hermeneutic circle as their pre-understanding is dialogically enhanced. In this, members take each other's action, or any other expression, as the document of, or evidence for, an underlying pattern of cultural meanings and relevances such that 'the underlying pattern (is not only) derived from its individual documentary evidences, but the individual documentary evidences, in their turn, are interpreted on the basis of "what is known about the underlying pattern". Each is used to elaborate the other' (Garfinkel, 1967, p. 78).

I shall return to the methodological implications of this view concerning the hermeneutic constitution of reality after consider-

Between interpretive and hermeneutic sociology 127

ing the consensual nature of social existence in a little more
detail.

Consensus and Garfinkel's experiments
To evidence the pre-understanding that sustains the everyday
constitution of social reality Garfinkel characteristically does not
try and emulate canonized scientific procedures in the pursuit
of hard data, but adopts a rather more hermeneutically informed
strategy which is intended not to provide empirically verifiable
statements but to aid his and our 'sluggish imagination'. His
(in)famous 'experiments' lead us to a more reflexive recognition
of what we know already but fail to take full account of.

The natural, taken-for-granted basis of our thinking and
doing is both pervasive and unstable and can itself best be
brought to light through our being confronted with events
that do not conform to our expectations. Ensuing surprise,
startlement, irritation, even crisis in our understanding of self
and others are clear indications that one or more of its supports
have been undermined or removed.

Garfinkel describes the rationale of his experiments in this
way: 'For the background expectancies to come into view one
must either be a stranger to the "life as usual" character of
everyday scenes, or become estranged from them' (1967, p. 37).
Outsiders and marginals tend to acquire a heightened perception
of the mores operative in social settings – which could be due to
distress suffered from being excluded or some uncertainty about
self and others arising out of unsuccessful attempts at integration,
'naturalization'(!) or the cunning playing-along with demands of
convention. In any case, perceived differences between self and
others lends itself to a reflexive examination of the reality
taken-for-granted by 'insiders'.

Agnes, a hermaphrodite, defines himself as a woman and has
to acquire a familiarity with the ways in which 'normal' members
assign sexual identity to themselves and others in order to find
acceptance. 'To speak seriously of Agnes as a practical method-
ologist is to treat in a matter of fact way her continuing studies
of everyday activity as members' methods for producing correct
decisions about normal sexuality in ordinary activities' (p. 180).

It is through being a non-member that the 'natural facts of
life' can appear as a 'managed production' which follows socially
recognized procedures; acquaintance with these, and their
competent employment, serves to mark off insider from outsider
and the various intermediary stages.

Trying to arrive at the basis of consensual reality from the
'inside', Garfinkel devised experiments in which students
estrange their family members by adopting modes of behaviour
'inappropriate' to family settings, especially an insistence on a
pronouncedly formal mode of conduct. Disorientation on the part
of the other members of the family was reduced as they provided
for themselves 'explanations' of the students' strange behaviour

128 *Between interpretive and hermeneutic sociology*

('he is overworked') and thereby re-integrated the latter into
the fold as well as reaffirming the stability and viability of their
accepted background expectancies.

Garfinkel's strategy can, however, not only be seen as
directed at the dialogically constituted nature of social reality
but also at evidencing the hermeneutic situatedness of the
sociologist/member as well.

The students involved were not only asked to disorient
members of their families but also to provide an objective account
of events. They found it difficult to look at their families with
the eye of a stranger. Yet, the exhortation to study social
phenomena 'objectively', i.e. as if the researcher was not part
of the object he studies, is central to objectivist methodologies.
How difficult it would prove if sociologists actually tried to
conform to this requirement and subject their own pre-
understanding to scrutiny or even tried to 'bracket it out', can
be inferred from Garfinkel's observation that 'students reported
that this way of looking was difficult to sustain. Familar objects
resisted students' efforts to think of themselves as strangers'
(p. 46).

Garfinkel's students can stand here for any student of society,
lay or professional. In fact, the radical nature of ethnomethodology derives from its adherence to this hermeneutic insight:
that sociologists, in line with the members they study, conduct
their affairs on the basis of a pre-understanding of social reality.
Consequently, the examination of how non-professional members
manage to produce and sustain for themselves and for others
a relatively stable conception of reality - and thereby constitute
it, since 'reality' has no existence outside accounting processes
- such an examination would also hold up a mirror to sociologists
and their self-understanding as scientists.

Objectivism could then simply be defined as the negation of the
proposition that underlies ethnomethodology, that 'rational
properties of indexical expressions and other practical actions
[are] contingent ongoing accomplishments of organized artful
practices of everyday life' (p. 11); the substitution or 'remedy'
of indexical expressions by an objective, 'literal', approach is
in any event 'unrealizably programmatic'.[2]

I should like to discuss the implications of the above quote
further with reference to the such central terms as 'indexicality'
and the 'documentary method of interpretation' which is linked
to it.

Indexicality
Garfinkel employs this term to refer to the contextuality of meaning familiar from earlier discussions when it was stated that
meaning contains a pragmatic moment; derives from the inter-
relationship of part and whole; contains more than is actually
expressed; involves the interpreter's pre-understanding. Since
the possibility of an objective study of social phenomena is

Between interpretive and hermeneutic sociology 129

predicated on the possibility of either by-passing or remedying the indexical nature of meaningful phenomena, it is of interest to refer to an experiment which demonstrates not only the difficulty inherent in the attempt to provide context-free accounts but also suggests that it may be impossible.

A group of students was asked to provide written accounts of everyday conversations, giving both a transcript of what had actually been said and their own version of what they thought had been talked about. It emerged that the former task was easily accomplished but that they found great difficulty in the second one, not being sure what to include. Garfinkel 'assisted', upon being approached for advice, by requiring their reports to fulfil certain criteria of objectivity - which made the task not only more difficult but virtually impossible.[3]

By insisting on such criteria as clarity, accuracy, and distinctiveness, Garfinkel evidenced the impossibility of substituting objective expressions for indexical ones. Students attempted to state what was meant by the participants of the conversation, filling-in items which were not uttered but implied or presupposed, background details relating to their intentions and their biographies, references to the pragmatic situation, events preceding the conversation, etc.

As Garfinkel required more objectivity, the frustration of his students grew in the face of a pedantic refusal to accept that their accounts gave a clear version of events. Their frustration was the greater the more 'obvious' the meaning-explication they achieved.

This experiment highlights the pervasiveness of indexicality.[4] The latter is not only apparent in the way members make sense of each other, but also in 'scientific' accounts of such activity. Lay and professional sociologists locate events, statements, etc. within a context and thereby render them meaningful. Both can, and have to, rely on pre-understanding which is tacitly assumed to be shared by all competent members. It is because such knowledge is taken-for-granted that it is so difficult to account for it and so irritating to be asked to do so.

This realization, if applied to the question of how sociologists can provide objective accounts yields the insight that indexicality cannot be remedied; even the most conscientious attempt at de-indexicalization cannot remove all elements of indeterminancy. As Garfinkel put it in relation to the experiments designed to bring to light this fact:

> The events that were talked about were specifically vague. Not only do they not frame a clearly restricted set of possible determinations but the depicted events include as their essentially intended and sanctioned features an accompanying 'fringe' of determinations that are open with respect to internal relationships, relationships to other events, and relationships to retrospective and prospective possibilities (1967, pp. 40-1).

130 *Between interpretive and hermeneutic sociology*

Documentary method of interpretation
The fact that indexical expressions employed in everyday life
cannot be transformed into non-contextual terms implies that
both members and sociologists take recourse to interpretive
procedures, one of which, and possibly the most pervasive, is
the 'documentary method of interpretation'. As was mentioned
above, this method follows the movement of the hermeneutical
circle; it also involves the interpreter/sociologist in an active
process as he tries to make sense of social life. The extent to
which he, in common with lay members, is involved creatively
emerges from another experiment, this time conducted by
Garfinkel and McHugh. I shall restrict myself to giving a very
brief summary of it.

When students were given 'yes' and 'no' answers in a random
sequence to questions they put to an 'advisor', they were
confronted with the need to make sense of what must have
initially appeared as some fairly surprising responses to problems that were of personal importance. This they managed to a
startling degree. They extracted sense from answers that were
in themselves meaningless, or at best oracular, and even in the
face of contradictory advice, did they not lose faith in the bona
fide status of the advisor and tried actively to 'extract' meaning.
The latter was easier, of course, if the 'advice' appeared normal
and predictable: 'Its "reasonable" character consisted of its
comparability with normative orders of social structure presumed
to be subscribed to and known between subject and advisor'
(1967, p. 94).

The result of this experiment, then, points to the way in
which members, and by implication sociologists, play an active
part in the constitution of 'reality'. Their methods not so much
duplicate in thought something 'out there', but actually act to
create for themselves and for others a meaningful universe. The
pervasive character of the documentary method of interpretation
emerges from Garfinkel's statement that

> it is recognizable for the everyday necessity of recognizing
> what a person is 'talking about' given that he does not say
> exactly what he means. . . . It is recognizable as well in
> deciding such sociologically-analyzed occurrences of events
> as Goffman's strategies for the management of impressions,
> . . . Parsons's value systems, . . . Merton's types of
> deviance, Lazarsfeld's latent structure of attitudes. (pp. 78-9)

THE ETHNOMETHODOLOGICAL CRITIQUE OF SOCIOLOGY

From within ethnomethodology emerged possibly the most force-
ful, hermeneutically oriented critique of conventional sociology.

Discussing the problem of measurement in sociology, Cicourel
notes that it 'presupposes a bounded network of shared meanings'

Between interpretive and hermeneutic sociology   131

(Cicourel, 1964, p. 14). This hermeneutic insight, i.e. that sociological discourse begins with the researcher's 'preselected and preinterpreted cultural meanings' (p. 14) is lacking in sociology, in particular its scientistic form which revolves largely around the measuring of social phenomena. It hereby takes for granted the correspondence between meaningfully structured objects and the results of the quantificatory methods applied to them as well as a 'theory of social order' which nevertheless is 'implied in the Lazarsfeld and Barten discussion of qualitative measurement' (p. 19). Such a pre-understanding is a precondition even for 'objective' research since it 'mediates, in a way which can be conceptually designated and empirically observed, the correspondence required for precise measurement' (p. 14).

It can be ignored only at the price of the researcher imposing his own definition on the object: if his theoretical concepts are not sufficiently precise

> he may be deluding himself by imposing methods that force incongruous relationships and false interpretations on his theory and data; and, two, the very measurement devices employed are inappropriate by the nature of their construction and so lead to measurement by fiat rather than to literal measurement. (1964, pp. 13-4)

The problem facing the researcher resides in the double hermeneutic operative in social science so that even seemingly objective activities such as measuring and theory-construction have to draw on the researcher's subjectivity. He brings into the relationship with the object a pre-understanding which can remain unproblematic only because it is culturally shared and taken for granted. Yet it is precisely this pre-understanding which allows the transformation of everyday events into scientific data. In fact, the latter have themselves to be seen as cultural products rather than mere givens.

Consequently, 'what members and researchers label "data" and "findings" can only be understood by reference to the background expectancies' (Cicourel, 1968, p. 8). Reliance on officially produced data merely 'passes the buck'. It may provide the researcher with a trouble-free conscience - but only at the expense of having to purchase someone else's preconceptions.

As Cicourel convincingly argues, most of the second-hand evidence which reaches the researcher under the guise of 'hard data' originates from within modern bureaucracies which collect information with the aim of efficient, rational organization in mind. These are the background expectancies, the pre-understanding, permeating the reifying thinking of the agencies which steer scientized socio-political evolution. They represent 'the very conditions for ordering and reporting the data of large-scale societal activities and have built into them the assump-

132 *Between interpretive and hermeneutic sociology*

tions which insure a quantitative product, irrespective of the structure of social acts originally observed and interpreted' (Cicourel, 1964, p. 36).

Hard data, then, far from eliminating the influence of common-sense assumptions, are themselves based on the common sense of a rationalized society. They appear mainly in two forms: as statistical and social rates and as social surveys.

Two interesting studies have brought to light the problems which pervade the former.

Cicourel, examining the production and use of official statistics, analysed the process in which justice is dispensed in the case of juvenile delinquents. He brought to light the negotiated character of the evidence used in deciding upon the nature of the offence.

In the course of a bargaining process between the parties involved a certain event undergoes redefinition on the basis of given rules. The latter comprise general procedural rules, yet in processing actual cases, 'members develop and employ their own theories, recipes and short cuts for meeting general requirements acceptable to themselves and tacitly or explicitly acceptable to other members' (Cicourel, 1968, p. 1).

The use of social rates, which emerge from official sources in the form of indisputable facts and figures, has been studied by Douglas (1967) in relation to Durkheim's use of official rates of suicide. He considers that the terms employed by Durkheim – e.g. egoism, altruism, anomie are unclear and used in an inconsistent way. But even more importantly, Douglas challenges the factual appearance of suicide rates by referring to the inferences made by coroners about the intentions underlying this act as they decide whether or not to classify it as suicide. It can, according to Douglas, be assumed that they are influenced by the general attitudes concerning suicide which, for example, may make them more reluctant to classify a case as suicide in cultures in which such an act is strongly disapproved of.

The second major source for hard data is the survey method. Here again the transformation of actors' meanings into data remains unreflexive and helps to blind the researcher to the constitutive role of his pre-understanding. In drawing up questionnaires and conducting interviews the researcher has to rely on, or presuppose the reality of, a shared agreement between himself and his object so that the question he poses will be understood as he intended it by all his respondents equally and their answer be understood by him. He therefore appears to be moving within a hermeneutic circle: his questions will be based on his pre-understanding of the subject matter and of his respondents – which then also acts as a framework for interpreting and processing their answers. 'In the course of this exercise we have no way of knowing how the actor accomplishes his answers, what is seen relevant or meaningful in the stimuli

Between interpretive and hermeneutic sociology 133

presented to him, or what he would do in actual social interaction' (Cicourel, 1968, p. 11).

Cicourel points to the necessity for hermeneutic reflection also
in relation to concept-formation in the context of his critique
of macro-sociology.

In the structural-functional approach the difficulties surrounding the production and use of quantitative data are compounded
by the additional commitment to the formulation of a sophisticated
theoretical framework. Here, too, the researcher's pre-
understanding is imposed on the object and its adequacy in
terms of a correspondence with the actor's self-understanding
is tacitly assumed. On this basis, patterns and structures are
discerned in social reality leading the researcher to posit a
stable set of properties which the actor is regarded to have
internalized giving his conduct its social dimension. The -
abstract - vocabulary employed by structural-functionalists
remains unexplicated: structures are posited and no consideration
is given to the processes which bring about social activities -
in fact, they are taken for granted and subsequently described
formally.

Cicourel's critique of scientistic and objectivist sociology is
hermeneutically based in that he considers that 'any and all
information imputed or extracted from members' descriptive
accounts requires the utilization and assumes the existence of
"background expectancies" or tacit knowledge' (p. 6).

LIMITATIONS OF ETHNOMETHODOLOGY IN RELATION
TO THE HERMENEUTIC PARADIGM

From among the many criticisms levelled at ethnomethodology I
would wish to consider two which have a bearing on the status
of ethnomethodology as a hermeneutically oriented approach. The
first of these affects the status of knowledge arrived at within
the hermeneutic paradigm in general - and is, in my view,
inappropriate; the second is concerned with the metascientific
underpinning of ethnomethodology.

Relativism
The most serious attack from within sociology on ethnomethodology
is directed at its non-scientific character. I will restrict myself
at this point to indicating the main positions within ethnomethodology towards what is often referred to as the 'infinite regress'
implied in the contextuality of knowledge.

At the danger of oversimplifying, a spectrum may be discerned
within ethnomethodology on the issue of 'relativism'.

One end would be occupied by, for example, McHugh (1974)
and Blum (1974) who, in an admirably consequential process of
reasoning, come to recognize the impossibility of trans-contextual
knowledge once it is accepted that sociologists employ the same

134 *Between interpretive and hermeneutic sociology*

accounting procedures as do lay members.

Garfinkel, who could be located in the middle of the spectrum, would wish to argue that ethnomethodology can be a non-relativist analysis of the practices through which members produce for themselves and others the appearance of stable phenomena. Yet, it is difficult to see on the basis of what criteria ethnomethodology can claim to avoid the contextuality of its analysis. Garfinkel does list fourteen criteria of rationality, ten of which pertain to the rationality of common sense and four to the rationality of science. The latter are those adhered to by conventional sociology.[5] Garfinkel considers these as inappropriate as they would force the rationalities emerging in everyday-life into a Procrustean bed. But then again, if the latter are the subject matter of ethnomethodology, as Garfinkel and his followers would maintain, then how can their study avoid the contextuality that 'afflicts' them?

The ambivalence apparent in Garfinkel's approach is resolved on the other end of the spectrum through the attempt to circumvent the double hermeneutic altogether by aiming at a reconstruction of the abstract rules which generate socially meaningful phenomena. Cicourel's (1970) search for the 'base rules' which underlie the 'general rules' of normative conventions would be an example here.

Whether such an approach can successfully shed all hermeneutic traces need not be discussed here. On the other hand, if we decide to study social phenomena in the role of a reflexive partner in ongoing communicative relationships then the context-dependency of knowledge would be a fact we have to learn to live with. The charge of 'relativism' could then, in a way, be 'shrugged-off' since it would be seen as being based on conceptions derivable from the model of a dichotomous relationship between subject and object which is inapplicable to the study of meaningful phenomena.

Furthermore, it might also be based on misconceptions about the possibility and nature of hermeneutically derived knowledge which can lay claim to being 'objective' - albeit in a different sense to the one applicable to the empirical-analytical sciences.

Within ethnomethodology there does exist a certain amount of confusion as to the nature and implications of the relationship between subject and object. I shall refer to some comments by Douglas (1971), who seems to contain those conflicting strands within his own thinking. He recognizes that, given the meaningful structure of the object, we have to 'modify our theory of knowledge and our conception of objectivity' (Douglas, 1971, p. 26), but he gives no systematic account of how this may be achieved in the course of his paper.[6] But when stressing the need for 'more objective' knowledge he conceives of it in scientistic terms. Where Dilthey and Schutz referred to some kind of commonality, be it the structure of Geist, Life, or consciousness, Douglas finds a naturalistic substratum as the

Between interpretive and hermeneutic sociology   135

condition for the possibility of objective knowledge: 'we can count on ultimate similarity in all human existence resulting from the encounter of our common animal forms with a common external world (so that) we do not face the necessity of accepting unresolvable conflicts in "objective" knowledge that could doom us to ultimate destruction' (1971, p. 44).

Not surprisingly, the lack of hermeneutic insight displayed on this matter is linked to a peculiarly objectivist account of the relationship between subject and object as he comments reproachfully that 'Schutz, after all, made very little use of any systematic observations of everyday life independent of his own involvement in that everyday life.' (p. 34, note 45)

Apart from showing uncertainty as to the implications of the double hermeneutic, the unclarified relationship between subject and object provides some hints as to the possible use of knowledge developed within the objectivist frame of references. Douglas recognizes a specific link between theory and practice:

> the commitment of the sociologist of everyday life to seeking useful knowledge, which involves the commitment to make that knowledge transituational ('objective'), has many fundamental implications for all their work (such as) concentrating much of one's efforts on those aspects of everyday life that promise to lend themselves best to the construction of such objective knowledge. (pp. 31-2)

Nominalist metascience
Serious limitations of the ethnomethodological programme attach to the ontological commitments of its phenomenalist position, i.e. 'the demand to confine the explanation of reality to the plane of phenomena alone and not to assume any metaphysical 'essence' behind the observable universe' (Bauman, 1973b, p. 20). Linked with it is a nominalist epistemology which has the effect that social reality 'crumbles into multitudes of essentially non-generalizable, endemically individual, experiences'. This charge is indeed justified and telling, and it indicates the point at which ethnomethodology and the hermeneutic paradigm part ways. Concomitant with the difficulty of conceiving of a dialogical relationship between subject and object grounded in more than fleetingly established agreement, ethnomethodology also loses out of sight the matrix of intersubjective meanings which supports and informs the accomplishments of members.

In contrast, the hermeneutic paradigm has evidenced features of social existence, variously referred to as tradition, language, consensus, which underlies not only the diffused object of ethnomethodology but also the activities of the researcher.[7]

In relation to a hermeneutically informed sociology these features are seen as sustaining the normative framework of communicative and instrumental interaction. The next chapter is therefore concerned with outlining an approach to sociology

136   *Between interpretive and hermeneutic sociology*

that recognizes the centrality of socially shared meanings for the reproduction of society and our understanding of it.

8 ELEMENTS OF A HERMENEUTIC SOCIOLOGY

Hermeneutic considerations have evidenced meaning as the central category in the study of social phenomena. In relation to it, sociological approaches could be differentiated according to whether, and how, they recognized the operation of the double hermeneutic that arises from it.

Scientistic sociology reduces meaningful social action to stimulated behaviour. As a consequence, 'society' as the object of sociology dissipates into molecular patterns formed by the random behavioural acts of atomized, i.e. monadically conceived, individuals.

Non-scientistic sociology does accept the meaningfulness of social phenomena, but in contrasting ways as being either subjectively or objectively constituted: interpretive or micro-sociology focuses on subjectively intended meaning at the expense of the supra-individual meaning-context of social actions. At the same time, the problem of meaning is 'solved' empiricistically through the consideration of meaning as something 'given'. Macro-sociology conversely reduces intentional actions to their structural context.

Apart from employing a restricted conception of 'meaning', both approaches exhibit another shortcoming if viewed from the perspective of the hermeneutic paradigm especially in relation to the hermeneutic dimension between the subject and object of sociology.[1] I used the term 'objectivist' to refer to approaches which conceive of this relationship in terms of the Cartesian dichotomy of subject and object and discussed its implications for the self-understanding of sociologists and sociological procedures.

I counter-posed objectivist elements in conventional sociology to the operation of the hermeneutic circle which I evidenced in the course of formulating a hermeneutic paradigm through the immanent critique of hermeneutical theory as the foundation of the Geisteswissenschaften - in which the problems besetting macro- and micro-sociology are already pre-figured.

The tenor of these discussions has often been polemical as I tried to prise hermeneutically relevant insights out of their objectivist shell. I should re-emphasize, therefore, at this stage that the explication of - hermeneutic - preconditions of doing sociology which brings to light what actually always happens as we understand does not detract from the validity of the results of the sociological enterprise. The critical-constructive aim here

138   *Elements of a hermeneutic sociology*

has been to make explicit the possibilities and limitations of sociological procedures; the benefit of such an understanding is that associated with gaining a better self-awareness on the part of the sociologist.

Hermeneutic sociology, as a (self-) reflexive way of doing sociology in which the double hermeneutic is fully recognized is already in action in the work of theorists which will be referred to in this chapter and who either do hermeneutically informed sociological work or conduct sociologically informed hermeneutic analyses of culture.

Such an approach to socially meaningful phenomena is more generally termed cultural sociology, i.e. that 'style of analysis . . . which insists on the salience of concern with life as well as society, concern with the role of ideas and symbols and the transmission of historicity, and a number of other matters which are best exposed by way of detailed case-studies' (Robertson, 1978, p. 7). The sociological aspect of such an analysis is given a more emphatic exposition in Mannheim's conception of 'cultural sociology', which he also refers to as a 'sociology of mind'; 'its primary aim . . . is the study of mental processes and their significations in their social context' (Mannheim, 1958, p. 88).

METATHEORETICAL PERSPECTIVE: WHAT 'MEANING'?

The hermeneutic paradigm stresses the commonality of understanding and hereby points to the grounding of acts of understanding in a shared 'tradition' which mediates different language-games.[2]

This insight is lacking in interpretive sociology in its focus on subjectively intended meaning, situated, i.e. localized, accomplishments, etc. A hermeneutic sociology would go beyond this limited conception in trying to grasp the general in the particular which is present in intentional action and which also transcends it.

The interpretation of meaningful action therefore follows the hermeneutical circle in its reference to the matrix of traditioned meaning which itself informs the motives of individual social actors. It is this intersubjective meaning-context which sustains social institutions and practices - and which eludes nominalistic interpretive sociology. Reference to an overarching meaning-context allows both the clarification of intended meaning and the recovery of meaning-contents not immediately accessible to the actor.[3]

Within conventional sociology it would appear that functional analyses of the supra-individual meaning-context of social action can overcome the limitations of interpretive sociology. Yet, the reduction of meaning to given systems of action cuts off intentions which point beyond existing arrangements. I would also like to refer to two further problems associated with the macro-

Elements of a hermeneutic sociology   139

sociological treatment of social action. First, social structures as seen from within this scheme, emerge as patterns of expectations of behaviour - which leads in Parsons's case to a near-behaviourist view as is apparent in the concept of 'sanctioned expectations'. The 'normative paradigm' (Wilson, 1971) is led to treating the meaning of action as an instance of a general law. Second, Mead's emphasis on the anticipatory moment in behaviour - which symbolic interactionism has fruitfully employed in re-affirming the active part played by actors in the formation and maintenance of social structures - acts as a pointer towards a dialogical conception of meaning. Intersubjectivity is consequently linked to the reciprocity of expectations of behaviour, which is to say that the meaning of social action 'emerges as identical meaning-expectation in the reciprocal reflexivity of the expectations of subjects who mutually recognize and accept each other' (Habermas and Luhmann, 1975, p. 194).

The category of meaning central to a hermeneutic sociology should therefore be seen as processual and relational. The communicative practices in which structures are ongoingly re-established are embedded within a larger socio-cultural context. Analyses of meaningful social phenomena, whether of macro or micro character, therefore proceed hermeneutically in that they take as their starting point the dialogically established self-understanding of social actors and interpret it as a particular in relation to the general that is manifested in it.

From this perspective, both macro and micro analyses of meaning contain a 'moment' of truth: the objective structural context of social interaction serves to delimit socio-cultural variation and choice and it defines what is socially possible in given historical situations. At the same time, choices can be made and changes initiated only by active individuals acting on the basis of their - socially - mediated - understanding of self, others and the societal context. It is on account of the dialectic between action and structure that 'meaning . . . is a sociological category and it is inseparable from some phase of sociation' (Mannheim, 1958, p. 65). 'As there exists no sociation without particular understandings, so there are no shared meanings unless they are derived from and defined by given social institutions' (1958, p. 18).

A processual conception of meaning can incorporate these static ones - apparent in the reference to objective and subjective meaning as something given - within a dialectical conception of social evolution: socialized individuals (re-)create the context of their actions. The 'figurations' (Elias) that emerge from the multiplicity of subjectively meaningful actions are, however, largely the unintended consequence of the latter, which may be due to the fact that in present and past historical circumstances individuals did not or could not act in full awareness and in solidarity; figurations also remain in a state of flux: they 'react back' in that any experience of their constraining value is

140 *Elements of a hermeneutic sociology*

absorbed into the pre-understanding of the actor and informs future actions which can be both affirmative and challenging.

> Structures can always in principle be examined in terms of their structuration as a series of reproduced practices. To enquire into the structuration of social practices is to seek to explain how it comes about that structures are constituted through action, and reciprocally how action is constituted structurally. (Giddens, 1976, p. 161)

METHODOLOGICAL CONSIDERATIONS

It has been stated that the double hermeneutic operative in sociology leads to a characteristic relationship between subject and object and thereby renders procedures employed in the natural sciences partially inadequate. I would like to clarify this fundamental issue in relation to empirical research and theory-formation within the hermeneutic paradigm.

Theory-formation
The Logic of Science conceives of 'data' as possible instances of general laws and as subsumable under a classificatory scheme. By contrast, the hermeneutic paradigm considers meaningful phenomena as individualizations of a general meaning-context. A hermeneutic sociology would consequently explicate the meaning of social phenomena from within an interpretive framework that depicts the matrix of intersubjective, i.e. socially shared, meanings that characterize a socio-historic complex. The formulation of such a framework is itself subject to the hermeneutic circle and emerges reflexively from a pre-understanding of social reality. Since it is historically oriented, i.e. considers past events in the light of the present and the latter in anticipation of a possible future, it necessarily contains hypothetical elements.

Given the sociologist's participation in the object, he is able to identify interpretively the meaning of social phenomena. It is only on the basis of a pre-understanding of social reality - which he shares with other members of society (his 'object') and which defines his competence as a full member - that his work can proceed: be it the hermeneutic clarification of social phenomena, the verstehen of the original intentions of actors, or their objectification in behaviourist, statistical, functionalist, or cybernetic methodologies. It is only its all-pervasive or 'universal' character which allows the hermeneutic dimension between subject and object to become taken for granted and remain unproblematic in sociology.[4]

In relation to theory and concept-formation this means that these activities will bear traces of their socio-historic context - and no more so than in precisely those schemes which purport to have formulated universally applicable concepts.[5] Recognition

Elements of a hermeneutic sociology 141

of the hermeneutic dimension in theory-formation furthermore brings to light a dialogical element apparent in it. Sociological theories are interpretations of social reality developed in the successive clarification of pre-understood meanings in contact with an object that can 'answer back' and endorse or reject proffered accounts. As a consequence, 'theory' cannot denote merely a system of logically connected statements that have withstood attempts at falsification and stand as corroborated as envisaged in the hypothetico-deductive model, but it represents a framework for the explication of meaning, for rendering explicit what has remained implicit, taken-for-granted, or mis-understood. It is a 'reading', an interpretation of the self-interpretation of others within a context.

Subjectively intended meaning is here considered in relation to the fabric of socially shared meanings which sustained and define the social setting of given actions. Forms of sociation can be interpreted in relation to the societal context in terms of their contribution to the maintenance of the latter; but in contrast to the reifying tendency apparent in structural-functionalism it is to be stressed that '"society", too, is a construct, for the acts of sociation which constitute society are inseparably fused with those acts in which ideas are conceived and re-interpreted' (Mannheim, 1968, p. 19).

Recognition of the contextuality and historicality of social phenomena also leads to a view of society itself in which ethnocentrism and hodiecentrism are overcome as a given society is located within an emerging global framework, and present arrangements are seen historically, i.e. as containing past conditions and future possibilities.

The interpretation of meaning of the three levels indicated above: individual, institutional, societal, can only proceed on the basis of some pre-understanding. Theories of society and of social evolution provide telling examples of the hermeneutic circle in sociological interpretation. As Mannheim observed,

> neither Hegel's nor Marx's terminal diagnoses are simply discovered, in the manner in which the Grimm brothers detected the Indo-European language family or Mendeleeff arrived at the periodicity of atomic weights. Rather both syntheses represent the fully developed versions of the author's initial points of view. The untenable character of the present social order is as much a volitional premise of Marx as is the finality of the state of 1830 an axiom of Hegel's system. (Mannheim, 1958, p. 42)

The element of transcendence in interpretation and the, 'anticipation of completeness' (Gadamer) can also be illustrated with reference to Marx's evolutionary scheme in which a projected future helps to render intelligible the present and its preceding epochs. Alternative schemes, such as Comte's three historical

142 *Elements of a hermeneutic sociology*

stages and Spencer's conception of a transition from military to industrial society, are equally infused by an idea of a more adequate form of social organization and bear witness to the historicality of sociological interpretation.

From the perspective of the Logic of Science, socio-hermeneutic interpretations are unscientific - if for no other reason than the fact that a scientific proof may not presuppose what is to be proved. Yet this is precisely what the hermeneutic circle implies.

Just as there are no 'raw data' available so there is no theory-independent reality which could be referred to in the testing of interpretations; we necessarily rely on pre-interpreted 'facts'. If socio-hermeneutic theory is a 'reading', then it cannot be verified or falsified but only clarified, i.e. made more comprehensive and comprehensible. Interpretations proffered cannot be judged in reference to a reality 'out there' but only in relation to their fruitfulness, i.e. their potential for opening-up new ways of seeing and thereby initiating new practices: 'understanding as an expansion of a form of life' (Bauman).

This does not imply the absence of criteria concerning the validity and objectivity of socio-hermeneutic interpretations, but only that they have to be conceived in dialogical terms. As in any reading, internal checks can be made: does it establish a mode or relatedness among the elements considered; do established typologies adequately account for particular phenomena or do they have to be revised - which may also require changes in the interpretive framework. At the middle and lower levels of interpretive work it is, of course, also a case of 'getting one's facts right' - even though the latter cannot serve by themselves as levers for unhinging a proffered interpretation.

Concept-formation
The dialogical element, or hermeneutic dimension, in socio-hermeneutic theory acts to overcome two equally unsatisfactory approaches: the first imposes concepts and categories on the object at the risk of misrepresenting it; the second relies solely on the concepts employed by the object and is thereby in danger of duplicating and perpetuating possible self-misconceptions of the object. The disregard of conceptual frameworks brought to bear in research can only have negative consequences for sociology. In opposition to the natural sciences where the ideal of detached observer and 'mute' object obtains - that is to say, the object is indifferent to the categories applied to it - it is crucial to recognize that in the social sciences the choice of categories is not immaterial to the eventual outcome and use of research findings.

Hermeneutic sociology would therefore try to formulate its concepts and categories dialogically, i.e. confront its own concepts with those employed by the object and vice versa. The necessity of mediating the language-game of the object with that of the sociologist whose language-game developed on the basis

Elements of a hermeneutic sociology 143

of his own pre-understanding of society, but was widened in contact with past and other contemporary thinking about it and enriched by his sensibility and reflexivity, this necessity also legitimizes a critical dimension in a hermeneutic sociology. Hermeneutical theory has, after all, always stressed that 'understanding' is also 'understanding better'.

Methods of research
In relation to sociological methods, hermeneutic reflection is concerned with their appropriateness - not in terms of a pre-established methodology but in view of the constitution of the object. It emerged that both interpretive and explanatory procedures can, and maybe have to, be employed given the dualistic nature of social reality as both meaningful and 'nature-like'.

Verstehen was defended as a legitimate method with great cognitive potential even though it was seen as a derivative of that understanding that permeates and sustains all social activity, even the use of objectifying methods. The dichotomy some theorists discerned between the human sciences and the natural sciences in view of their irreconcilable methods is consequently untenable: firstly, as Dilthey had observed, explanatory accounts find a place in the sphere of human conduct while natural scientists draw on their capacity to understand;[6] secondly, since both interpretive and generalizing objectifying methods are employed on the basis of a preceding understanding, the abovementioned dichotomy had better be seen as a bifurcation, a parting of intellectual ways from a common basis, i.e. the pre-reflexive participation in the life-world.

In sociology this has the implication that we approach a meaningfully structured object as members of it. As far as the use of methods is concerned I would therefore single out participant observation as particularly appropriate. A hermeneutic sociology would benefit from elevating this everyday process in which the sociologist is unavoidably involved to a more self-reflexive level.

Participant observation is employed by both sociologist and layman and, in any case, precedes 'objective' observation. As is the case in the relationship between verstehen and pre-understanding, objective observation is possible only on the basis of a body of pre-knowledge acquired in the course of having participated in the life-world.

Participant observation is not a 'soft option', but requires constant self-reflection and learning. It is dialogical in that subject and object remain in communicative contact in the course of which a fusion of horizons may occur: the sociologist has to become socialized into the particular form of life of his object while being able to widen the 'horizon' of the latter through offering a differing account of a given situation.[7]

Symbolic interactionists see participant observation as being ideally suited to the demands of a 'naturalistic' inquiry. It allows

144   Elements of a hermeneutic sociology

researchers to avoid errors caused by misconceptions of the
object and it sensitizes them to incongruencies, implications,
nuances in the observed phenomena leading to an ongoing
revision of theoretical assumptions - and maybe even of the
initial research programme. In Blumer's view, contact with
informed members can be of immense value and 'a small number
of such individuals . . . is more valuable many times over than
any representative sample' (Blumer, 1969, 1, p. 41).

But in contrast to symbolic interactionists, who seem to
advocate this method mainly for the explorative stage, I would
regard it as important for all levels of sociological work: as far
as the 'spade-work' is concerned, participant observation lends
itself to on-the-spot testing of low-level empirical hypotheses
and the verification of data the sociologist may have 'dug up'.
At the same time, experiences of apparently isolated phenomena
may, if reflected upon, give insight into intersubjective meaning-
contexts and thereby clarify the interpretative framework itself.

This conception of the status of participant observation differs
from the one cast in an objectivist mould which considers it as a
procedure in which neither subject nor object are changed. In
the latter case, the sociologist is asked to assume the role of
something like a 'participant outsider'. It seems that such a
position was assumed by the first and second generations of
anthropologists as they tried to render field research scientifically respectable. In their case, the distance between cultures
helped to secure an element of distantiation - possibly maintained
and strengthened by the people under study - which could easily
be mistaken for objectivity. But it appears that this status of
participant outsider exacted its price in the form of personal
frustrations of various kinds, as Malinowski's 'off the record'
self-observations would indicate.

In sociological research such deliberate self-alientation -
which is co-extensive with the objectification of the object - is
apparent in cases where the observer does not identify himself
or has to rely on other forms of deception to achieve his aim.
The extreme case here again highlights implications inherent
in this kind of distorted dialogue: the spy who acquires information under cover against the interests of those involved.

METASCIENTIFIC ISSUES: SUBJECTIVITY, SUBJECTIVISM
AND THE SUBJECT OF SCIENCE

In scientistic philosophies of science objectivity is predicated
on the separation of subject and object in the scientific process
and the consequent elimination of 'subjectivist' elements.
Intersubjectivity of knowledge, the hallmark of objective findings, is here seen as the interchangeability of the subject of
science and therefore implies that all arbitrary and idiosyncratic
elements have been removed. Only through the exclusion of the

Elements of a hermeneutic sociology   145

scientist's subjectivity could the adequatio and rem, the correct
depiction of the object, be made possible.

Critical rationalists are prepared to concede a more active part
to the subject. As the shift in focus from the logic of verification
to that of discovery suggests, an adequate account of how
science develops necessitates reference to such imponderables
as creativity, insight, genius.

An early statement of this view is contained in Polanyi's work
(1964) which stresses the psychological and sociological dynamic
underlying the growth of knowledge. Phenomenologically oriented
philosophers of science stress the telenoesis, i.e. a purposive
cognitive process, guiding concept and theory-formation, the
selection of research strategies and metascientific precepts.
Sinha, for example, regards the development of knowledge to be
due to a ceaseless intellectual effort in conjunction with the
creative imagination of the theorist; it also incorporates the
interpretation he gives of selected items of information and the
meaning he extracts from them. This 'tellic principle in the
personality of a theorist gives him the necessary guidance in
the construction of a theory' (Sinha, 1968, p. 225).

While recognizing the subject's influence on the process of
science, some hermeneuticians are equally concerned with tread-
ing a path between a rejection of subjectivism and the recognition
of the constitutive role of subjectivity. Theorists who would
subscribe to the view that presuppositionless knowledge is
impossible are at particular pains to 'draw the line somewhere'
and do so usually in relation to the dichotomy of descriptive
and evaluative statements, the contexts of discovery and
verification, value-relation and value-freedom, the sociologist
as citizen and as scientist. This view entails the belief that the
hermeneutic dimension can be cut and a definite caesura be
inserted where inevitable subjectivity ends and arbitrary subjectivism takes its course unchecked.

Hermeneuticians such as Betti, Hirsch and Crane provide a
coherent counter-position to scientistic conceptions. Betti, for
example, strongly asserted the possibility of hermeneutical interpretations to attain the status of '(relatively) objective' knowledge. But in his case, this element of objectivity is predicated
on the interpreter's ability to limit methodically the effectiveness
of the hermeneutic circle in the recovery of the author's
intended meaning. By contrast, I have tried to show that the
researcher's hermeneutic situatedness ('historicality'), permeates all aspects of his work and that even the mathematically
oriented social sciences cannot rid themselves of the pre-
understanding that guides them. In general, the use of canonized
procedures and formalizations merely provides a veneer of
objectivity underneath which subjectivist elements - from idio-
syncrasies to class bias to ethnocentrism - can be the more
virulent for remaining hidden; openly acknowledged as inevitable
'prejudices' such elements would, on the other hand, become

146 *Elements of a hermeneutic sociology*

more controlable and fruitful in the course of their dialogical progression through the hermeneutic circle.

Far from issuing a carte blanche to the social researcher working within the hermeneutic paradigm to conduct his work in accordance with his particular ideological predilections, this insight into the place of 'prejudices' imposes a great burden on him. It is not enough for him to confess openly his commitment and then continue with a clear conscience: he has to maintain an open mind and accept, if not actively look for, refutations of his preconceived ideas. Making a mistake in the interpretation of the self-interpretations of others weighs far more heavily than committing a technical error in the application of scientific methods. Such interpretations contain a moral dimension so that here 'error is cowardice . . . a lack of coming clean with oneself', in Nietzsche's harsh words. Or as Taylor put it,

> These sciences cannot be 'wertfrei'; they are moral sciences . . . their successful prosecution requires a high degree of self-knowledge, a freedom from illusion, in the sense of error which is rooted and expressed in one's way of life; for our incapacity to understand is rooted in our self-definitions, hence in what we are. (Taylor, 1971, p. 51)

Turning again to the 'subject' of science, the hermeneutic dimension here refers to the ongoing formation of a consensus among practitioners in which criteria for valid knowledge, worthwhile objects of research, etc., are developed and applied. The subject of science should therefore be seen as the scientific community - which in the social sciences includes, potentially, the object as well: society as the - potential - subject-object in the (self-)clarification about processes of social self-formation.

The charge of 'subjectivism' could here, ironically, be levelled at the monadic conception of the subject of science prevalent in the Neo-Kantian tradition, in which I would include not only Weber but also Betti and Popper. Neo-Kantianism, and to some extent phenomenology, presupposes the situationless, a-historic subject of transcendental philosophy. Linguistic and hermeneutic thinking on this matter has, by contrast, turned to the ground which sustains the monadic subject and refers to a 'form of life', 'tradition', 'language', the sociality of communicative action.

CONCLUSION

BETWEEN AND BEYOND IDEALISM AND REIFICATION – TOWARDS A HERMENEUTIC-DIALECTICAL SOCIOLOGY

So far, the hermeneutic paradigm has largely been used as a yardstick to which the sociological approaches considered do not seem to measure up. It would therefore be appropriate to ask whether it may not itself rest on certain idealizations concerning the object of sociology. Such self-reflection is required in order to not impose yet another 'correct' view on an unclarified subject matter.

HERMENEUTICS AND SOCIOLOGY IN A CAPITALIST SOCIETY

To the extent that social phenomena are meaingfully structured they can be approached and studied hermeneutically. Yet do all social relationships proceed on a dialogical basis and allow the clarification of meaning through the medium of socially available language in cases of 'mis-understanding'? Or is the object of sociology characterized by fundamental disjunctures which cannot be accounted for hermeneutically and which remain in existence precisely through the systematic distortion of dialogical processes? In the latter case, it is language itself which is afflicted, thereby rendering it inadequate for the purpose of making sense of oneself and one's social existence. If this is so, then hermeneutic sociology can only give a limited account of social reality; it has to 'take its word' and refrain from inquiring into mechanisms that may be operative behind common-sensically available meaning.

Habermas[1] has argued against the universality of language since 'the metainstitution of language is apparently itself dependent on social processes that cannot be dissolved into normative contexts.' . . . The non-normative forces that penetrate into language as a metainstitution derive both from systems of domination and societal labour (Habermas, 1971a, pp. 187-8).

These non-normative factors which impinge upon meaningful action are historically specific. The level of economic development circumscribes the degree to which society can be freed from toil and the repression of needs. Yet within the space of freedom allowable on the basis of having achieved the required material preconditions, group interest still operates to the effect of maintaining historically obsolete forms of domination. This 'surplus repression' (Marcuse) rests on either brachial force or the manipulation of consciousness.

148 *Conclusion*

The cultural hegemony exercised by privileged groups reinforces, and is itself sustained by, the economic structures of contemporary society - and it is the task of the former to 'patch up' the discrepancy between norms which formally 'guarantee' equality among citizens and inequalities issuing from the asymmetric relationship between owners and producers which is mediated by the operation of a market which is no longer 'free' and has never been 'fair'.

It should be obvious that conditions in which sections of society are systematically disadvantaged cannot provide a climate in which the hermeneutic paradigm can flourish; that is to say, communicative processes which help sustain social disjunctures can only be 'pseudo-dialogical'. The sole reliance on hermeneutic methods in such conditions would rest on a premature idealization of the object of sociology and the transparency of processes within it - both to the actors concerned and to their sociological observers. It is that transparency which is lacking on account of the fact that the fate of social actors is still under the control of forces over which they have no direct and no sufficient influence.

The relationship between dominant and dependent groups is non-normative in that public debate concerning the legitimacy of vested interests, the dialogical determination of the rights and wrongs of existing privileges in the light of what is materially possible, is prevented and suppressed. The 'excommunication' of needs which cannot be satisfied without social transformation is based on a closing of the universe of discourse, a narrowing of horizons in which meanings transcending the present disappear from view and in which the 'possible' and 'different' are redefined in terms of what already is and as more of the same.

Such 'one-dimensionality' (Marcuse) is apparent on the level of social intercourse in that instrumental action is now predominant and 'the other' is objectified.

It may be possible to correlate the degree to which social processes are reified with the degree to which objectifying methods are appropriate. Conditions in which men act under the dictates not only of nature but also of a 'second nature', that is, of man's social environment appearing as unchangeable, uncontrollable and sometimes as menacing as 'first' or physical nature, provide the material basis for the introduction of causal and statistical methods into social science. Causal approaches imply that human behaviour has to be explained rather than 'understood', i.e. the motives underlying behaviour are operative in a causal way rather than in the form of reasons that have been formed consciously and that are immediately intelligible as such to others; the application of statistics can only be successful if people do behave in regular, if not stereotypical, fashion.

Marx's discussion of the 'internal laws of capitalist production' considers 'natural' processes as the expression of a form of social reproduction in which its authors can no longer recognize

Conclusion 149

their agency and intentions. Objectifying methods are tailor-made for the study of unconscious social processes - but they also act to perpetuate such a state of affairs by failing to grasp its historic character. This point is well developed in Lukács's analysis of the domination of the commodity form of objects in capitalist society.

The commodity form, i.e. the reduction of objects to their exchange value in disregard of their use value, brings with it the consideration of these objects and all dealings with them solely in relation to their exchange value - which, of course, is quantifiable. All processes within capitalist society are, as a consequence, directed at the rationalization of all aspects of life for the purpose of increasing the exchange value at the expense of all qualitative considerations: 'The capitalist process of rationalization, based on private economic calculation, requires that every manifestation of life shall exhibit this very interaction between details which are subject to laws and a totality ruled by chance. It presupposes a society that is so structured' (Lukács, 1971, p. 102) Commodity-relation has become the 'universal category' and its universality Lukács comprehends as the structure of reification. He thereby extends Marx's socio-economic analysis to the whole of socio-historical and cultural life. The theoretical necessity of the universality of the commodity-structure he refers to as the most general and abstract basis of bourgeois thought.

The critique offered by Lukács also encompasses the field of science. Its methodological tenets are seen as in complete conformity with the society they help to reproduce. Scientistic social science and reified objects are linked together like Siamese twins, each requiring the other to remain in existence.

Adorno was to argue in a similar vein when he referred to manifestations of the dominance of exchange over use value which are apparent in the standardization of contemporary life through the effects of the concentration of economic power. Again, scientistic sociology is seen as contributing to the increasing reification of social life where 'factuality wins the day; cognition is restricted to its repetition; and thought becomes mere tautology' (Horkheimer and Adorno, 1973, p. 27).

ASPECTS OF A HERMENEUTIC-DIALECTICAL SOCIOLOGY

A hermeneutically informed sociology which also takes cognizance of the objective context in which communicative processes occur can best be defined as 'dialectical'. The interpenetration of objective and subjective moments of social reality is reflected on the level of methodology in which intended and objective meaning are related to one another. Such an endeavour is 'critical' in a sense which goes beyond the critical analysis of meaning developed in hermeneutical theory since it implies recourse to conditions

150 Conclusion

which have an effect on, while not being immediately traceable in, communicative processes.

Social analysis has to find a way between idealizing the conditions under which communication takes place and hypostatizing given socio-economic and political constraints. It has to recognize in its approach that action-orienting understanding - within the object, among sociologists, and between the two - may be inadequate or distorted. In relation to the object, this could mean that the meaning of social phenomena can, and should be interpreted within a framework that includes reference to the objective context of social reproduction. At the same time, empirical regularities have to be seen as manifestations of historical forces which, though mediated through the consciousness of actors, are able to assert themselves 'behind their backs', which also means that non-normative determinants of social action can become effective only through entering the orientations of actors. If this view is correct, then a hermeneutic-dialectical sociology cannot avoid methods and concepts which can reflect such relationships which may preclude the formation of a true consensus among members - and thereby undermine the universality of the hermeneutic dimension. In such conditions a hermeneutic-dialectical sociology will try to mediate hermeneutically grounded self-understanding and the objective context in which it is formed in the attempt to examine and resolve cases of systematically distorted communication.

Hermeneutic-dialectical sociology consequently aims to conduct theoretically guided empirical analyses which are directed at evidencing the causal mechanisms operative in the continuation of systematic social inequality in the face of ideological mystifications of that state of affairs; it also, and foremost, hopes to establish an empirically grounded framework for the interpretation of social pathologies, so as to be able to explain and assign truly social significance to empirically significant findings. And was stressed repeatedly throughout this book, empirical research is guided by a - normative - pre-understanding of the object; the 'facts' that emerge from it come to life only within a theoretical framework. Statistics about inequality become significant the moment they are related to normative concepts so that, for example, wide and systematic differentials lose their supposedly functional appearance once they are seen as the manifestation of 'hidden mechanisms' and as incompatible with the notion of a 'good society'.

A hermeneutic-dialectical analysis is necessarily critical and is guided by an interest in emancipation. An awareness of the quasi-causal repressive mechanisms underlying social action would deprive the latter of their motivating force, which they acquire through being unconscious determinants of action, and lead to a questioning of the legitimacy of social arrangements that are based on the continued surplus repression of needs. While it may not by itself lead to the transformation of historically

Conclusion 151

obsolete domination, such an awareness provides the preconditions for emancipatory action in which knowledge and political
will are fused.

Such critical interpretations are dependent on a theoretical
framework which depicts the history of social groups or classes
with reference to the level of material production, political
domination, and cultural tradition.[2] Such a framework, which
could be viewed as a 'societal physiognomy of appearances'
(Adorno), itself emerges hermeneutically: it incorporates and
develops reflexive accounts of everyday occurrences and it is
guided by the idea of a good life which acts as a point of
reference for the cognitive imagination of a state of affairs in
which objective possibilities existing in the present are fully
realized. This hermeneutic-dialectical theory would provide a
foil for the interpretation of instances and results of distorted
communication in that it allows the sociologist to 'fill in' aspects
of the life-history of social agents which are not accessible to
them. The dialectical moment is here represented in the evidencing of a history of repression which is brought to light and,
once accepted as valid by the 'object', is deprived of its unconscious force as intersubjectivity and self-understanding is
achieved. Since this process of enlightenment occurs on the
basis of previous suffering and, at the same time, in the face
of resistance on the part of the 'object' as illusions - which had
been invested with a great amount of emotional commitment -
are gradually dismantled, it obviously represents more than a
mere remedying of a defective language-game; successful critical
interpretation here leads to a change not only on the level of
cognition but also to a change in the affective-motivational basis
of social action. While hermeneutic interpretation may lead to a
widening of horizon, hermeneutic-dialectical interpretation may
lead to a new way of seeing, to a change in one's interpretation
of self and others.

As I mentioned, the formulation of a critical-interpretive framework which can overcome systematically distorted communication
is itself a hermeneutic process in that its concepts derive from
the reflexive development of everyday interpretations. This is
to say, the terminology employed may overarch the concepts
employed by members, but with one proviso: the latter must
'in principle have the possibility to transcend their linguistic
self-understanding through critical self-reflection and thereby
become members of the communicative community to which the
sociologist belongs' (Apel, 1973, II, p. 27, note 15).

It should also be stressed that the recognition that the results
of the critical enterprise are intimately tied to the level of self-
reflection achieved by the sociologist need not imply a reversion
away from the hermeneutic relationship between two - potential
- subjects to a subject/object scheme; it may be more appropriate
to see the sociologist as a primus inter pares, or as the Socratic
'midwife', rather than as an absolute authority or expert.

152   Conclusion

The relatively 'privileged' position of the critical sociologist also has a bearing on the verification of interpretations which again deviates from the one envisaged in the hermeneutic paradigm. A framework for critical interpretations remains relatively 'fixed' rather than being subjected to the hermeneutic circle and striving for a 'fusion of horizons'. Practical hypotheses or suggested interpretations derivable from it are, furthermore, in a sense verifiable; their validity is tested in their application and its result, i.e. whether or not they lead to self-reflection and a change in life-practice - mere acceptance of the proferred account is not a sufficient criterion. But, conversely, its rejection need not necessarily imply a failure on the part of theory since it may be due to continuing resistance to enlightenment.

The 'difficulties' attaching to the formulation and use of a critical theory of society - i.e. its tentative character as opposed to the fixedness of empirical theory - have two further consequences which are consonant with the hermeneutic paradigm: on the methodological level it leads to a recognition of the contextuality of hermeneutic-dialectical interpretations which are developed in the course of their application so that the contexts of discovery and verification are linked; and since we can never know whether the state of freedom anticipated in critical theory is in fact realizable in the way projected, or indeed at all, the social practice of critical sociology can only be 'experimental' - it cannot take the form of a putting into practice of a blueprint in some kind of large-scale social engineering.

This caveat in relation to the practical intentions of hermeneutic-dialectical sociology need not, of course, detract from its commitment to its 'project': the initiation of emancipatory action. It is this self-reflexive awareness of the theory and practice nexus which in fact marks it off most clearly from the other approaches to sociology discussed in this work. From the perspective of hermeneutic-dialectical sociology their use-contexts are essentially tied to the perpetuation of present arrangements.

Scientistic sociology, especially in the form of 'administrative research', serves to 'dissolve institutional congestions within bureaucratic society' (Habermas, 1972, p. 295) as they occur in the day-to-day running of society by social technocrats; yet these congestions are themselves the result of the scientization of political practice. Macro-approaches, and in particular systems theory, reflect and perpetuate the subservience of subjective intentions to supra-individual learning processes as they depict social activities as aspects of the self-steering of societal systems; the defiant quest for a meaningful life must here appear as 'selfish', or at best as hopelessly romantic. Interpretive and hermeneutic sociology lose sight of the determinants of action operating through distorted language and behind the backs of individuals and groups. For this reason they remain largely on a contemplative level of social practice, expanding our understanding but not changing it.

Conclusion 153

Yet it may be the case that it is precisely such a change which is not only socially desirable but a precondition for solving global problems which are already impinging on our lives and making our future increasingly problematic. Only through freeing communicative processes from obsolete domination through a release of our hermeneutic imagination can we be in a position to tackle internal social problems and thereby also to progress towards a lessening of the dangers of international confrontation and possible self-extinction.

NOTES

CHAPTER 1 SCIENTISM AND HERMENEUTICS: TWO CLAIMS
TO UNIVERSALITY

1 According to Schütz, as quoted in the 'Translator's Introduction' to
Husserl (1970a, p. xxix).

2 Dasein and the Lebenswelt appear to be congruent concepts. It is, however,
important to recognize that they emerged in different universes of discourse. Gadamer, for example, argues that Husserl's analysis of the life-
world should not be seen merely as a response to 'Being and Time' since
it represents the culmination of an immanent thought process that revolves
around the attempt to evidence the ultimate ground of true knowledge.
Gadamer at the same time points to Husserl's concern about the great
popularity Heidegger's work had achieved in a dark period of German
history. The motivation to undertake the task of establishing a transcendental phenomenology may have been generated by the awareness of an
upsurge in relativism, if not irrationalism. The urgency of tone in part I
of Husserl (1970a) seems to bear out Gadamer's view.

3 Illustrating the contrasting conceptions of 'the thing' implied by the adoption
of the 'mathematical' view, Heidegger refers to the doctrine of motion in
Aristotle and Newton. In Aristotelian physics any body in motion is conceived of as moving according to its particular nature: material bodies
seek the earth and flames move upwards because their natural place is
either 'below' or 'above'. Their nature, furthermore, causes earthly bodies
to move in a rectilinear way and heavenly bodies to move in circles. In
short, 'the kind of motion follows from the kind of being' (Heidegger, 1967,
p. 85).

By contrast, Newton's first axiom states that 'every body continues in
its state of rest or uniform motion in a straight line unless it is compelled
to change that state by force impressed upon it'. In the principle of inertia
the new, mathematical, view of nature is given its full expression; it
abolishes the distinction between earthly and heavenly bodies and with it
the higher status of circular motion and it leads to a change in the concept
of place. The result of these and other formulations amounts to no less than
a change in the concept of 'nature': 'no longer the inner principle out of
which the motion of the body follows . . .' (1967, p. 88).

4 'Wissenschaftliche Weltauffassung: Der Vienna Circle', reproduced in
Neurath (1973, p. 308). It was dedicated to Moritz Schlick at the occasion
of his appointment to a post at Bonn (which he eventually turned down)
and in the course of this event helped to establish the 'Circle' as a group
with a specific programme. See in particular Kraft (1953) for an account of
its history.

5 Carnap (in Schilpp, 1963, p. 48) refers to 'sympathy for Hilbert in the
Vienna Circle because of his emphasis on the hypothetico-deductive method
and his work on the construction and analysis of formal systems'.

6 See Apel, 'Die Entfaltung der sprachanalytischen Philosophie und das
Problem der Geisteswissenschaften', in Apel (1973, II, pp. 28-95) for a
detailed account.

7 As Horkheimer (1937a) has remarked, 'metaphysics' here includes all
thought that escapes the narrow confines of empirically verifiable statements.
The favourite example used to illustrate the meaningless of metaphysics
employed by Carnap was Heidegger's dictum: 'das Nichts nichtet'.

8 References are to Wittgenstein (1961).

Notes to pages 3–36   155

9   This term is from C.I. Lewis, 'Experience and Meaning', in: Feigl and Sellars (1949, p. 129).
10 I shall refer to Peirce in a more systematic context further on.
11 I am relying here on Carnap's exposition in his autobiographical essay in Schilpp (1963).
12 As a point of - revealing - gossip, the editors of a volume on Neurath recall that he made frequent interjections of 'Metaphysics!' during the 'Circle's' reading and discussion of the 'Tractatus', to the irritation of Schlick who finally told him he was interrupting the proceedings too much. Hans Hahn, as conciliator, suggested to Neurath to say just 'M' instead. After much humming Neurath made another suggestion 'I think it will save time and trouble if I say 'non-M' every time the group is *not* talking metaphysics' (Neurath, 1973, pp. 82-3).
13 This Carnap attempted in his 'Logical Syntax'.
14 In Feigl and Sellars (1949, pp. 373-84).
15 See Carnap (1963, p. 53).
16 The Vienna group made, and is still making, a profound impression on the philosophy of science in the United States as reference to names such as Carnap, Hempel, Nagel, Lazarfeld testifies. Neurath emigrated to England.
17 In How to make our ideal clear, 'Popular Science Monthly', vol. 12, 1878, pp. 286-302; reproduced in Whyte (1955, p. 142).
18 The technicalities of this central concept are not at issue here and are developed in Chomsky (1957). Summarily speaking, the transformational grammar converts deep into surface structures by means of transformations and it consists of three parts: phase-structure, transformational component and morphophonemic component. Chomsky (1965) introduces some reconceptualizations and a new semantic component. See Lyons (1975, esp. ch 5) for an outline.
19 See Barbel Inhelder, 'Some Aspects of Piaget's Genetic Approach to Cognition', in: Furth (1969, p. 23). For a comprehensive account, see Gruber and Vonèche (1977).
20 John Searle, in conversation with Bryan Magee, in 'Listener' 30 March 1978, p. 39; for a further account see also Apel (1973).
21 Kisiel (1974) applies this term to approaches which focus on the socio-historical and psychological dimension in the history and growth of science. Popper is here seen as the progenitor of a movement which also includes, among others, Toulmin (1953), Polanyi (1964), Hanson (1965), Kuhn (1970), Lakatos and Musgrame (1970), Feyerabend (1975).
22 Carnap may be correct when he states that 'Popper's conception . . . is not as fundamentally opposed to my conception and that of logical empiricism in general as he thinks . . . Popper's problem of demarcation consists in the task of explicating the boundary between science and pseudo-science. Our aim, on the other hand, is to explicate the boundary between the empirical realm, which comprises both science and pseudo-science, and the realm of meaningless pseudo-statements' (Carnap in Schilpp, 1963, p. 877).
23 A more consistently rationalist conception of the growth of science has been developed by Bachelard. Referring to the conceptualization employed in micro-physics, Bachelard states that 'we have reached a level of knowledge at which the scientific objects are what we make them, no more and no less. . . . We are *realizing* by degrees our theoretical thought' (Bachelard, L'activité rationaliste de la physique contemporaine, quoted in Lecourt, (1975, p. 58). In addition to the view that science develops in a process of production, Bachelard emphasizes its 'dialectical' dimension: concepts are generated in order to approximate the object of study as it unfolds in empirical research - which itself is seen as a process of the realization of the object, or the 'materialization of theory'. See Lecourt (1975) for an outline.
24 Kuhn (1970) states that the term 'mass' means something different in Newton's and in Einstein's physics since in the latter it is seen as materialized energy. This point, which parallels Heidegger's argument about the

156 *Notes to pages 37-53*

relationship between Aristotle and Newton, contradicts the gradualist belief in the deducibility of new from old theories.

CHAPTER 2 THE RISE OF A SCIENCE OF SOCIETY AND ITS NORMATIVE PRESUPPOSITIONS

1 From this point of view, it would be more appropriate to regard Saint-Simon as the 'father' of sociology, since it is with him that the technocratic intentions underlying the science of society find their first exposition and justification; see Gouldner (1971). In commencing my discussions with Comte, I take into account the subsequent history of sociology which is more generally traced back to this theorist.
2 'The Positive Philosophy of August Comte', pp. 7-8; quoted in Mandelbaum (1971, p. 376, note 187).
3 See Habermas (1968, p. 96).
4 See Caird (1893, pp. 68-75).
5 The conceptual framework of positivist sociology does, of course, centre on a perceived similarity between social and organic systems - whatever different ontological status is given to this similarity. As far as the origins of sociology are concerned it is, of course, Spencer whose introduction of the terms 'structure' and 'function' assured him a central place in the pantheon of sociology. For the striking overlap on this point between positivist sociology and German Romanticism - which provided Durkheim with organicist conceptions - see the next chapter.
6 Britton (1969, p. 117) traces this distinction back to Mill's doctrine of meaning and the distinction between connotation and denotation and further notes its connection with the distinction between real and merely apparent inference which, in turn, leads to Mill's theory of deduction and induction.
7 From the introduction to his article in the 'Encyclopedia Britannica' on Education, quoted in Britton (1969, p. 9).
8 Durkheim's sociology, which in Davy's view is that 'Philosophy which would contribute to giving the Republic a basis and inspiring in it rational reforms while giving to the nation a principle of order and a moral doctrine' (quoted in Lukes (1973, p. 46)), seems to relate closely to Mill's programme.
9 Rex, who refers to an 'academic domestication' in this context, considers that the ensuing sterility necessarily acquires 'pathological traits'. See Rex (1974).
10 Lundberg, The Future of the Social Sciences, 'Scientific Monthly', October 1941; quoted in Bauman (1976, p. 37).
11 See Homans (1961) for a seminal outline of this approach.
12 See Lynch (1975) for an account of their interconnections.
13 When referring to the behaviourist approach to sociology it is really neo-behaviourism one is discussing. The transition to the latter is marked by the same reasoning that had led Carnap to allow for non-observable terms in science. In mathematical models of learning it became apparent that a 'stimulus' may not be directly observable and that only 'responses' and 'reinforcement' were so. Neo-behaviourism consequently allows the supplementation of the stimulus-response scheme by unobservable internal structures. See Suppes (1975) for a further account.
14 Pirandello, 'Six Characters in Search of an Author'.

CHAPTER 3 THE DEVELOPMENT OF A NON-SCIENTISTIC SOCIOLOGY IN THE CONTEXT OF THE GEISTESWISSENSCHAFTEN AND IDEALIST PHILOSOPHY

1 This term is from Giddens (1976) who explicates it in the following way: 'Sociology, unlike natural science, stands in a subject-subject relation to its "field of study", not a subject-object relation; it deals with a pre-interpreted world; the construction of social theory thus involves a double hermeneutic that has no parallel elsewhere; and finally the logical status of generalizations is in a very significant way distinct from that of natural scientific laws' (Giddens, 1976, p. 146).
2 For an outline of the origin of hermeneutics see Bleicher (1980, ch. 1).

Notes to pages 55–91   157

Jameson (1972) has translated Dilthey's seminal essay on this topic, The Rise of Hermeneutics. See also: Bauman (1978, ch. 1).

3 B. Groethuysen, Vorbericht des Herausgebers, in Dilthey (1964-6, vol. VII, p. viii).

4 One immediate consequence of this position is a rejection of the dualism of the sciences based solely on the difference between ideographic and nomothetic methods. The distinction made by Windelband and Rickert now falls within the Geisteswissenschaften and can consequently not serve the purpose of differentiating the latter from the natural sciences. Weber at a later stage, too, stated in opposition to his Neo-Kantian teachers that just as the natural sciences contain ideographic statements so the 'cultural sciences' contain nomothetic ones (see: Weber, 1951, p. 190) - which would parallel Dilthey's rejection of the simple dichotomy of explanation and understanding. The historian, for example, would draw on causal explanations when referring to the influence of socio-cultural milieu or given psychological drives on certain events.

5 'Fateful' for two reasons: (a) by cutting off German intellectual life from Western (i.e. liberal-democratic) traditions, thereby engendering a supercilious and self-righteous attitude which fed nationalistic sentiments; (b) the 'sublimation' of political frustration into the veneration of 'historical forces' paralysed academia when faced with their malignant manifestation - where it did not actually help smooth their path.

6 Note in Dilthey's copy of Mill's Logic, quoted in: Misch, Vorwort des Herausgebers, in: Dilthey, (1964-6, vol. V, p. ixxiv).

7 Dilthey's harmonistic view of the socio-historical context of interpretive understanding is decidedly late-romanticist in its organic conception of society. Lukács's view, in 'Die Zerstörung der Vernunft', which sees Dilthey as a reactionary, may be too harsh, yet the failure to take cognizance of the class-division, and with them the division of 'truth', that had by then emerged, has clear ideological implications.

8 For a fuller treatment of Betti's epistemology, see Bleicher (1980, pt I, ch. 1 and Betti's text 'Hermeneutics as the general methodology of the Geisteswissenschaften', in Reading I).

9 References in this section are to Betti (1967).

10 It is significant of Betti's subjective-idealist approach that he should conceive of barriers to communication solely in individualistic terms at the expense of a recognition of objective forces in society which are operative 'behind the backs' of social actors. See ch. 8 and the conclusion in this book for a critique of the subjective-idealist approach to sociology.

CHAPTER 4 TOWARDS A HERMENEUTIC PARADIGM FOR SOCIOLOGY

1 References are to Gadamer, 'Wahrheit and Methode', 1975 and to the translation, 'Truth and Method', where two numbers appear; reference to the German text only indicates own translation.

2 See Bultmann (1950).

3 See Heidegger (1949).

4 Gadamer (1975, p. xxiv) states that when coming across Wittgenstein's concept it 'seemed to me quite natural'.

5 Cf. 'Gesammelte Aufsätze zur Wissenschaftslehre', (1951, p. 536, pp. 541-6).

CHAPTER 5 OBJECTIVE INTERPRETATION IN MACRO-SOCIOLOGY AND THE HERMENEUTIC DIMENSION

1 See Weber, Objectivity in the Social Sciences, in Weber (1949).

2 See Weber, Fundamental Concepts in Sociology, in Weber (1949).

3 See Parsons (1970b, esp. p. 838) for an account of the integration of Freud into the action schema.

4 Parsons states that in his view Weber 'went so far as to deny the legitimacy of the formulation of a generalized theoretical system as an aim of theoretical analysis in social science. This denial seems to rest on a failure on Weber's part to carry his criticism of certain aspects of German idealist

158 *Notes to pages 91-111*

social thought to its logical conclusion'. Parsons (1947, p. 109, note 33).
See further Parsons's Introduction to his translation of Weber's 'Wirtschaft
und Gesellschaft' in Weber (1947, pp. 10-12).

5 For a further discussion of the hermeneutic situatedness of theorizing, see
ch. 8 in this book and the third section of this chapter, 'System, structure
and meaning'.

6 See Saussure (1966) and Culler's (1974) exposition of the latter.

7 See Barthes, Myth Today, in Barthes (1972, pp. 109-59) for a lucid outline
of the semiological approach.

8 Barthes (1972, p. 113) explains the terms sign, signifier and signified in
this way: 'the signifier is empty, the sign is full, it is a meaning . . . take
a black pebble: I can make it signify in several ways, it is a mere signifier;
but if I weight it with a definite signified (a death sentence, for instance,
in an anonymous vote), it will become a sign'.

9 Formal analysis does not require the expurgation of history and even less
the establishing of an ontological priority of form or system over process
or change, as other structuralist thinkers imply. 'On the contrary: the
more a system is specifically defined in its forms, the more amenable it is to
historical criticism. To parody a well-known saying, I shall say that a little
formalism turns one away from History, but that a lot brings one back to
it' (Barthes, 1972, p. 112).

10 See: Sève (1972) for a general statement of the elements and assumptions
of the structuralist method.

11 This point was made by Boudon (1969, pp. 299-301), especially in view of
the 'arbitrary radicalization' of a mathematical method for which Foucault,
in particular, is responsible.

12 See in particular Foucault (1970), who introduces the important concept of
épistémé, i.e. the epistemological structure of an epoch, which is regarded
as the object of the human sciences and which forms the 'historical a
priori' (p. 158).

13 Althusser, however, refuses to be labelled a 'structuralist' - even though
he is generally included in this category; see: Althusser and Balibar
(1975, pp. 7, 226, 319) for his distanciation from what he calls 'structuralist
ideology'.

14 One would think here of Lukács, Korsch and also Adorno.

15 'The Hegelian totality is the essence behind the multitude of its phenomena,
but the Marxist totality is a decentred structure in dominance' (Althusser
and Balibar, 1975, p. 322).

16 This point is made in Leach (1970, p. 20).

17 See Structure and Hermeneutics, in Ricoeur (1969b).

18 Ricoeur has since formulated a synthesis of structural-explanatory and
hermeneutic accounts of meaningful phenomenon in terms of the 'hermeneutic
arch'. See Bleicher (1980, p. iv) for a more detailed account of Ricoeur's
contribution.

CHAPTER 6 THE DILEMMA OF INTERPRETIVE SOCIOLOGY

1 'Dilemma': 'a position where each of two alternative courses is eminently
undesirable. . . . The argument was called a "horned syllogism", and the
victim compared to a man certain to be impaled on one or other of the horns
of an infuriated bull' ('Chamber's Twentieth Century Dictionary'). The two
'horns' in relation to interpretive sociology are 'subjectivism' and 'objectivism'.

2 Glaser and Strauss (1977) in their concern with the discovery of grounded
theory, i.e. one that overcomes the limitations of both the 'verification'
model of theorizing and 'Grand' theory which is generated by logical deduction from a priori assumptions, in a similar way stress comparative analysis
as the most suitable method for sociological research (1977, esp. ch. 2).

3 Thomas and Znaniecki (1918, vol. II, pp. 1822-3), quoted in Blumer (1969,
6, p. 120). The documents used by the authors include letters, newspaper
reports, autobiographies, etc.

Notes to pages 112-34   159

4   It is indicative that Blumer should use a natural scientist, Charles Darwin, as an example of the use of the method of exploration. See Blumer (1969, 1, pp. 41-2).
5   It should be noted that Blumer himself regards the term symbolic inter-actionism as 'unfortunate', but does not explain why; See Blumer (1969, p. 1).
6   The required neutrality of the social scientist contrasts with hermeneutic concerns, as Schutz himself recognized: when dealing with social objects. 'I am not satisfied with the pure knowledge of the existence of such objects; I have to understand them, and this means I have to be able to interpret them as possible relevant elements for possible acts or reaction I might per-form within the scope of my life plans' (Schutz, 1962, p. 9). This is a very good statement of the unity of understanding and application emphasized by Gadamer.
7   See Bauman (1973b) for an early recognition of the antinomy of a sociology purportedly basing itself on Husserl's phenomenology.
8   See Habermas (1973a, pp. 215-21) and (1975, pp. 174-9).
9   'I agree with Professor Nagel that the social sciences, like all empirical sciences, have to be objective in the sense that their propositions are sub-jected to controlled verification and must not refer to private uncontrollable experience' (Schutz, 1962, p. 64).
10 In Schutz's work these presuppositions are already apparent in the found-ational social relationship, the 'thou-orientation'. Here, the objective communicative context of action, 'society', is bracketed and the individual, be he an ordinary member or the observing social scientist, is conceived ego-logically. The latter point then leads to the advocacy of introspective approaches to the study of social processes.
11 The relationship between subject and object has to be seen as 'analogous to the participation of the natural scientist with his fellow workers in the activities of scientific investigation' (Winch, 1973, pp. 87-8).
12 Winch does not differentiate between these as far as understanding them is concerned.

CHAPTER 7 BETWEEN INTERPRETIVE AND HERMENEUTIC SOCIOLOGY: THE CASE OF ETHNOMETHODOLOGY
1   See, for example, the definition given of a 'member': 'we do not use the term to refer to a person. It refers instead to mastery of natural language' (Garfinkel and Sacks, 1978, p. 236).
2   Garfinkel in fact lists seven times which clarify the distinction between indexical and objective expressions and discusses their implication for the status of ethnomethodology.
3   'As I progressively imposed accuracy, clarity, and distinctiveness, the task became increasingly laborious. Finally, when I required that they assume I would know what they actually talked about only from reading literally, they gave up with the complaint that the task was impossible' (Garfinkel, 1967, p. 26).
4   Cicourel employs the definition of measurement used by the physicist Norman Campbell: 'the assignment of numbers to represent properties' (Cicourel, 1964, p. 10).
5   In particular the means-ends scheme familiar from Weber's attempt to provide an objective account of subjectively meaningful phenomena, as well as the stress on semantic clarity. It also points at moral problems associated with Garfinkel's refusal to deal with his students in a sincere way - which is, of course, one of the 'dialogue-constitutive rules' outlined by Habermas referred to in ch. 1, pp. 32-3.
6   Douglas's uncertainty about the conditions for the possibility of objective knowledge is at times hidden by the vacuity of some of his statements, e.g. 'As our knowledge grows, we can focus our attention more on increasing our objectivity about fundamentals and worrying less about all of the other factors' (1971, p. 31).

160 *Notes to pages 135-43*

7 It is interesting to note that one theorist close to ethnomethodology has recognized the hermeneutic situatedness in the observation that 'Ethnomethodologists in sociology rarely study primitive peoples; they study present-day Americans. This difference is more than a matter of taste. In their theorizing ethnomethodologists rely heavily on their knowledge of American culture learned by being members of the culture' (Churchill, 1971, p. 182).

CHAPTER 8 ELEMENTS OF A HERMENEUTIC SOCIOLOGY

1 Differences in relation to the meaning of meaning are paralleled by differences in relation to a model of man: scientistic sociology does not see any qualitative difference between human and non-human objects; macrosociology sees man as malleable and, in a sense, insignificant in societal terms; interpretive sociology, in opposition, considers social agents as independent, self-determing agents; this monadic, liberalistic view of man is superseded in hermeneutic sociology where the individual - be it the 'object' of research or the researcher himself - is from the outset seen as interwoven in a network of mutual relationships, thereby overcoming the dichotomy of individual/society on both the substantive and metascientific level.

2 This point is well expressed by Gadamer: 'Every word emerges from within a middle and refers to a whole. Every word lets the whole of a language to which it belongs resonate and lets appear the whole of the vision of the world which underlies it. Consequently, every word brings . . . with it something unsaid to which it presents an answer and which is indicated by it.' (1975, p. 434). (In the context of my discussions read 'action' for 'word' and 'socio-cultural context' for 'language'.)

3 I would therefore, cautiously heretical, 're-interpret' Gadamer's notion of the 'anticipation of perfection' by regarding the present, and with it the 'truth of tradition', as incomplete. 'Completeness' or 'perfection' would then be seen as an 'active utopia' (Bauman) which we can anticipate in our - cognitive - 'day dreams' (Bloch), i.e. the view of something better which already exists as a potential in the present. See the conclusion for a further development of this position.

4 Habermas (1973a, pp. 144-8) and Taylor (1971, pp. 32-45) give telling examples of the - unrecognized - hermeneutic dimension in Abel's rejection of the 'operation called verstehen' and of the ethnocentrism apparent in American political science, respectively.

5 Mills (1959, ch. 8) gives a good account of the historic element in structural-functionalist concepts; see also Taylor 1971, note 5).

6 'Every guide to understanding, and so every hermeneutical aid to understanding, must itself be treated as an explanation. Explanation of this sort may take the form of inclusion under hypothetical laws, but it is not limited to this form. In particular, where the objects to be explained are unique structures, as in a historical event, laws have only limited explanatory force compared with interpretation, which can reveal the individual structure of the complex of events. On the other hand, such an interpretation is itself an explanation when it meets a need for understanding, and in the light of such an explanation - if it is informative - what was previously unintelligible can be understood' (Pannenberg, 1976, p. 157).

7 'He asked his friends to explain what they were doing and why, and this forced them to reflect on their behaviour. They also corrected his faux pas by telling him the proper way to act, and this induced them to formulate the rules they had been following. Later in the study he discussed his observation and ideas with them, and finally they read his book about them and saw themselves through his eyes. All these things changed their behaviour and Whyte saw the changes.' (Diesing, 1972a, p. 160, in discussing Whyte, 1955).

Notes to page 147   161

CONCLUSION: BETWEEN AND BEYOND IDEALISM AND REIFICATION - TOWARDS A HERMENEUTIC-DIALECTICAL SOCIOLOGY

1   The following discussions draw heavily on Habermas's work, especially
Habermas (1968, chs 3, 9, 10; 1973b, ch. 1; 1973c, pp. 48-104; (Habermas
and Luhmann, 1975, pp; 142-285).
From this perspective, a traditional 'materialist' analysis is essentially
flawed in that it fails to deal adequately with cultural tradition and normative
structures which overarch instrumental actions and learning processes in
the sphere of material production; they are here either reduced to the
latter or explained in their function and development in relation to material
processes. In my view, ideas are not - only - a reflection of the material
base, and nor are they - just - the ideas of the ruling class.
   I would at the same time consider it inappropriate to label a hermeneutic-
dialectical approach 'idealist' on account of the inclusion of hermeneutic
procedures.
   'Idealist', as I use the term, refers to a disregard of the socio-historical
context of social action - thereby idealizing the scope for intentional action
in given circumstances. Conversely, a hermeneutic-dialectically 'materialist'
analysis would consider all aspects that 'matter' without prejudging a priori
which these are and whether any of them have to be assigned primacy or
even sole determinancy.
   In present circumstances, socio-cultural aspects are clearly not immaterial to the understanding of social phenomena - in addition to an analysis
of constraints issuing from their natural ('first nature') and 'thing-like'
('second nature') context. To distinguish this approach, which takes
cognizance of the constitution of the object in the formulation of methodological tenets, I would differentiate within the term 'materialist' between
the following:
'mat(t)erialist' views are based on the failure to distinguish between
methodological and ontological arguments and in relation to the latter maintain the 'Mind over Matter' scheme; in relation to social analysis, this would
take the form of a reductionist position in which social phenomena are
explained as reflections of a mat(t)erialist base (thereby representing a
per-version of idealist identity philosophy).
'materialist', in the traditional Marxist sense, would eschew the metaphysical
speculation underlying the above notion. Applied to sociology, this method
would, however, carry with it a commitment to seeing the economic sub-
structure as primary in social evolution and regarding the socio-cultural
framework as a dependent variable.
'material-ist' analysis, as in a hermeneutic-dialectical sociology, considers
all aspects material to the phenomenon under study and can grant an independent logic to the socio-cultural framework, but it would also include a
reference to economic and political factors in the analysis of what degree
of freedom is historically possible. See again Habermas (1976, ch. 1,
section 2) and (1975, esp. pp. 250-90) for the source of these views.

BIBLIOGRAPHY

Abel, T. (1974a,) The operation called verstehen, in Truzzi (1974); originally in 'American Journal of Sociology', 1948, 54, pp. 211-8.
Abel, T. (1974b), A reply to Professor Wax, in Truzzi (1974).
Abel, T. (1975), Verstehen I and Verstehen II, 'Theory and Decision', 6, i.
Adorno, T, et. al. (1976), 'The Positivist Dispute in German Sociology', Heinemann, London.
Althusser, L., and Balibar, E. (1975), 'Reading Capital', New Left Books London.
Apel, K.-O. (1972), Communication and the foundation of the humanities, 'Acta Sociologica', 25, 7-26.
Apel, K.-O. (1973), 'Transformation der Philosophie', 2 vols, Suhrkamp, Frankfurt.
Aron, R. (1971) 'Main Currents in Sociological Thought', vol. II, Penguin, Harmondsworth.
Austin, J.L. (1970), 'How to do Things with Words', Oxford University Press.
Baker, K.M. (1975), 'Condorcet', University of Chigago Press.
Barthes, R. (1972), 'Mythologies', Paladin.
Bauman, Z. (1973a) The structuralist promise, 'British Journal of Sociology', 24, i.
Bauman, Z. (1973b), On the philosophical status of ethnomethodology, 'Sociological Review', 21, 5-23.
Bauman, Z. (1976), 'Towards a Critical Sociology', Routledge & Kegan Paul, London.
Bauman, Z. (1978), 'Hermeneutics and Social Science', Hutchinson, London.
Becker, H. (1967), Whose side are we on? in 'Social Problems', 14, pp. 239-47.
Becker, H., and Greer, B. (1960), Participant observation and interviewing: a comparison, 'Human Organization', 18, Fall 20-32.
Bergmann, G. (1954), 'The Metaphysics of Logical Positivism', Longmans, New York.
Berlin, I. (1976), 'Vico and Herder', Hogarth Press, London.
Bernstein, R. (1976), 'Restructuring of Social and Political Theory', Blackwell, Oxford.
Betti, E. (1967), 'Allgemeine Auslegungslehre als Methodik der Geisteswissenschaften', J.C.B. Mohr, Tübingen; translated from 'Teoria Generale della Interpretazione', 2 vols, Dott. A. Giuffrè, Milan, 1955.
Bleicher, J. (1980), 'Contemporary Hermeneutics', Routledge & Kegan Paul, London.
Bloch, E. (1959), 'Das Prinzip Hoffnung', Suhrkamp, Frankfurt.
Blum, A. (1974), 'Theorising', Heinemann, London.
Blumer, H. (1969), 'Symbolic Interaction', Prentice-Hall, Englewood Cliffs, N.J. (1 The methodological position of symbolic interactionism; 2 Sociological implications of the thought of G.H. Mead; 3 Society as symbolic interaction; 6 An appraisal of Thomas and Znaniecki's 'The Polish Peasant in Europe and America'; 7 Sociological analysis and the 'variable'; 8 What is wrong with social theory?).
Blumer, H. (1978), A note on symbolic interactionism, in Wells (1978).
Boudon, R. (1969), Le structuralism, in Klibansky (1969).
Boudon, R. (1972), The sociology crisis, 'Social Science Information', 11, iii.
Braybrooke, D. (ed.) (1965), 'Philosophical Problems of the Social Sciences', Macmillan, New York.
Brittan, A. (1973), 'Meaning and Situations', Routledge & Kegan Paul, London.

162

Bibliography 163

Britton, K. (1969) 'John Stuart Mill. Life and Philosophy', Dover, New York.
Bubner, R., et al. (eds), 'Hermeneutik und Dialektik', 2 vols, J.C.B. Mohr, Tübingen.
Buckley, W. (1967), 'Sociology and Modern Systems Theory', Prentice-Hall, Englewood Cliffs, N.J.
Bultmann, R. (1950), Das Problem der Hermeneutik, 'Zeitschrift für Philosophie und Kirche', 47, 19-31.
Bunge, M. (1964) (ed.), 'The Critical Approach to Science and Philosophy', Collier-Macmillan, London.
Caird, E. (1893), 'The Social Philosophy and Religion of Comte', James Maclehose, Glasgow, 2nd edition.
Carnap, R. (1928), 'Der Logische Aufbau der Welt', Weltkreis Verlag, Berlin.
Carnap, R. (1933), Über Protokollsätze, 'Erkenntnis', 3.
Carnap, R. (1936), Testability and meaning, 'Philosophy of Social Science', 3, iv, and 4, i.
Carnap, R. (1950), Empiricism, Semantics, and Ontology, 'Revue International de Philosophy', 4.
Castelli, E. (ed.) (1973), 'Ideologie et Demythisation', Aubier, Paris.
Chomsky, N. (1957), 'Syntactic Structures', Mouton, Press, Amsterdam.
Chomsky, N. (1959), Review of Skinner's Verbal Behaviour, 'Language', 35, i; extracts in Chomsky (1971).
Chomsky, N. (1965), 'Aspects of the Theory of Syntax', MIT Press.
Chomsky, N. (1969a), Language and philosophy, in Hook (1969).
Chomsky, N. (1969b), Linguistics and politics, 'New Left Review', 57, 21-34.
Chomsky, N. (1971), 'Chomsky: Selected Readings', ed. P.B. Allen, and P. van Buren, Oxford University Press.
Chomsky, N. (1972), 'Problems of Knowledge and Freedom', Barrie & Jenkins, London.
Churchill, L. (1971), 'Ethnomethodology and measurement, 'Social Forces', 50, December.
Cicourel, A. (1964), 'Method and Measurement in Sociology', Free Press, Chicago.
Cicourel, A. (1968), 'The Social Organization of Juvenile Justice', Wiley, New York.
Cicourel, A. (1970), Basic and normative rules in the negotiation of status and role, in Dreitzel (1970).
Cicourel, A. (1973) 'Cognitive Sociology', Penguin, Harmondsworth.
Clammer, J. (1976), Wittgensteinism and the social sciences, 'Sociological Review', 24, iv.
Comte, A. (1848), 'A General View of Positivism', trans. J.H. Briggs, Reeves & Turner, London (2nd edition 1880).
Culler, J. (1974), 'Saussure', Fontana, London.
Denzin, N. (1969), Symbolic interactionism and ethnomethodology: a proposed synthesis, 'American Sociological Review', 34, December.
Denzin, N. (1971), The logic of naturalistic enquiry, 'Social Forces', 50.
Denzin, N. (1978), The methodological implications of symbolic interactionism for the study of deviance, in Wells (1978); originally in 'British Journal of Sociology', 25, 1974, 269-82.
Descartes, R. (1946), 'A Discourse on Method', J.M. Dent, London.
Diesing, P. (1972a), Subjectivity and objectivity in the social sciences, 'Philosophy of the Social Sciences', 2, 147-65.
Diesing, P. (1972b), 'Patterns of Discovery in the Social Sciences', Routledge & Kegan Paul, London.
Dilthey, W. (1964-6), 'Gesammelte Schirften', B.G. Teubner, Leipzig and Berlin, (Stuttgart) (vol. I, ed. B. Broethuysen, 6th edn, 1966; vol. V, ed. G. Misch, 4th edn, 1964; vol. VII, ed. B. Groethuysen, 4th edn, 1965).
Douglas, J. (1967) 'The Social Meaning of Suicide', Princeton University Press, New Jersey.
Douglas, J. (1971), 'Understanding Everyday Life', Routledge & Kegan Paul, London.

164 *Bibliography*

Dreitzel, H.P. (1970), 'Recent Sociology', vol. 2, Macmillan, New York.
Dreitzel, H.P. (1972), Social science and the problem of rationality, 'Politics and Society', 2, ii, 165-82.
Duncan, G. (1973), 'Marx and Mill', Cambridge University Press.
Durkheim, E. (1965), 'The Rules of Sociological Method', Free Press, New York.
Durkheim, E. (1975), 'Sociology and Philosophy. With an Article on Durkheim's Life and Work by T. Parsons', Collier-Macmillan, London.
Elias, N. (1977), Zur Grundlegung einer Theorie sozialer Prozesse, 'Zeitschrift für Soziologie', 6, ii, 127-49.
Feigl, H., and Sellars, W. (eds) (1949), 'Readings in Philosophical Analysis', Appleton, New York.
Feyerabend, P. (1975), 'Against Method', New Left Books, London.
Feyerabend, P. (1980), Democracy, elitism, and scientific method, 'Inquiry', 23, 3-18.
Filstead, W. (ed.) (1970), 'Qualitative Methodology: Firsthand Involvement With the Social World', Markham, Chicago.
Fletcher, R. (1971), 'John Stuart Mill: A Logical Critique of Sociology', Michael Joseph, London.
Foucault, M. (1970), 'The Order of Things', Tavistock, London.
Fowler, R. (1971),'Introduction to Transformational Syntax', Routledge & Kegan Paul, London.
Freud, S. (1975), 'The Future of an Illusion', 'Standard Edition', Hogarth, London, vol. 21.
Furth, H.G. (1969), 'Piaget and Knowledge', Prentice-Hall, Englewood Cliffs, New Jersey.
Gadamer, H.G. (1967), 'Kleine Schirften', 3 vols, J.C.B. Mohr, Tübingen; translations from it in D. Linge, 'Philosophical Hermeneutics', University of California Press, 1976.
Gadamer, H.G. (1975), 'Wahrheit und Methode', J.C.B. Mohr, Tübingen, translated into English as 'Truth and Method' Sheed & Ward, London.
Garfinkel, H. (1967), 'Studies in Ethnomethodology', Prentice-Hall, Englewood Cliffs, New Jersey.
Garfinkel, H., and Sacks, H. (1978), On formal structures of practical actions, in Wells (1978), 294-311.
Giddens, A. (1974), 'Positivism and Sociology', Heinemann, London.
Giddens, A. (1976), 'New Rules of Sociological Method', Hutchinson, London.
Giddens, A. (1977), 'Studies in Social and Political Thought', Hutchinson, London.
Glaser, B., and Strauss, A. (1977), 'The Discovery of Grounded Theory', Aldine, Chicago.
Godelier, M. (1966), Comments on the concepts of structure and contradiction, 'Alethia', 4, 178-88.
Godelier, M. (1972), The thought of Marx and Engels today and tomorrow's research, 'International Journal of Sociology', 2, ii-iii.
Goffman, E. (1961), 'Encounters', Penguin, Harmondsworth.
Goldmann, L. (1973), 'The Philosophy of the Enlightenment', Routledge & Kegan Paul, London.
Gouldner, A. (1968), The sociologist as partisan, 'American Sociologist', 3, 103-16.
Gouldner, A. (1971), 'The Coming Crisis of Western Sociology', Heinemann, London.
Gouldner, A. (1974), Marxism and social theory, 'Theory and Society', 1, 17-35.
Gross, L. (ed.) (1959), 'Symposium on Sociological Theory', Harper & Row, New York.
Gruber, H., and Vonèche, J. (eds) (1977), 'The Essential Piaget', Routledge & Kegan Paul London.
Habermas, J. (1968), 'Erkenntnis und Interesse', Suhrkamp, Frankfurt, translated into English as 'Knowledge and Human Interests', Heinemann, London, 1972.

Bibliography 165

Habermas, J. (1971a), 'Der Universalitätsanspruch der Hermeneutik', in K.-O.
Apel et al., 'Hermeneutik, Dialektik und Ideologiekritik', Suhrkamp, Frankfurt, 1971; trans. in Bleicher (1980).
Habermas, J. (1971b), 'Theorie und Praxis', Suhrkamp, Frankfurt, 4th rev.
ed.; translated into English as 'Theory and Practice', Heinemann, London,
1974.
Habermas, J. (1973a), 'Zur Logik der Sozialwissenschaften', Suhrkamp,
Frankfurt.
Habermas, J. (1973b), 'Legitimationsprobleme im Spätkapitalismus', Suhrkamp,
Frankfurt; translated into English as 'Legitimation Crisis', Heinemann, London.
Habermas, J. (1973c), 'Technik und Wissenschaft als Ideology', Suhrkamp,
Frankfurt.
Habermas, J. (1973d), 'Kultur und Kritik', Suhrkamp, Frankfurt.
Habermas, J. (1973e), Wahrheitstheorien, in 'Festschrift für W. Schulz', Neske.
Pfullingen.
Habermas, J. (1974), 'Zwei Reden, Suhrkamp', Frankfurt; with D. Henrich.
Habermas, J. (1976), 'Zur Rekonstruktion des Historischen Materialismus',
Suhrkamp, Frankfurt.
Habermas, J., and Luhmann, N. (1975), 'Theorie der Gesellschaft oder
Sozialtechnologie', Suhrkamp, Frankfurt.
Hanson, N.R. (1965), 'Patterns of Discovery: an Inquiry into the Conceptual
Foundation of Science', Cambridge University Press.
Harrison, J. (1976) 'Hume's Moral Epistemology', Clarendon Press, Oxford.
Heap, J. and Roth. P.H. (1973), On phenomenological sociology, 'American
Sociological Review', 38, June, 254-67.
Heidegger, M. (1949), 'Sein und Zeit', Neomarius, Tübingen, 6th edn, translated into English as 'Being and Time', Harper & Row, New York, 1962.
Heidegger, M. (1962), 'Die Technik und die Kehre', Neske, Pfullingen.
Heidegger, M. (1967), 'What is a Thing?', Henry Regenery, Chicago.
Hempel, C. (1949), The logical analysis of psychology, in Feigl and Sellars
(1949).
Hempel, C. (1950), The function of general laws in history, 'Journal of
Philosophy', 39.
Hirsch, E. (1967), 'Validity in Interpretation', Yale University Press.
Hirsch, E. (1972), Three dimensions of hermeneutics, 'New Literary History',
3, ii.
Hochberg, H. (1959a), Physicalism, Behaviorism and Phenomena, 'Philosophy
of Science', 26, 93-103.
Hochberg, H. (1959b), Axiomatic systems, formalization, and scientific theories,
in Gross (1959).
Homans, G. (1961), 'Social Behavior: Its Elementary Forms', Harcourt, New York.
Hook, S. (ed.) (1969) 'Language and Philosophy', New York University Press.
Horkheimer, M. (1937a), Der neueste Angriff auf die Metaphysik, 'Zeitschrift
für Sozialforschung', 6, i, 4-51.
Horkheimer, M. (1937b), Traditionelle und kritische Soziologic, 'Zeitschrift
für Sozialforschung', 6, ii, 245-94.
Horkheimer, M. and Adorno, T. (1973), 'Dialectic of Enlightenment', Allen
Lane, London.
Huber, J. (1978a), Symbolic interaction as a pragmatic perspective: the basis
of emergent theory, in Wells (1978), 109-19.
Huber, J. (1978b), Reply to Blumer: but who will scrutinize the scrutinizers?,
in Wells (1978), 123-5.
Hume, D. (1962), 'A Treatise on Human Nature', Fontana, London, Book I.
Husserl, E. (1970a), 'The Crisis of European Sciences and Transcendental
Phenomenology', Northwestern University Press, Evanston.
Husserl, E. (1970b), 'Logical Investigations', Routledge & Kegan Paul, London,
2 vols. trans. from 2nd German edition, 1913.
Jameson, F. (1972), The rise of hermeneutics, 'New Literary History', 3, ii.
Johnson, H. (1961), 'Sociology: A Systematic Introduction', Routledge & Kegan
Paul, London.

166 *Bibliography*

Kaplan, A. (1964), 'The Conduct of Inquiry', Chandler, San Francisco.
Kisiel, T. (1971), Zu einer Hermeneutik naturwissenschaftlicher Entdeckung, 'Zeitschrift für allgemeine Wissenschaftstheorie', 2.
Kisiel, T. (1974), Comments on Heelan's 'Hermeneutics of Experimental Science', 'Zeitschrift für allgemeine Wissenschaftstheorie', 5, i.
Klibansky, R. (ed.) (1969), 'Contemporary Philosophy, A Survey', La Nuova Editrice, Firenze, vol. III.
Koestler, A. (1967), 'The Ghost in the Machine', Pan, London.
Kolakowski, L. (1972), 'Positivist Philosophy', Penguin, Harmondsworth.
Kraft, V. (1953), 'The Vienna Circle. The Origin of Neo-Positivism', Philosophical Library, New York.
Kuhn, M. (1964), Major trends in symbolic interaction theory in the past 25 years, 'Sociological Quarterly', 5, i, 61-84.
Kuhn, T. (1970), 'The Structure of Scientific Revolutions, Chicago University Press, 2nd enlarged edn with Postscript.
Lakatos, I., and Musgrave, A. (eds) (1970), 'Criticism and the Growth of Scientific Knowledge', Cambridge University Press.
Leach, E. (1970), 'Lévi-Strauss', Fontana, London.
Lecourt, D. (1975), 'Marxism and Epistemology, Bachelard, Canguilhem and Foucault', New Left Books, London.
Lévi-Strauss, C. (1968), 'Structural Anthropology', Penguin, Harmondsworth, vol. I.
Lévi-Strauss, C. (1977), Structural Anthropology, Penguin, vol. II.
Lorenzen, P. (1970), Szientismus versus Dialektik, in Bubner et al. (1970).
Louch, A. (1963), The very idea of a social science, 'Inquiry', 6, 273-86.
Louch, A. (1965), On misunderstanding Mr. Winch, 'Inquiry', 7, 212-16.
Louch, A. (1966), 'Explanation and Human Action', University of California Press.
Lukács, G. (1962), 'Die Zerstörung der Vernunft', Luchterhand, Berlin.
Lukács, G. (1971), 'History and Class Consciousness', Merlin Press, London.
Lukes, S. (1973), 'Émile Durkheim. His Life and Work', Allen Lane, London.
Lundberg, G. (1939), Contemporary Positivism in Sociology, 'American Sociological Review', 4, February.
Lundberg, G. (1964), 'Foundations of Sociology', David McKay, New York.
Lynch, F. (1975), Is there a behaviorist bandwagon?, 'American Sociologist', 10, 84-51.
Lyons, J. (1975), 'Chomsky', Fontana, London.
McHugh, P. et al. (1974), 'On the Beginnings of Social Inquiry', Routledge & Kegan Paul, London.
Mandelbaum, M. (1971), 'History, Man, and Reason', Johns Hopkins University Press, Baltimore.
Mannheim, K. (1958), 'Essays in the Sociology of Culture', Routledge & Kegan Paul, London.
Marcuse, H. (1964), 'One-Dimensional Man', Abacus, London.
Marcuse, H. (1968), 'Negations', Penguin, Harmondsworth.
Marcuse, H. (1972), 'Eros and Civilization', Abacus, London.
Marx, K. (1974), 'The German Ideology', Lawrence & Wishart, London.
Marx, K. (1975), 'Early Writings', ed. L. Coletti, Penguin/New Left Books, London.
Mead, G.H. (1934), 'Mind, Self and Society: from the Standpoint of a Social Behaviourist', University of Chicago Press.
Mead, G.H. (1936), The problem of society – how we become selves, in 'Movements of Thought in the 19th Century', University of Chicago Press.
Mead, G.H. (1938), 'The Philosophy of the Act', ed. C. Morris, University of Chicago Press.
Mehan, H., and Wood, H. (1975), 'The Reality of Ethnomethodology', Wiley, New York.
Merton, R. (1957), The role-set: problems in sociological theory, British Journal of Sociology', 8.
Merton, R., Broom, L., Cottrel, L.S. (eds) (1959), 'Sociology Today',

Bibliography 167

Basic Books, New York.
Mill, J.S. (1970), 'A System of Logic', Longmans, London.
Mills, C.W. (1959), 'The Sociological Imagination', Oxford University Press.
Morris, C. (1938), Introduction, to Mead (1938).
Morris, C. (1951), The science of man and unified science, 'Proceedings of the American Academy of Arts and Science', vol. 80, 37-44.
Morris, C. (1963), Pragmatism and logical empiricism, in Schilpp (1963).
Natanson, M. (1966), The Phenomenology of A. Schutz, 'Inquiry', 9, 147-55.
Neurath, O. (1933), Protokollsätze, 'Erkenntnis', 3, 204-14.
Neurath, O. (1973), 'Empiricism and Sociology', ed. Marie Neurath, Riedel, Dortrecht.
Outhwaite, W. (1975), 'Understanding Social Life', Allen & Unwin, London.
Palmer, R. (1969), 'Hermeneutics', Northwestern University Press, Evanston.
Pannenberg, W. (1976), 'Theology and the Philosophy of Science', Darton, Longman & Todd, London.
Parsons, T. (1947), 'The Theory of Social and Economic Organization', Oxford University Press.
Parsons, T. (1968), 'The Structure of Social Action', Free Press, New York.
Parsons, T. (1970a), 'The Social System', Routledge & Kegan Paul, London.
Parsons, T. (1970b), On social systems building: A personal history, 'Daedalus', 99, 4, 826-81.
Parsons, T. (1978), The concept of society: the components and their inter-relation, in Wells (1978).
Pavlov, I. (1927), 'Conditioned Reflexes', Oxford University Press.
Pelz, W. (1974), 'The Scope of Understanding in Sociology', Routledge & Kegan Paul, London.
Polanyi, M. (1964), 'Personal Knowledge', Harper Torchbooks, New York.
Popper, K. (1959), 'The Logic of Scientific Discovery', Hutchinson, London.
Popper, K. (1962), Die Logik der Sozialwissenschaften, 'Kölner Zeitschrift für Soziologie und Sozialpsycholgie', 14, 233-48.
Popper, K. (1966), 'The Open Society and Its Enemies', 2 vols, Routledge and Kegan Paul, London.
Popper, K. (1972), 'Objective Knowledge. An Evolutionary Approach', Clarendon Press, Oxford.
Popper, K. (1974), 'Conjectures and Refutations', Routledge & Kegan Paul, London.
Quine, W. (1961), 'From a Logical Point of View', Harvard University Press.
Quine, W. (1969), Linguistics and philosophy, in Hook (1969).
Quine, W. (1970), 'The Web of Belief', Random House, New York.
Radnitzki, G. (1970), 'Contemporary Schools of Metascience', Akademieforlaget, Goteborg.
Rex, J. (1974), 'Sociology and the Demystification of the Social World', Routledge & Kegan Paul, London.
Ricoeur, P. (1969a), Philosophie et langage, in Klibansky (1969).
Ricoeur, P. (1974), 'The Conflict of Interpretations. Essays in Hermeneutics', ed. Don Ihde, Northwestern University Press, Evanston.
Ricoeur, P. (1971), The Model of the text: meaningful action considered as a text, Social Research, 38, iii.
Riedel, M. (1978), 'Verstehen oder Erklären?', Klett-Cotta, Stuttgart.
Robertson, R. (1978), 'Meaning and Change', Blackwell, Oxford.
Rose, A. (1962), 'Human Behavior and Social Processes', Routledge & Kegan Paul, London.
Rose, G. (1978), 'The Melancholy Science. An Introduction to the Thought of Theodor W. Adorno', Macmillan, London.
Rucker, D. (1969), 'The Chicago Pragmatists', University of Minnesota Press.
Saussure, F. de (1966), 'Course in General Linguistics', McGraw-Hill, New York.
Scheffler, I. (1974), 'Four Pragmatists', Routledge & Kegan Paul, London.
Schilpp, P. (ed.) (1963), 'The Philosophy of Rudolf Carnap', Cambridge University Press.
Schlick, M. (1949), Meaning and verification, in Feigl and Sellars (1949).

168 *Bibliography*

Schutz, A. (1962), 'Collected Papers', vol. I, M. Nijhoff, The Hague.
Schutz, A. (1964), 'Collected Papers', vol. II, M. Nijhoff, The Hague.
Schutz, A. (1966), 'Collected Papers', vol. III, M. Nijhoff, The Hague.
Schutz, A. (1972), 'The Phenomenology of the Social World', Heinemann, London.
Schutz, A. (1974), 'The Structures of the Life-World', Heinemann, London.
Searle, J.R. (1970), 'Speech Acts: An Essay in the Philosophy of Language',
  Cambridge University Press.
Sève, L. (1972), Structural and dialectical method, 'International Journal of
  Sociology', 2, ii-iii, 196-214.
Sinha, A. (1968), Foundations of Scientific Theory, in 'Akten des 14.
  Internationalen Kongress für Philosophie', Vienna.
Skinner, B.F. (1957), 'Verbal Behavior', Appleton-Century-Croft, New York.
Skjervheim, H. (1974), Objectivism and the study of man, 'Inquiry', 17, 213-39,
  and 18, 265-302.
Stouffer, S., et al. (1949), 'Studies in Social Psychology in World War II', 4
  vols, Princeton University Press, New Jersey.
Suppes, P. (1975), 'From Behaviorism to neo-behaviorism, 'Theory and Decision',
  6, iii.
Taylor, C. (1971), Interpretation and the sciences of Man, 'Review of Meta-
  physics', 25 Sept., 3-51.
Therborn, G. (1976), 'Science, Class and Society', New Left Books, London.
Thomas, W, and Znaniecki, F. (1918), 'The Polish Peasant in Europe and
  America', Knopf, New York.
Thompson, M. (1963), 'The Pragmatic Philosophy of C. S. Peirce', University
  of Chicago Press.
Thorns, D. (ed.)(1976), 'New Directions in Sociology', David & Charles, London.
Toulmin, S. (1953), 'The Philosophy of Science: An Introduction', Hutchinson,
  London.
Truzzi, M. (ed.)(1974), 'Subjective Understanding in the Social Sciences',
  Addison-Wesley, Massachusetts.
Turner, R. (1962), Role-taking: Process versus Conformity, in Rose (1962).
Turner, R. (ed.) (1974), 'Ethnomethodology', Penguin, Harmondsworth.
Watson, J.B. (1928) 'The Ways of Behaviorism', Morton, New York.
Weber, M. (1947), 'The Theory of Social and Economic Organization', Oxford
  University Press.
Weber, M. (1949), 'The Methodology of the Social Sciences', ed. E.A. Shils
  and H. Finch, Free Press, Chicago.
Weber, M. (1951), 'Gesammelte Aufsätze zur Wissenschaftslehre', J.C.B. Mohr,
  Tübingen.
Weinberg, J. (1936), 'An Examination of Logical Positivism', Kegan Paul, London.
Wellmer, A. (1969), 'Kritische Gesellschaftstheorie', Suhrkamp, Frankfurt;
  translated into English as 'Critical Theory of Society', Seabury, New York,
  1972.
Zimmerman, D., and Wieder, L. (1971), Ethnomethodology and the problem of
  Social order: comment to Denzin, in Douglas (1971), pp. 285-95.

Name index

Abel, T., 160
Adorno, Th., 149–50, 158
Althusser, L., 96, 158
Apel, K.O., 28, 33, 80, 124, 151, 154–5
Aristotle, 87, 154, 156
Aron, R., 91-2
Austin, J.L., 32

Bachelard, G., 155
Bacon, F., 7, 36, 43, 46, 74
Barthes, R., 93, 158
Bauman, Z., 49, 90, 94, 121, 135, 142, 156–7, 159–60
Becker, H., 112
Bentham, J., 43
Bergmann, G., 21
Berkeley, G., 41-2
Betti, E., 52, 64–7, 70–1, 81–7, 112, 146, 157
Blau, P.M., 50
Bleicher, J., 156-8
Bloch, E., 160
Blum, A., 133
Blumer, H., 106–14, 116, 144, 159
Boudon, R., 158
Britton, K., 156
Bultmann, R., 66, 74, 76, 157

Carnap, R., 15-27, 154-6
Caird, E., 40-1, 156
Campbell, N., 159
Chomsky, N., 30-1, 95-6, 155
Churchill, L., 160
Cicourel, A., 130-3, 158
Comte, A., 39, 40-2, 44-6, 54, 57, 69, 141, 156
Condorcet, M. de, 46
Crane, R.S., 145
Culler, J., 158

Darwin, C., 159
Denzin, N., 113
Descartes, R., 7, 10, 13, 82
Diderot, D., 45
Diesing, P., 160
Dilthey, W., 23, 48, 52–65, 69–70, 81, 83, 88, 105, 115, 122, 124, 134, 143, 157

Douglas, J., 113, 132, 134, 159
Dreitzel, H.P., 92
Duhem, P.M., 27
Durkheim, H., 47, 90, 132, 156

Einstein, A., 155
Elias, N., 139
Engels, F., 96
Erdmann, J.E., 56

Feigl, H., 25, 155
Feyerabend, P., 5, 155
Foucault, M., 95-6, 158
Frege, G., 14, 102
Freud, S., 157

Gadamer, H.-G., 34, 70, 72-7, 79-82, 84-7, 141, 154-5, 157, 159-60
Galileo Galilei, 8, 86
Galton, F., 50
Garfinkel, A., 126-35, 159
Glaser, B., 113-14
Godelier, M., 96-9
Goffman, E., 130
Gouldner, A., 47, 112
Groethuysen, B., 157

Habermas, J., 28, 32-4, 38, 53, 80, 91-2, 121, 124, 139, 147, 152, 156, 159-61
Hanson, N.R., 30, 155
Hegel, G.W.F., 60, 62, 74-6, 141
Heidegger, M., 3, 10-13, 66, 70-1, 74, 76-81, 117, 154-5, 157
Hempel, C., 23-5, 116, 155
Hilbert, D., 15
Hirsch, E., 83
Hochberg, H., 15
d'Holbach, P.H., 45
Homans, G., 50, 156
Horkheimer, M., 149, 154
Huber, J., 112
Hume, D., 39, 42,
Husserl, E., 7-11, 43, 62, 67, 74, 77, 115, 117-18, 120, 154, 159

Inhelder, B., 155

Jameson, F., 157

170 Name index

Jaspers, K., 66
Johnson, H., 50

Kant, I., 8, 11, 28, 35, 40-1, 63, 121
Kaplan, A., 34
Kisiel, T., 155
Korsch, K., 97, 158
Kraft, V., 19, 154
Kuhn, Th., 36, 87, 155

Lakatos, I., 155
Lazarsfeld, P., 114, 130-1, 155
Leach, E., 158
Leibnitz, G.W., 15-16
Lévi-Strauss, C., 1, 93-7, 99, 100-2
Lewis, C.I., 155
Locke, J., 41-2
Lorenzen, P., 33
Luhmann, J., 92, 139
Lukács, G., 149, 157-8
Lukes, S., 156
Lundberg, G., 48-9, 156

McHugh, P., 130, 133
Magee, B., 155
Maistre, J. de, 45
Mannheim, K., 54, 138-9, 141
Marcuse, H., 147-8
Marx, K., 44, 54, 95-6, 141, 148-9
Mill, J.S., 19, 41-3, 48, 50, 54, 56, 62,
  156-7
Mills, C.W., 160
Misch, G., 157
Mead, G.H., 106-7, 139, 159
Merton, R., 114, 130
Morris, C., 26

Nagel, E., 116, 155, 159
Neurath, O., 14, 16, 18, 20-6, 48, 154
Newton, I., 154-6
Nietzsche, F., 54, 146

Pannenberg, W., 160
Parsons, T., 89, 90-1, 105, 130, 139,
  157-8
Pavlov, I., 30
Pearson, E.S., 50
Peirce, C., 19, 26-8
Piaget, J., 31, 155
Polanyi, M., 145, 155
Popper, K., 34-5, 146, 155

Quetelet, L.A., 50
Quine, W., 26-8, 30

Ranke, L. von, 54, 85
Reichenbach, H., 19
Rex, J., 156
Rickert, H., 157
Ricoeur, P., 53, 101-3, 158
Robertson, R., 138
Rothacker, E., 56
Rousseau, J.-J., 45
Russell, B., 14-17

Sacks, H., 159
Saint-Simon, C.H. de, 156
Saussure, F. de, 93, 158
Schleiermacher, F., 68, 83
Schlick, M., 17, 19-20, 154-5
Schütz, A., 115-23, 125, 134-5, 154,
  159
Searle, J., 32, 155
Sève, L., 98-9, 158
Simmel, G., 68
Sinha, A., 145
Skinner, B.F., 30
Spencer, H., 57, 142, 156
Stouffer, S., 109
Strauss, A., 113-14, 158
Suppes, P., 156

Taylor, Ch., 53, 146, 160
Thomas, W., 111, 158
Toulmin, S., 155
Troubetzkoj, N.S., 93

Watson, J.B., 30
Weber, M., 37, 47, 88-90, 92, 105,
  115, 117, 119-23, 146, 157-9
Weinberg, J., 18
Whitehead, A.N., 15-16
Whyte, W., 160
Wieder, L., 126
Wilson, T.P., 139
Winch, P., 122-4, 159
Windelband, W., 157
Wittgenstein, L., 20, 29, 154,
  157

Zimmerman, D., 126
Znaniecki, F., 111, 113, 158

Subject index

academic sociology, 47
anthropology, 59
art, 55, 59, 62, 77
astronomy, 43

behaviourism, 28-31, 50, 88, 116, 140;
  neo-behaviourism, 156
biography, 62
biology, 23-4
bourgeoisie, 4

canons of interpretation, 67
commodity-relation, 149
communicative interaction, 5
community of investigators, 27-8;
  of scientists, 28-9, 35, 146
confirmation, 19-20
connotation, 156
consensus, 33, 127

Dasein, 10-13, 71, 74
denotation, 156
discourse, theoretical, 34
documentary interpretation, 126-8,
  130
double hermeneutic, 2, 52, 63, 80, 92,
  103-4, 112, 114-15, 119, 121-2,
  124-5, 131, 134, 137-40

Empiricism, 18-20, 29, 50
Encyclopedism, 19
England, 61, 155
Enlightenment, 37, 46, 70-1, 81, 83
ethnology, 59
ethnomethodology, 2, 125-36, 159-60
ethology, 43
existentialism, 65
exploration, 110, 159

falsification, 18, 35
France, 61
functionalist sociology, 2

game, 78, 82-3
Geisteswissenschaften, 48, 52-4, 65,
  69-71, 81-2, 85, 88, 105, 115, 137,
  154, 157
Germany, 49, 54, 57, 89
Grand theory, 113

grounded theory, 113, 158

hermeneutic circle, 11, 66, 82, 94, 126,
  132, 137-8, 140-2, 145-6, 152
hermeneutic consciousness, 81
hermeneutic dimension: in science,
  28-9, 33, 36, 49, 52, 78; in social
  reproduction, 1, 3; in sociology,
  1-2, 55, 63-4, 70, 91, 112, 116,
  120-2, 137, 140-2, 146
hermeneutic imagination, 1, 7, 153
hermeneutic paradigm, 2, 49, 70,
  106, 111, 113, 115, 124-5, 135,
  137, 140, 146, 152
hermeneutic philosophy, 82
hermeneutic sociology, 2, 137-46, 152
hermeneutic-dialectical (critical) sociology, 2, 147, 150, 152, 161
hermeneutical theory, 81, 88, 121, 137,
  143, 149
hermeneutics vs scientism, 3, 33
historicality, 74-5, 83-4, 101, 141-2,
  145
historical school, 54, 85
historism, 70-2, 87
history, 55, 62, 77

ideal type, 89; personal, 119;
  objective, 119
ideographic method, 157
indexicality, 128-30, 159
inspection, 110
instrumental rationality, 4
interpretive sociology, 2, 52, 105,
  116-17, 124-5, 137-8, 152, 158, 160
intersubjectivity, 117, 120-1, 125-7,
  139, 144, 151; transcendental intersubjectivity, 118, 122
Israel, 101

language, distorted, 147-8
language: ideal, 17, 22; ordinary, 18;
  physical, 22-4, 27; theoretical, 16,
  25-6; thing, 23-5, universal, 22
language-acquisition: behaviourist
  theory, 28-30; rationalist theory, 30-1
language-game, 122, 124, 138, 142, 151
life-world (Lebenswelt), 9, 74, 78,
  115, 118, 121, 125-7, 143, 154

172 *Subject index*

linguistic competence vs communicative competence, 32-3
linguistics, 93, 98-9
literature, 55
Logical Empiricism, 17, 19, 22, 48, 92
Logic of Inquiry, 35
Logic of Science, 14, 16, 21, 28, 34-6, 87, 140, 142

macro-sociology, 88, 92, 105, 109-10, 115, 122, 133, 137, 160
Marxism, 97
material production, 151, 161
meaningfulness, criterion of, 14-20, 26, 35
metaphysics, 12, 14, 16-17, 45, 48; vs science, 16, 20-1, 28, 39, 40
micro-sociology, 88, 137
moral science, 56-7, 146
motive, 119, 138, 148

neo-Kantianism, 68, 81-2, 89, 146, 157
neo-Positivism, 14, 16, 26-7
Nominalism, 18, 135-6, 138
nomothetical method, 157

objective frame of reference, 115
objectivism, 80-1, 87, 103, 115-16, 124, 158; defined, 52, 128
objectivity: in interpretation, 64, 66, 71, 76, 84, 87, 103, 120-1, 129, 134, 144-5; (relative) objectivity, 84, 86; in science, 74, 78, 80

paradigm, 36
participant observation, 143
phenomenological sociology, 114
phenomenology, 117, 146, 154, 159
Physicalism, 21, 23-5, 48
political domination, 151
political economy, 55
Positivism, 37, 39, 44-8
positivist sociology, 38, 47, 156
practical knowledge, 53, 55, 87; vs instrumental knowledge, 54
Pragmatism, 26-9
pre-understanding, 66, 74, 79, 83, 114, 126-8, 131-2, 140-3, 150
protocol sentences, 21-2
psychology, 58-9, 62

rationalism, 42
rationalization, 37, 149
Reason, 8, 35, 45-6, 62, 70-1, 83, 95; vs Life, 62-3
reification, 149
relativism, 66, 81, 93, 124, 133-4, 154
religion, 54, 60, 62, 98
Renaissance, 46

role, 90, 107-8
Romanticism, 156

science, and social development, 4-5, 7
scientistic philosophy of science, 7, 13, 27, 33, 50, 144
scientistic sociology, 2-4, 10, 38, 40, 47, 49-52, 64, 105, 109-10, 115, 122, 125, 133, 137, 149, 152, 160
scientism: defined, 3; vs hermeneutics, 2, 3, 20, 64
semiology, 93
sensitizing concepts, 110
sign, 158
social studies, 122
structural-functionalism, 103, 107, 109, 115, 133, 141, 160
structuralism, 89, 92, 95, 97, 99, 103
structuralist sociology, 2
subjective frame of reference, 115, 117
subjectivism, 63, 65-6, 81, 113, 116, 145-6, 158
subjectivity, 65, 71, 78, 81, 131, 145; principle of, 105-6, 108, 115, 123
subject-object, 13, 17, 49, 52, 63, 67-8, 70, 80-5, 103, 111, 114, 120-2, 124, 134-5, 137, 140, 143-4, 151, 159
surplus repression, 147
survey method, 109-10
symbolic interactionism, 106-15, 143, 159
systems theory, 91, 152

technocracy, 7, 46-7
technology, 12-13
testability, 20
theology, 37, 39, 45, 86
'Thomas's postulate', 116
totality, 62, 149
transformational grammar, 155

United States, 155
unity of science, 21-3, 25-6, 43, 50, 87, 92-3
USSR, 49

value-interpretation, 89
value-orientation, 89
verifiability, 18; vs confirmation, 19
verification, 16-18, 27
verstehen, 55, 65-6, 70, 116, 143; vs explanation (erklären), 20, 66, 140, 157
Vienna Circle, 14-20, 23, 26, 28, 35, 48, 154